WHAT IS ENLIGHTENMENT?

WHAT IS ENLIGHTENMENT?

EXPLORING THE GOAL OF THE SPIRITUAL PATH

Edited by John White

PARAGON HOUSE

NEW YORK

1995 Edition published in the United States by

Paragon House
370 Lexington Avenue
New York, NY 10017

Library of Congress Cataloging-in-Publication Data

What is enlightenment? : exploring the goal of the spiritual path /
edited by John White.
     p.   cm.
    Originally published: Los Angeles : J.P. Tarcher, c1984.
    Includes bibliographical references and index.
    ISBN 1-55778-726-3 (pbk.)
    1. Spiritual life. I. White, John Warren.
BL624.W44   1995
291.4'2—dc20   95-7514
                                    CIP

Manufactured in the United States of America

CONTENTS

To *Homo noeticus,*
the higher humanity now being born,

To the saints, seers and sages of history
whose selfless service helped prepare the birthplace,

And to you, the readers,
who are the bridge.

Understanding others is wisdom,
Understanding yourself is enlightenment.

Lao Tse

ACKNOWLEDGEMENTS

"From Self to Cosmic Consciousness" is reprinted from *Cosmic Consciousness* by Richard Maurice Bucke. Copyright © 1901, 1923 by E. P. Dutton, Inc.

"This Is It" is reprinted from *This Is It and Other Essays on Zen* by Alan W. Watts. Copyright © 1960 by Alan W. Watts. Reprinted by permission of Pantheon Books, a Division of Random House, Inc.

"The Perennial Philosophy" is reprinted from pages vii–xi ("Introduction") and page 21 ("That Art Thou," Chapter 1) in *The Perennial Philosophy* by Aldous Huxley. Copyright © 1944, 1945 by Aldous Huxley. Reprinted by permission of Harper & Row, Publishers, Inc., Mrs. Laura Huxley, and Chatto and Windus Ltd.

"The Unitive Life" is reprinted from *Mysticism* by Evelyn Underhill. Published by E. P. Dutton & Co., Inc., 1961.

"The Sacred Unconscious" is reprinted from *Beyond Health and Normality: Explorations in Exceptional Psychological Well-Being* by Roger N. Walsh and Deane H. Shapiro. Copyright © 1983 by Van Nostrand Reinhold Co., Inc. Reprinted by permission of the publisher.

"Meher Baba and the Quest of Consciousness" originally appeared as "The Quest of Consciousness" (Chapter 2) in *The Mastery of Consciousness: An Introduction and Guide to Practical Mysticism and Methods of Spiritual Development as given by Meher Baba*, compiled and edited by Allan Y. Cohen. Copyright © 1977 by Ira G. Deitrick. Copyright © 1977 by Adi K. Irani for selected quotations from Meher Baba. Reprinted by permission of Allan Y. Cohen and Harper & Row, Publishers, Inc.

"Love, Freedom and Enlightenment: An Interview with J. Krishnamurti" is an original article. Copyright © 1984 by John White.

"Oneness and the Teaching of Sri Aurobindo" originally appeared as "Oneness" (Chapter 11) in *Sri Aurobindo, or the Adventure of Consciousness* by Satprem. Copyright © 1968 by Sri Aurobindo Ashram Trust, Pondicherry, India 605002. Reprinted by permission of the Trust.

Acknowledgments

"Enlightenment and the Judeo-Christian Tradition" is expanded from "Jesus, Evolution and the Future of Humanity" by John White, a lecture published in the September-October 1981 issues of *Science of Mind* magazine.

"Ten Seasons of Enlightenment: Zen Ox-herding" is excerpted from "Ten Seasons of Enlightenment" (Chapter 4) in *Coming Home* by Lex Hixon. Copyright © 1978 by Alexander P. Hixon, Jr. Reprinted by permission of Doubleday & Company, Inc.

"Exceptional Mental Health: Ancient Images and Recent Research" by Roger N. Walsh is an expansion of "The Ten Perfections: Qualities of the Fully Enlightened Individual as Described in Buddhist Psychology" (Chapter 8) in *Beyond Health and Normality: Explorations in Exceptional Psychological Well-Being* edited by Roger Walsh and Deane H. Shapiro. Chapter 8 is copyright © 1983 by Van Nostrand Reinhold Co., Inc. and reprinted by permission of the publisher. "Exceptional Mental Health" is copyright © 1984 by Roger N. Walsh and printed by permission.

"The True Aim of Yoga" originally appeared in *Psychic* magazine, January/February 1973. Reprinted by permission of the Kundalini Research Foundation, 475 Fifth Avenue, New York, NY 10016.

" 'Human, all too human' and Beyond" is an original article written especially for this book. Copyright © 1984 by Dane Rudhyar and published by permission of the author.

"The Mood of Enlightenment" is reprinted from *The Enlightenment of the Whole Body* by Da Avabhasa. Copyright © 1978 by the Johannine Daist Communion. All rights reserved.

"The Ultimate State of Consciousness" originally appeared in *Journal of Altered States of Consciousness*, Vol. 2, No. 3, 1975–1976. Reprinted by permission of the author.

"The Seven Stages of Life" is reprinted from *What Is the Conscious Process?* by Da Avabhasa (The Dawn Horse Press). Copyright © 1983 by The Johannine Daist Communion. All rights reserved.

PREFACE

THIS BOOK is a kind of sequel to my first book, *The Highest State of Consciousness*, which was published in 1972. *Highest State* was appropriate for its time and sold well during the decade of its life, but the passing years dated some of its selections and revealed their overall unevenness. Clearly, the book served a useful purpose. Just as clearly, however, its usefulness came to an end and it properly went out of print.

What Is Enlightenment? contains three of the thirty-three selections (Bucke, Huxley, and Watts) from *Highest State*. I chose them for this book because of their seminal importance to the now-global quest for higher consciousness and self-transcendence, and because they have a timeless quality that sets them somewhat apart from the rest of *Highest State*.

The other selections in *What Is Enlightenment?* are, I trust, fully appropriate to the theme-title. I have tried to avoid the shortcomings I came to see in the earlier book by striving for greater balance and brevity, bearing in mind the words of Ecclesiastes: "Of making many books there is no end, and much study is a weariness to the flesh." I hope this book serves its purpose by being a companion and able assistant as you follow your path in life. The *journey* is the real teaching, but written teachings record others' journeys and can thereby enrich your own. May yours be rich indeed.

INTRODUCTION

WHAT IS enlightenment? The question has been asked throughout history by people looking for the meaning of existence. So precious has such understanding seemed, so important for their happiness that men and women of all ages have devoted themselves exclusively to finding an answer, despite hardship, privation, and even, at times, social ostracism. Their search has been motivated by a hunger for self-knowledge: Who am I? Why am I here? Where am I going? What is life all about? These are all aspects of the fundamental question: What is enlightenment?

Today an increasing number of seekers are following in the steps of their predecessors. There is restlessness and dissatisfaction with the status quo, which has provided neither answers nor happiness. In addition, the age-old question is now being asked by consciousness researchers in science and by the merely curious who hear vague but alluring stories about something called enlightenment which makes living blissful and worthwhile. In fact, so widespread is the urge to know about enlightenment that, for the first time in history, people and organizations claiming to understand it have developed into a thriving field of commerce. The enlightenment industry is big business. Ads proclaim everywhere, it seems, that no longer is the search relegated to years of arduous discipline in remote sanctuaries. Today, enlightenment is for everyone.

EGO AND THE ENLIGHTENMENT INDUSTRY

Now, it is true in the ultimate sense that enlightenment *is* for everyone. That, thank God, is precisely the point toward which all creation drives. But one of the unfortunate aspects of all the commercialism has been devaluation of the term "enlightenment." A surge of books, articles, tapes, lectures, and seminars on enlightenment offers conflicting opinions, claims, and counter-claims about it. There has also been a veritable explosion of psychotechnologies and consciousness-altering devices claiming to induce mystical, transformative, and "enlightened" states. Hypnotic tape recordings, past life recall sessions, alpha and theta brainwave training, out-of-body astral sounds, various meditation systems, sensory isolation flotation tanks— these are typical of the wares being offered today in spiritual supermarkets. However, the spiritual "consumer" should ask: Do they have any value? If so, how much? What are they useful for?

All these products and services and systems just mentioned have value of a limited sort—value for the novice, value for the person just beginning to become aware of the higher ranges of being that are culturally denied and educationally excluded in western society. They are capable of delivering experiences that open our window on reality a bit wider than normal. They can show the limitations of everyday consciousness and the possibility of something beyond it. But the critical point to be understood is this: the value of mystical and transformative states is not in producing some new experience but in *getting rid of the experiencer*. Getting rid, that is, of the egocentric consciousness which experiences life from a contracted, self-centered point of view rather than the free, unbound perspective of a sage who knows he or she is infinity operating through a finite form.

WHAT ENLIGHTENMENT IS NOT

Now, if the last statement sounds too vague (most statements about enlightenment do), perhaps it would help to be specific about what enlightenment is not. It is not an altered state of consciousness, whether induced through meditation, drugs, sex, or any other mind-altering psychotechnology. As one contributor to this anthology, transpersonal psychologist Ken Wilber, said in the (now-deleted) abstract of his essay, "The Ultimate State of Consciousness . . . is known not one among many but one without a second . . . [it] is not an altered state of consciousness, for there is no alternative to it."

Neither is enlightenment a dazzling display of psychic phenomena or paranormal powers. Nor is it a vision that transports you to some celestial realm. It is not sitting immobile in trance while experiencing an inner world of fascinating colors and sounds or alternatively, a complete blankness of mind. Enlightenment can include all that but it also infinitely transcends all that. *Anything* less than ultimate is not the answer, and all phenomena are passing, non-ultimate. And, *caveat emptor*, that applies to nearly everything offered by the enlightenment industry.

So as all the excitement about quick fixes, bliss machines, effortless systems and instant ego cures winds down without noticeable results, as the froth of commercialism subsides and people begin to see deeper into the nature of self-transformation and the spiritual quest, they are left confused and dissatisfied. And again the question arises: What is enlightenment?

THE PERENNIAL WISDOM

If that has been the perennial question, the answer has been called the perennial wisdom. This is the goal of the spiritual journey: radical understanding that gets to the heart of human experience, illuminating every facet, removing all doubt about the meaning of existence and the nature of reality. It is not so much a matter of factual knowledge as feeling-wisdom; not omniscience, but certitude.

That is what this book is all about. It brings together some of the best material from the vast body of literature about enlightenment so you can get a clear picture of the wisdom of the ages. In my various anthologies on higher human development over the years, I have sought to offer in one volume a comprehensive collection so that the reader gets a solid introduction to an important subject or theme without having to wade through huge stacks of material or to expend great time and energy in a literature search. That is my intention here. By reading this book you can gain an accurate concept of enlightenment—an intellectually sound understanding that is, in effect, a map of reality. (A word of caution, however: the map is not the territory. To put it another way, pictures of pancakes do not satisfy hunger. The term "enlightenment" is, after all, a word at a great distance from what it refers to. So I'll say more about maps of reality later.)

The perennial wisdom is unchanging; truth is one. That is agreed on by the sages of all major religions and sacred traditions, all hermetic philosophies, genuine mystery schools and higher occult paths. Enlightenment is the core truth of them all. Even more broadly, it is the essence of life—the goal of all growth, development, evolution. It is the discovery of what we ultimately are, the answer to the questions: Who am I? Why am I here? Where am I going? What is life all about?

THE PARADOX OF BEING AND BECOMING

Paradoxically the answer we seek is none other than what we *already are* in essence—Being, the ultimate wholeness that is the source and ground of all Becoming. *Enlightenment is realization of the truth of Being.* Our native condition, our true self is Being, traditionally called God, the Cosmic Person, the Supreme Being, the One-in-all. (Incidentally, some enlightened teachers—Buddha was one—prefer to avoid theistic terms in order to communicate better. Their intent is to bypass the deep cultural conditioning that occurs through such language and blocks understanding.) We are manifestations of Being, but like the cosmos itself, we are also in the process of Becoming—always changing, developing, growing, evolving to higher and higher states that ever more beautifully express the perfection of the source of existence. Thus, we are not only human beings; we are also human becomings. Enlightenment is understanding the perfect poise of being-amid-becoming.

The truth of all existence and all experience, then, is none other than the seamless here-and-now, the already present, the prior nature of that which seeks and strives and asks: Being. *The spiritual journey is the process of discovering and living that truth.* It amounts to the eye seeing itself—or rather, the I seeing its Self. In philosophical terms, enlightenment is comprehending the unity of all dualities, the harmonious composite of all opposites, the oneness of endless multiplicity and diversity. In psychological terms, it is transcendence of all sense of limitation and otherness. In humanistic terms, it is understanding that the journey is the teaching, that the path and the destination are ultimately one. In theological terms, it is comprehending the union of God and humanity. In ontological terms, it is the State of all states, the Condition of all conditions that transcends the entire cosmos yet is also everyday reality, since nothing is apart from it or ever can be.

When we finally understand that Great Mystery, we discover our true nature, the Supreme Identity, the Self of all. That direct perception of our oneness with the infinite, that noetic realization of our identity with the divine is the source of all happiness, all goodness, all beauty, all truth. The experience is beyond time, space, and causality; it is beyond ego and all socially conditioned sense of "I." Knowing ourselves to be timeless, boundless, and therefore cosmically free ends the illusion of separateness and all the painful, destructive defenses we erect, individually and societally, to preserve the ego-illusion at the expense of others. The *Maitrayana Upanishad* puts it this way: "Having realized his own self as the Self, a person becomes selfless. . . . This is the highest mystery."

INVOLUTION, EVOLUTION AND RETURN TO GODHEAD

Although we are essentially Being, we are not static. We are also active, also Being-in-the-process-of-Self-induced-change, which is traditionally called Becoming or cosmic evolution. However, *evolution* is only one aspect of that mysterious process underlying creation. The other is *involution*—that "breathing out" by God, that "emptying" or kenosis which brings forth the cosmos and involves divinity in matter so that it may work itself through stages of growth in awareness, from nescience through simple consciousness, self consciousness and cosmic consciousness to that Great Remembrance-Resurrection of itself as none other than the One-in-all.

We are *involved in matter* to become *evolved as Spirit*. We are developing individually and as a race, through the levels of existence—physical, mental and spiritual—that are in their ultimate nature simply gradations of God, the Great Chain of Being. Original creation of the cosmos was the materialization of Spirit; all that follows is the spiritualization of matter, in all worlds, high and low. Thus, we are ultimately God in a Self-imposed drama—a drama in which a part of God "forgets" itself, believes itself to be "lost" and thereby is motivated to seek reunion with the Whole, the One Without a Second. The process in which we become lost and forget our god-nature is involution, the fall from grace and bliss; the process in which we find ourselves and remember our true condition is evolution, the conscious return to godhead. When you understand that, you begin to live what a contributor to this book, Sri Aurobindo, calls "the life divine."

EXISTENCE IS THE PLAY OF GOD

From the cosmic perspective, the situation we find ourselves in is a drama in which we are sleepwalking actors. We go through life unaware of the fact that everything is the play of God (pun intended). To awaken from that drama is enlightenment. You discover that God is the author, actor and stage for an infinitely playful—and therefore delightful—drama. But what do you do after you wake up? Why, just the same as in daily living: you go about your business and get on with what must be done in the world—in all worlds. You become, in a sense, a co-creator with God in "saving" the universe by doing what you can to help others see the light and love of divinity shining in all things—indeed, *as* all things.

Enlightenment, then, is an endless process—not simply a one-time event. True, there are quantum leaps in awareness that mark the spiritual path, as "maps of reality" developed by sacred traditions show, but one white-light experience does not a mystic make, nor a saint. Even the most spiritually elevated people have found there are states of being beyond their present level of development. This lifetime is sufficient to reach enlightenment but not to complete it. Self-realization is not the same as self-transformation. As Sri Aurobindo puts it, god-realization is a "middle term" in the process of higher human development. Thus, self-realization, however radical, is not the end of the human journey. Higher states of development await, calling us to further transformation in our evolutionary destiny. Understood, however, that all such future stages of Becoming are nevertheless expressions of infinitely and eternally present Being and this our ultimate identity is in the words of another contributor, the spiritual teacher Da Love-Ananda, (formerly Da Free John) "always already God." Always, that is, already enlightened.

NAMES AND SYMBOLS FOR ENLIGHTENMENT

Enlightenment has been given many names. Buddha means "the enlightened one"; Christ and Messiah also mean that. St. Paul called it "the peace of God that passeth understanding" and Richard Maurice Bucke named it "cosmic consciousness." In Zen it is *satori*, in yoga it is *samadhi* or *moksha*, in Sufism it is *fana* or *tawhid*, in Taoism it is *wu* or The Ultimate Tao. Gurdjieff labeled it "objective consciousness," Sri Aurobindo spoke of the Supermind, mystery schools and occult paths speak of "illumination," "liberation," and "self-realization." Likewise, enlightenment has been symbolized by many images: the thousand-petaled lotus of Hinduism, the Holy Grail of Christianity, the clear mirror of Buddhism, Judaism's Star of David, the yin-yang circle of Taoism, the mountaintop, the swan, the still lake, the mystic rose, the eternal flame.

And enlightenment has been described by saints, sages and scholars in many ways. For example, Ken Wilber, whom many regard as the foremost theorist of transpersonal psychology and whom I regard as the Einstein of consciousness research, offers this summary of the final chapter of his brilliant *Eye to Eye*:

> The Ultimate State of Consciousness is universally described in mystical literature as union with the Absolute, where the Absolute is known not as one among many but one without a second. Further, it is specified that to know the Absolute is to be the Absolute. It follows that the Ultimate State of Consciousness is itself the Absolute, and thus the Ultimate State is not a state of consciousness set apart from other states, not one state among many, but rather one state without a second—that is to say, absolutely all-inclusive. Hence, the Ultimate State of Consciousness is not an altered state of consciousness, for there is no alternative to it.

Likewise, Da Love-Ananda has commented at great length on the subject. His point of view, elaborated in his discourses and writing, is succinctly given in this excerpt from *The Bodily Sacrifice of Attention*.

> The usual man or woman thinks that Enlightenment is the having of a vision. Enlightenment is the most subtle, or tacit, unspeakable understanding. It is the Bodhicitta, the ultimate realization of Being, the ultimate Wisdom. On

its basis, all kinds of radiant transformations may develop, but the Realization itself is so fundamental, so tacit, so simple, so direct, so obvious, so transcendental, that it is not identified with any phenomenon of experience or knowledge. The means of the transmission of this Realization is an awakened individual, the Spiritual Master, but the Realization is most tacit, perfect, simple, direct, and obvious. When you come to the point of acknowledging the Divine Identity and Condition of manifest existence, then you are Enlightened.

Thaddeus Golas, author of the brief but wise *The Lazy Man's Guide to Enlightenment*, describes it like this: "Enlightenment is any experience of expanding our consciousness beyond its present limits. We could also say that perfect enlightenment is realization that we have no limits at all . . ." And to paraphrase still another contemporary source, Maharaj-ji, the guru of ex-Harvard professor of psychology Ram Dass, enlightenment is never casting anyone out of your heart—i.e., living as infinite and unconditional love, the way God loves.

ENLIGHTENMENT IS BEYOND WORDS AND SYMBOLS

Regardless of the name or symbol, however, and no matter how poetic and inspiring the verbal description, there is no substitute for direct experience. Enlightenment is ineffable—beyond words, images and concepts; it cannot be grasped by intellect, logic, analysis, or any aspect of our egoic-rational-mental being, no matter how keen and penetrating the mind, no matter how cunning the intelligence. A symbol conceals as much as it reveals and words are only *about* truth—they are not truth itself. They are therefore only guides, not guarantees. Reading about enlightenment is not a substitute for practice of a spiritual discipline or a sacred tradition. There must be actual experience; pictures of pancakes do not satisfy hunger.

To experience enlightenment yourself, then, the only thing that absolutely must be "read" is the Great Mystery, and for that you read with the eye of contemplation, not the eye of reason, and certainly not with the various glittering goods of the enlightenment industry. Furthermore, no matter how hard you seek, no matter how great your effort, enlightenment can never be achieved—only discovered. And for that we are all dependent on what spiritual traditions call grace.

But grace abounds—amazing grace. As Jesus said, if you ask for bread, you will not be given stones. Seek and you shall find. Knock and it shall be opened unto you. A universal intelligence provides everything you need every step of the way. Its entire purpose is simply to awaken you to your true nature. Enlightenment, or the kingdom of heaven, is your birthright.

WALKING THE PATH TO ENLIGHTENMENT

Claiming our birthright, however, is no easy matter. Grace falls like rain on everyone, but also like rain, it can only be received by a vessel properly prepared to "catch" it. The preparation involves a change of consciousness. Without that, we are mere stones from which the rain slides off; with it, we become worked stone hollowed into urns or chalices that can retain what falls from heaven.

Nor is claiming our birthright a straightforward matter. On the spiritual path there are many side trails that are essentially deadends, if not traps. There are also periods of chaotic upheavals in the mind, moments of insight and partial breakthrough, intervals of exhaustion and utter apathy, and times of intense struggle and doubt when faith in the ultimate importance of the spiritual journey alone carries you stumblingly forward. What can we say about this process of finding our true self?

Sacred traditions emphasize right living and awareness of the present moment, rather than offering minute descriptions of higher worlds intended for intellectual study. That is not to say they have no such descriptions—they do, as I show in Appendix I, which is concerned with maps of reality.

But if you were to ask a Zen master, for example, to explain satori, he might stoop down, pick up a rock and hand it to you, or he might bark like a dog or do something else equally startling. Such behavior is intended to help you burst through your ordinary state of awareness which is so thing-oriented and language-bound, so conditioned by culture. Or he might puzzle you with a koan—an apparently unsolvable riddle—which goes like this: "Before enlightenment, I chopped wood and carried water. After enlightenment, I chopped wood and carried water."

What is the spiritual seeker to understand by such "crazy wisdom"? The answer is this: reality is unchanging, but *your perception* of reality changes as you change consciousness. As the rishis of ancient India said: knowledge is structured in consciousness. The difference before and after enlightenment, therefore, is in you—not in reality. The limitation is in you—your consciousness—and when that limitation is transcended, you perceive existence differently and therefore relate to it in a new way. Your sense of identity changes. You experience the cosmos as unified and intimately one with your own essential being, rather than experiencing yourself as a separate, isolated physical form apart from all the rest of existence.

MAPS THAT GUIDE YOU ALONG THE PATH

But is it that simple? No. Although, as the *Brihadaranyaka Upanishad* declares, "By understanding the Self, all this universe is known," the discovery of Self-as-all is far from simple. What more can be said about this process of coming to see things as they are—infinite?

Another Zen koan is appropriate here. "Before I came to Zen, mountains were only mountains, rivers only rivers, trees only trees. After I got into Zen, mountains were no longer mountains, rivers no longer rivers, trees no longer trees. But when enlightenment happened, mountains were again only mountains, rivers again only rivers, trees again only trees."

Here you can see the same perspective as in the other koan, but there is an additional element—the suggestion of an intermediate stage of growth in the process of enlightenment. If you follow this notion of stages of growth, you find that sacred traditions have very soundly mapped the major landmarks on the spiritual journey. Their "maps" are called, in contemporary language, esoteric/transpersonal psychologies.

In ascending through the higher realms of mind, which are stages of growth as you evolve in consciousness, it can be an enormous help to have a guidebook—something that offers sound advice and trustworthy directions. Of course, as another contributor to this book, Krishnamurti, has said, truth is a pathless land. Or as Thaddeus Golas, author of the brief and witty *The Lazy Man's Guide to Enlightenment*, puts it, enlightenment doesn't care how you get there. All this is perfectly true, but why reinvent the wheel? There are already time-tested and world-honored maps of reality for bringing spiritual travelers through the mazes of mind and labyrinths of inner space with relative ease and safety. The spiritual traveler should take advantage of the best guidance available when the self-realization journey is begun. Appendix I is intended to facilitate access to that guidance.

HUMILITY, SELFLESS SERVICE AND UNCONDITIONAL LOVE

As I said, from the cosmic perspective the human situation is a kind of sleepwalking from which you awaken by grace and no small effort of your own. But it is nothing to be proud of. Since you and all things are ultimately one, a genuine realization of God-as-yourself does not give you exclusive status, however intelligent, talented, charismatic or otherwise distinguished you may be. You realize you are nobody special because, beneath outward form and name, everyone else is also you as expressions of the One Great Being. Thus, the true response to self-realization is humility.

The true response is also selfless service—the behavioral reflection of unconditional love. When you realize your true Self, you automatically respond to the call of humanity. That call, however unconsciously uttered, is: show me the way to God. Thus, the enlightened are more involved in human society than any other group is, even though they may live retiringly or reclusively, because they alone see the truth, beauty and love at the heart of existence. They alone live in accord with that perception to help others change consciousness and thereby discover the essential perfection of all things. Purpose, meaning, direction in life, understanding, happiness— that is what all people are searching for, however ignorantly. And that is what the enlightened seek to help others find, patiently, humbly, lovingly, without concern for a reward or recognition, status or power because ultimately it is all being done for oneself. "By their fruits ye shall know them."

SAVING THE WORLD

Planet Earth today is facing unprecedented threats to life. But those dangers looming over us—socioeconomic, environmental, nuclear/military—are, ironically, productions of our own minds—our ignorance and our self-centeredness. Now, a problem cannot be solved at the level that generated it. And therefore resolution of the dangers facing humanity requires getting beyond the usual mind or self-sense. Political action, social programs, humanitarian work and so forth are good but not enough. Only transformed consciousness can transform the world. The ultimate action, then, is no action at all except to change consciousness. That is what this book is all about.

Enlightenment is liberation, freedom. But so long as one person is not free, no one is free. That is why, throughout history, the truly enlightened have always taken upon themselves a mission of devoted service to the world. Self-realization leads to a transformation of one's total being—both inner awareness and outer behavior. The illusion of separate self melts away. There is a marvelous release from all the corrosive scheming, manipulation, and defensiveness people go through—or rather "e-go" through— to protect their illusory self-image from the truth of existence. Self-pity, self-righteousness, anger, lust, envy, sloth, and so forth evaporate—egoing, egoing, egone! What is left has a human form to ordinary perception. It eats, sleeps, walks, and functions like other human beings. As the koan says, it continues to chop wood and carry water. But the personal has changed into the universal by the recognition of one's total union with the infinite. Energy and intelligence are freed to make heavy work light and to be creative in tasks and relationships. Saintliness and sageliness emerge. Life becomes simple and unitive. The world becomes wonderful, the ordinary becomes extraordinary. Circumstances previously regarded as a problem become a challenge, even an exciting opportunity to learn and to grow and to relieve a bit of the world's burden. There may be unpleasant circumstances, there may be difficult circumstances, but there is no aversion to them and no suffering from them.

THE KEY TO UNDERSTANDING
AND HAPPINESS

Understanding is a function of your state of consciousness. So is happiness. As long as there is an "other" in your consciousness, there will be a limit to your understanding and happiness. Ignorance and suffering are directly proportional to the degree of ego or self-centeredness you bring to your circumstances. But when there is no one but the One, when you are the Self of all, you are infinitely fulfilled, infinitely assured, infinitely happy. In such a state, existence itself is seen to be inherently blissful. Then whatever occurs in your life and whatever you are required to do is perfectly acceptable. Your mere being contributes to the liberation of all and the salvation of the world.

There are many paths up the mountain to enlightenment, as this book shows. But when the paths get to the top, they all come together in the realization that truth is one. That is when the ego dies and you are reborn into life, into reality, as this book also shows. In the enlightened condition, you discover that you are not just the traveler—you are also the path and the mountain. That is why Jesus died on the cross with forgiveness in his heart. That is why *bodhisattvas*, Buddhist saints, vow not to accept final enlightenment until all sentient beings are ready for it first. And it is possible for you to *real*ize that right now because it is your very condition at every moment.

What is enlightenment? Look around you. Everything is yourself. That is it—just that. So open your "I" and see the wonder of chopping wood and carrying water. And then lovingly share it with others.

Now, spiritual traveler, read on . . .

FROM SELF TO
COSMIC CONSCIOUSNESS

R I C H A R D   M .   B U C K E

Cosmic Consciousness, written in 1901, is one of a handful of classic texts that helped give rise to the global consciousness movement now occurring. (William James' 1902 *Varieties of Religious Experience* was another.) In 1872, at age 35, a Canadian psychiatrist named Richard M. Bucke experienced an extraordinary moment of illumination and thereafter devoted himself to the study of the phenomenon that so profoundly altered his life for the better. Surveying human history, he found and described more than a dozen instances of people who displayed what he called cosmic consciousness, a new faculty entering the human race through evolution. He also found several dozen "lesser, imperfect, and doubtful" instances which he likewise cataloged. Among those in full cosmic consciousness, according to Bucke: Buddha, Krishna, Jesus, St. Paul, Plotinus, Mohammed, Dante, St. John of the Cross, William Blake, Walt Whitman, and Madame Guyon.

In this selection, Bucke discusses the characteristics of cosmic consciousness. Two things are worth noting here. First, Bucke's writing style is somewhat foreign to modern sensibilities, but was nevertheless graceful and appropriate for its time. Don't let his stylized use of "he" or "a man" for "the human being" or "people" be an obstacle to appreciating the message.

Second, although Bucke comments that cosmic consciousness "appears in individuals mostly of the male sex," he was not a male chauvinist. He lists three females in the "lesser, imperfect, and doubtful" section, and toward the end of the book comments that he knows a living woman who is a genuine case of cosmic consciousness but who wishes to remain anonymous. It is sad but understandable that Bucke should find so few recorded instances of enlightened women simply because recorded history tended at that time to be male history, ignoring half the human race through a patriarchal bias toward men and men's activities. Ongoing research has begun to rectify the situation (see Appendix 2.) Bucke, however, did the best he could at the time, and the world is all the better for his courageous statement.

I

IF WE ARE RIGHT in [the] assumption [that human evolution has not ceased] new faculties will from time to time arise in the mind as, in the past, new faculties have arisen. This being granted, let us assume that what in this book is called Cosmic Consciousness is such a nascent . . . faculty. And now let us see what we know about this new sense, state, faculty, or whatever it may be called. And, first, it may be noted that the new sense does not appear by chance in this man or that. It is necessary for its appearance that an exalted human personality should exist and supply the preconditions for its birth. In the great cases especially is there an exceptional development of some or all of the ordinary human faculties. Note particularly, since that case in unmistakably known to us, the singular perfection of the intellectual and moral faculties and of the special senses in Walt Whitman. It is probable that an approximation to this evolutionary excellence is necessary in all cases. Then certainly in some, probably in all, cases the person has an exceptional physique—exceptional beauty of build and carriage, exceptionally handsome features, exceptional health, exceptional sweetness of temper, exceptional magnetism.

II

The faculty itself has many names, but they have not been understood or recognized. It will be well to give some of them here. They will be better understood as we advance. Either Gautama [Buddha] himself, or some one of his early disciples, called it "Nirvâna" because of the "extinction" of certain lower mental faculties (such as the sense of sin, fear of death, desire of wealth, etc.) which is directly incident upon its birth. This subjugation of the old personality along with the birth of the new is, in fact, almost equivalent to the annihilation of the old and the creation of a new self. The word "nirvâna" is defined as "the state to which the Buddhist saint is to aspire as the highest aim and highest good." Jesus called the new condition "the Kingdom of God" or the "Kingdom of Heaven," because of the peace and happiness which belong to it, and which are perhaps its most characteristic features. Paul called it "Christ." He speaks of himself as "a man in Christ," of "them that are in Christ." He also calls it "the Spirit" and "the Spirit of God." After Paul had entered Cosmic Consciousness he knew that Jesus had possessed the Cosmic Sense and that he was living (as it were) the life of Jesus—that another individuality, another self, lived in him. This second self he called Christ (the divinely sent deliverer), identifying it not so much with the man Jesus, as with the deliverer which was to be sent and which had been sent in his person, who was both Jesus (the ordinary Self Conscious man) and Messiah (the herald and exemplar of the new, higher race). The duplex personality of men having Cosmic Consciousness will appear many times as we proceed and will be seen to be a constant and

2

prominent phenomenon. Mohammed called the Cosmic Sense "Gabriel," and seems to have looked upon it as a distinctly separate person who lived in him and spoke to him. Dante called it "Beatrice" ("Making Happy"), a name almost or quite equivalent to "Kingdom of Heaven." Balzac called the new man a "specialist" and the new condition "Specialism." Whitman called Cosmic Consciousness "My Soul," but spoke of it as if it were another person; for instance:

> *O soul repressless, I with thee and thou with me. . . .*
> *We too take ship O soul. . . .*
> *With laugh and many a kiss . . .*
> *O soul thou pleasest me, I thee.*

Bacon (in the Sonnets) has treated the Cosmic Sense so emphatically as a distinct person that the world for three hundred years has taken him at his word and has agreed that the "person" in question (whatever his name may have been) was a young friend of the poet's! . . .

III

It has already been incidentally mentioned that when a race enters upon the possession of a new faculty, especially if this be in the line of the direct ascent of the race as is certainly the case with Cosmic Consciousness, the new faculty will necessarily be acquired at first not only by the best specimens of the race but also when these are at their best—that is, at full maturity and before the decline incident to age has set in. What, now, are the facts in this regard as to the coming of the Cosmic Sense?

They may be summarized in a few words as follows: Of thirty-four cases, in which illumination was instantaneous and the period at which it occurred was with some degree of certainty known, the age at which the person passed into Cosmic Consciousness was in one instance twenty-four years; in three, thirty years; in two, thirty-one years; in two, thirty-one and a half years; in three thirty-two years; in one, thirty-three years; in two, thirty-four years; in eight, thirty-five years; in two, thirty-six years; in two, thirty-seven years; in two, thirty-eight years; in three, thirty-nine years; in one, forty years; in one, forty-nine years; and, in one, fifty-four years. . . .

IV

Cosmic Consciousness, then, appears in individuals . . . of good intellect, of high moral qualities, of superior physique. It appears at about that time of life when the organism is at its high-water mark of efficiency, at the age of thirty to forty years. It must have been that the immediate precursor of Cosmic Consciousness—Self Consciousness—also appeared at first in mid-life, here and there, in isolated cases, in the most advanced specimens of the race, becoming more and more nearly universal (as the race grew up to it), manifesting itself at an earlier and earlier age, until (as we see) it declares itself now in every fairly constituted individual, at about the age of three years.

Analogy, then, would lead us to believe that the step in promotion . . . also awaits the whole race—that a time will come when to be without the faculty in question will be a mark of inferiority parallel to the absence at present of the moral nature. The presumption seems to be that the new sense will become more and more common and show itself earlier in life, until after many generations it will appear in each normal individual at the age of puberty or even earlier; then go on becoming still more universal, and appearing at a still earlier age, until, after many thousands of generations, it shows itself immediately after infancy in nearly every member of the race.

V

It must be clearly understood that all cases of Cosmic Consciousness are not on the same plane. Or, if we speak of Simple Consciousness, Self Consciousness and Cosmic Consciousness as each occupying a plane, then, as the range of Self Consciousness on *its plane* (where one man may be an Aristotle, a Cæsar, a Newton, or a Comte, while his neighbor on the next street may be intellectually and morally, to all appearance, little if at all above the animal in his stable) is far greater than the range of Simple Consciousness *in any given species* on its plane, so we must suppose that the range of Cosmic Consciousness (given millions of cases, as on the other planes) is greater than that of Self Consciousness, and it probably is in fact very much greater both in kind and degree: that is to say, given a world peopled with men having Cosmic Consciousness, they would vary both in the way of greater and less intellectual ability, and greater and less moral and spiritual elevation, and also in the way of variety of character, more than would the inhabitants of a planet on the plane of Self Consciousness. Within the plane of Cosmic Consciousness one man shall be a god while another shall not be, to casual observation, lifted so very much above ordinary humanity, however much his inward life may be exalted, strengthened, and purified by the new sense. But, as the Self Conscious man (however degraded) is in fact almost infinitely above the animal with merely Simple Consciousness, so any man permanently endowed with the Cosmic Sense would be almost infinitely higher and nobler than any man who is Self Conscious merely. And not only so, but the man who has had the Cosmic Sense for even a few moments only will probably never again descend to the spiritual level of the merely Self Conscious man; but twenty, thirty, or forty years afterwards he will still feel within him the purifying, strengthening, and exalting effect of that divine illumination, and many of those about him will recognize that his spiritual stature is above that of the average man.

VI

The hypothesis adopted by the present writer requires that cases of Cosmic Consciousness should become more numerous from age to age, and not only so but that they should become more perfect, more pronounced. What are the facts? Putting aside minor cases, such as must have appeared and been forgotten by hundreds in the last few millenniums, of those given above at least thirteen, are so great that they can never fade from human memory— namely: Gautama [Buddha], Jesus, Paul, Plotinus, Mohammed, Dante, Las Casas, John Yepes, Francis Bacon, Jacob Behmen, William Blake, Balzac, and Walt Whitman.

From Gautama [Buddha] to Dante we count eighteen hundred years, within which period we have five cases. Again, from Dante to the present day we count six hundred years, in which we have eight cases. That is to say, while in the earlier period there was one case to every three hundred and sixty years, in the later there was a case to each seventy-five years. In other words, Cosmic Consciousness has been 4.8 times more frequent during the latter period than it was during the former. And before the time of Gautama [Buddha]? There were probably no, or few and imperfectly developed, cases.

We know that at present there are many of what may be called lesser cases, but the number of these cannot be compared with the number of similar cases in the past, for the reason that the latter are lost. It must also be remembered that the thirteen "great cases" given above are only perhaps a small fraction of cases just as great which have occurred since the time of Gautama [Buddha], for probably only a small proportion of the "great cases" undertake and carry through work which ensures them remembrance. How easily might the memory even of Jesus have been obliterated from the minds of his contemporaries and followers almost before it was born. Many today think that, all else granted, if he had not been immediately followed by Paul, his work and name would have expired together almost with the generation that heard him speak. . . .

VII

It seems that in every, or nearly every, man who enters into Cosmic Consciousness apprehension is at first more or less excited, the person doubting whether the new sense may not be a symptom or form of insanity. Mohammed was greatly alarmed. I think it is clear that Paul was, and others to be mentioned further on were similarly affected.

The first thing each person asks himself upon experiencing the new sense is: Does what I see and feel represent reality or am I suffering from a delusion? The fact that the new experience seems even more real than the old teachings of Simple and Self Consciousness does not at first fully reassure him, because he probably knows that delusions, when present, possess the mind just as firmly as do actual facts.

True or not true, each person who has the experience in question eventually, perforce, believes in its teachings, accepting them as absolutely as any other teachings whatsoever. This, however, would not prove them true, since the same might be said of the delusions of the insane.

How, then, shall we know that this is a new sense, revealing fact, and not a form of insanity, plunging its subject into delusion? In the first place, the tendencies of the condition in question are entirely unlike, even opposite to, those of mental alienation, these last being distinctly amoral or even immoral, while the former are moral in a very high degree. In the second place, while in all forms of insanity self-restraint—inhibition—is greatly reduced, sometimes even abolished, in Cosmic Consciousness it is enormously increased. The absolute proof of this last statement can be found in the lives of the men here cited as examples In the third place (whatever the scoffers of religion may say) it is certain that modern civilization (speaking broadly) rests (as already said) very largely on the teachings of the new sense. The *masters* are taught by it and the rest of the world by them through their books, followers and disciples, so that if what is here called Cosmic Consciousness is a form of insanity, we are confronted by the terrible fact (were it not an absurdity) that our civilization, including all our highest religions, rests on delusion. But (in the fourth place), far from granting, or for a moment entertaining, such an awful alternative, it can be maintained that we have the same evidence of the objective reality which corresponds to this faculty that we have of the reality which tallies any other sense or faculty whatever. Sight, for instance: You know that the tree standing there across the field, half a mile away, is real and not an hallucination because all other persons having the sense of sight to whom you have spoken about it also see it; while if it were an hallucination it would be visible to no one but yourself. By the same method of reasoning do we establish the reality of the objective universe tallying Cosmic Consciousness. Each person who has the faculty is made aware by it of essentially the same fact or facts. If three men looked at the tree and were asked half an hour afterwards to draw or describe it the three drafts or descriptions would not tally in detail, but in general outline would correspond. Just in the same way do the reports of those who have had Cosmic Consciousness correspond in all essentials, though in detail they doubtless more or less diverge (but these divergences are fully as much in our misunderstanding of the reports as in the reports themselves). So there is no instance of a person who has been illumined denying or disputing the teaching of another who has passed through the same experience. . . .

VIII

As has been either said or implied already, in order that a man may enter into Cosmic Consciousness he must belong (so to speak) to the top layer of the world of Self Consciousness. Not that he need have an extraordinary intellect (this faculty is rated usually far above its real value and does not seem nearly so important, from this point of view, as do some others), though he must not be deficient in this respect, either. He must have a good physique, good health, but above all he must have an exalted moral nature, strong sympathies, a warm heart, courage, strong, and earnest religious feeling. All these being granted, and the man having reached the age necessary to bring him to the top of the Self Conscious mental stratum, some day he enters Cosmic Consciousness. What is his experience? Details must be given with diffidence, as they are only known to the writer in a few cases, and doubtless the phenomena are varied and diverse. What is said here, however, may be depended on as far as it goes. It is true of certain cases, and certainly touches upon the full truth in certain other cases, so that it may be looked upon as being provisionally correct.

  a. The person, suddenly, without warning, has a sense of being immersed in a flame, or rose-colored cloud, or perhaps rather a sense that the mind is itself filled with such a cloud or haze.

  b. At the same instant he is, as it were, bathed in an emotion of joy, assurance, triumph, "salvation." The last word is not strictly correct if

taken in its ordinary sense, for the feeling, when fully developed, is not
that a particular act of salvation is effected, but that no special "salvation" is needed, the scheme upon which the world is built being itself
sufficient. It is this ecstasy, far beyond any that belongs to the merely
Self Conscious life, with which the *poets,* as such, especially occupy
themselves: As Gautama [Buddha], in his discourses, preserved in the
"Suttas"; Jesus in the "Parables"; Paul in the "Epistles"; Dante at the
end of the "Purgatorio" and beginning of "Paradiso"; Shakespeare in
the "Sonnets"; Balzac in "Seraphita"; Whitman in the "Leaves"; Edward Carpenter in "Towards Democracy"; leaving to the *singers* the
pleasures and pains, loves and hates, joys and sorrows, peace and war,
life and death, of Self Conscious man; though the *poets* may treat of
these, too, but from the new point of view, as expressed in the
"Leaves": "I will never again mention love or death inside a house"—
that is, from the old point of view, with the old connotations.

Simultaneously or instantly following the above sense and emotional
experiences there comes to the person an intellectual illumination quite
impossible to describe. Like a flash there is presented to his consciousness a clear conception (a vision) in outline of the meaning and drift of
the universe. He does not come to believe merely; but he sees and
knows that the cosmos, which to the Self Conscious mind seems made
up of dead matter, is in fact far otherwise—is in very truth a living
presence. He sees that instead of men being, as it were, patches of life
scattered through an infinite sea of nonliving substance, they are in
reality specks of relative death in an infinite ocean of life. He sees that
the life which is in man is eternal, as all life is eternal; that the soul of
man is as immortal as God is; that the universe is so built and ordered
that without any peradventure all things work together for the good of
each and all; that the foundation principle of the world is what we call
love, and that the happiness of every individual is in the long run
absolutely certain. The person who passes through this experience will
learn in the few minutes, or even moments, of its continuance more
than in months or years of study, and he will learn much that no study
ever taught or can teach. Especially does he obtain such a conception of
the whole, or at least of an immense *whole,* as dwarfs all conception,
imagination or speculation, springing from and belonging to ordinary
Self Consciousness, such a conception as makes the old attempts to
mentally grasp the universe and its meaning petty and even ridiculous.

This awakening of the intellect has been well described by a writer
upon Jacob Behmen in these words: "The mysteries of which he
discoursed were not reported to him, he *beheld* them. He saw the root

of all mysteries, the *Ungrund* or *Urgrund,* whence issue all contrasts and discordant principles, hardness and softness, severity and mildness, sweet and bitter, love and sorrow, heaven and hell. These he *saw* in their origin; these he attempted to describe in their issue and to reconcile in their eternal results. He saw into the being of God; whence the birth or going forth of the divine manifestation. Nature lay unveiled to him—he was at home in the heart of things. His own book, which he himself was (so Whitman: 'This is no book; who touches this touches a man') the microcosm of man, with his three-fold life, was patent to his vision."

d. Along with moral elevation and intellectual illumination comes what must be called, for want of a better term, a sense of immortality. This is not an intellectual conviction, such as comes with the solution of a problem, nor is it an experience such as learning something unknown before. It is far more simple and elementary, and could better be compared to that certainty of distinct individuality, possessed by each one, which comes with and belongs to Self Consciousness.

e. With illumination the fear of death which haunts so many men and women at times all their lives falls off like an old cloak—not, however, as a result of reasoning—it simply vanishes.

f. The same may be said of the sense of sin. It is not that the person escapes from sin; but he no longer sees that there is any sin in the world from which to escape.

g. The instantaneousness of the illumination is one of its most striking features. It can be compared with nothing so well as with a dazzling flash of lightning in a dark night, bringing the landscape which had been hidden into clear view.

h. The previous character of the man who enters the new life is an important element in the case.

i. So is the age at which illumination occurs. Should we hear of a case of Cosmic Consciousness occuring at twenty, for instance, we should at first doubt the truth of the account, and if forced to believe it we should expect the man (if he lived) to prove himself, in some way, a veritable spiritual giant.

j. The added charm to the personality of the person who attains to Cosmic Consciousness is always, it is believed, a feature in the case.

k. There seems to the writer to be sufficient evidence that with Cosmic Consciousness, while it is actually present, and lasting (gradually passing away) a short time thereafter, a change takes place in the appearance of the subject of illumination. This change is similar to that caused in a person's appearance by great joy, but at times (that is, in pronounced cases) it seems to be much more marked than that. In these great cases in which illumination is intense the change in question is also intense and may amount to a veritable "transfiguration." Dante says that he was "transhumanized into a God." There seems to be a strong probability that could he have been seen at that moment he would have exhibited what could only have been called "transfiguration."

The passage from Self to Cosmic Consciousness, considered from the point of view of the intellect, seems to be a phenomenon strictly parallel to the passage from Simple to Self Consciousness.

As in the latter, so in the former, there are two chief elements:

a. Added consciousness.
b. Added faculty.
a. When an organism which possesses Simple Consciousness only, attains to Self Consciousness, it becomes aware for the first time that it is a separate creature, or *self* existing in a world which is apart from it. That is, the oncoming of the new faculty instructs it without any new experience or process of learning.
b. It, at the same time, acquires enormously increased powers of accumulating knowledge and of initiating action.

So when a person who was Self Conscious only, enters into Cosmic Consciousness—

a. He knows without learning (from the mere fact of illumination) certain things, as, for instance: (1) that the universe is not a dead machine but a living presence; (2) that in its essence and tendency it is infinitely good; (3) that individual existence is continuous beyond what is called death. At the same time:
b. He takes on enormously greater capacity both for learning and initiating.

X

The parallel holds also from the point of view of the moral nature. For the animal that has Simple Consciousness merely cannot possibly know anything of the pure delight in simply living that is possessed (at least part of the time) by every healthy, well-constituted young or middle-aged man or woman. "Cannot possibly," for this feeling depends on Self Consciousness and without that can have no existence. The horse or dog enjoys life while experiencing an agreeable sensation or when stimulated by an agreeable activity (really the same thing), but cannot realize that everyday calm in the enjoyment of life, independent of the senses, and of outward things, which belongs to the moral nature (the basic fact, indeed of the *positive* side of this), starting, as may be truly said, from the central well-spring of the life of the organism (the sense of *bien-être*—"well-being") that belongs to man as man and is in truth one of his valued heritages. This constitutes a plane or plateau, in the region of the moral nature, upon which the sentient creature steps when passing, or as it passes, from Simple to Self Consciousness.

Corresponding with this moral ascent and with those steps, above noted, taken by the intellect from Simple to Self, and from Self to Cosmic Consciousness, is the moral ascent that belongs to the passage from Self to Cosmic Consciousness. This can only be realized, therefore only described, by those who have passed through the experience. What do they say about it? Well, read what Gautama [Buddha] and the illuminati of the Buddhists tell us of Nirvâna; namely, that it is the "highest happiness." Says the unknown, but unquestionably illumined writer, in the Mahabbharata: "The devotee, whose happiness is within himself, and whose light [of knowledge] also is within himself, becoming one with the Brahman, obtains the Brahmic bliss." Note the dicta of Jesus on the value of the "Kingdom of Heaven," to purchase which a man sells all that he has; remember the worth that Paul ascribes to "Christ," and how he was caught up into the third heaven; reflect on Dante's "transhumanization" from a man "into a God," and on the name he gives the Cosmic Sense: Beatrice—"Making Happy." Here, too, is his distinct statement of the joy that belongs to it: "That which I was seeing seemed to me a smile of the universe, for my inebriation was entering through the hearing and through the sight. O joy! O ineffable gladness! O life entire of love and of peace! O riches secure without longing!" See what Behmen says on the same subject:" "Earthly language is entirely insufficient to describe what there is of joy, happiness, and loveliness contained in the inner wonders of God. Even if the eternal Virgin pictures them to our minds, man's constitution is too cold and dark to be able to express even a spark of it in his language." Observe Elukhanam's oft-repeated exclamation: "Sando-siam, Sandosiam Eppotham"—"Joy, always joy." And again Edward Carpenter's "All sorrow finished," "The deep, deep ocean of joy within," "Being filled with joy," "singing joy unending." Above all, bear in mind the testimony of Walt Whitman—testimony unvarying, though given in ever-varying language, and upon almost every page of the "Leaves," covering forty years of life: "I am satisfied—I see, dance, laugh, sing." "Wandering, amazed at my own lightness and glee." "O the joy of my spirit—it is uncaged—it darts like lightning." "I float this carol with joy, with joy to thee, O death." And that forecast of the future taken from his own heart—that future "when through these states walk a hundred millions of superb persons"—that is, persons possessed of the Cosmic Sense. And finally: "The ocean filled with joy—the atmosphere all joy! Joy, joy, in freedom, worship, love! Joy in the ecstasy of life: Enough to merely be! Enough to breathe! Joy, Joy! All over joy!"

XI

"Well," someone will say, "if these people see and know and feel so much, why don't they come out with it in plain language and give the world the benefit of it?" This is what "speech" said to Whitman: "Walt, you contain enough, why don't you let it out, then?" But he tells us:

> *"When I undertake to tell the best I find I cannot,*
> *My tongue is ineffectual on its pivots,*
> *My breath will not be obedient to its organs,*
> *I become a dumb man."*

So Paul, when he was "caught up into paradise," heard "unspeakable words." And Dante was not able to recount the things he saw in heaven. "My vision," he says, "was greater than *our speech*, which yields to such a sight." And so of the rest. The fact of the matter is not difficult to understand; it is that speech (as fully explained above) is the tally of the Self Conscious intellect, can express that and nothing but that, does not tally and cannot express the Cosmic Sense—or, if at all, only insofar as this may be translated into terms of the Self Conscious intellect.

XII

It will be well to state here (partly in recapitulation) for the benefit of the reader . . . briefly and explicitly, the marks of the Cosmic Sense. They are:

   a. The subjective light.
   b. The moral elevation.
   c. The intellectual illumination.
   d. The sense of immortality.

e. The loss of the fear of death.

f. The loss of the sense of sin.

g. The suddenness, instantaneousness, of the awakening.

h. The previous character of the man—intellectual, moral, and physical

i. The age of illumination.

j. The added charm to the personality so that men and women are always (?) strongly attracted to the person.

k. The transfiguration of the subject of the change as seen by others when the Cosmic Sense is actually present.

. . . everything in this universe, at any moment, is exactly where it should be; it may not suit us, it may not be convenient to us, but it is a fact once you grant that there is a divine Will which is effectuating itself, that governs. When you look at one point or two points in the large process, you may find things disharmonious, but from another point of view things are as they are all in the melting pot; they are in the midst of a process and at the right moment they will emerge into the intended pattern. All the dualities, all the opposites in the universe are temporary formations; we do not need to plead for God when critics point to the existence of sorrow, pain and evil—they are incidentals, they are temporary formations. The sense of evil, the sense of injustice, of suffering were not there before the human mind with its ego arrived on the scene. And they will not be there once man transcends this mind of ego and desire. They are temporary phenomena of which men are apt to make too much. The existence of these temporary phenomena cannot stand in the way of recognizing the existence of an Omnipresent Reality.

M.P. PANDIT

THIS IS IT

A L A N   W.   W A T T S

Some people mistakenly regard the quest for enlightenment as infantile regression or otherworldly escapism. It is none of that. Enlightenment, Alan Watts points out here, is the very essence of what is happening here and now throughout the cosmos. It therefore includes all planes and worlds, from the gross material to the exalted and ethereal, but at the same time it transcends them. Enlightenment is that state of awareness which lights all creation, making it clear and understandable, accessible to vision by the inner eye. And what the inner eye sees is this: I am the universe; I am present everywhere. Thus it is paradoxical that the enlightened, although beyond the entire realm of space, time and causality in their consciousness, are at the same time more *in* the world than anyone else. When you realize yourself to be infinite and eternal, when you have nowhere to go and nothing to seek, you become, in the most fundamental sense, here and now, completely at home in the universe.

In this selection Watts elucidates the relationship between ordinary awareness and cosmic consciousness, and shows that enlightenment is none other than your everyday mind, but *realized as such*. Where does mind end? Where does self end? They don't—they are infinite and eternal. In truth, then, the ordinary is extraordinary. Enlightenment is simply surrendering yourself to what is already the case. Here-and-now is It, perfect in all its apparent imperfection. As a wise yogi once said, there is nothing wrong with the world but your attitude toward it. If the creation is perfect, if you are in essence already perfectly enlightened, the question of how to experience enlightenment is not primarily a matter of "What should I do in the future to get it?" but rather, "What am I *presently* doing that prevents me from realizing It is so right now?" The answer: everything about us that is ego-based, separative, and resistant to recognizing the intelligence that lives in us all—the Love, as Dante put it at the end of *The Divine Comedy*, "to which all creation moves."

THE MOST IMPRESSIVE FACT in man's spiritual, intellectual, and poetic experience has always been, for me, the universal prevalence of those astonishing moments of insight which Richard Bucke called "cosmic consciousness." There is no really satisfactory name for this type of experience. To call it mystical is to confuse it with visions of another world, or of gods and

14

angels. To call it spiritual or metaphysical is to suggest that it is not also extremely concrete and physical, while the term "cosmic consciousness" itself has the unpoetic flavor of occultist jargon. But from all historical times and cultures we have reports of this same unmistakable sensation emerging, as a rule, quite suddenly and unexpectedly and from no clearly understood cause.

To the individual thus enlightened it appears as a vivid and overwhelming certainty that the universe, precisely as it is at this moment, as a whole and in every one of its parts, is so completely *right* as to need no explanation or justification beyond what it simply is. Existence not only ceases to be a problem; the mind is so wonder-struck at the self-evident and self-sufficient fitness of things as they are, including what would ordinarily be thought the very worst, that it cannot find any word strong enough to express the perfection and beauty of the experience. Its clarity sometimes gives the sensation that the world has become transparent or luminous, and its simplicity the sensation that it is pervaded and ordered by a supreme intelligence. At the same time it is usual for the individual to feel that the whole world has become his own body, and that whatever he is has not only become, but always has been, what everything else is. It is not that he loses his identity to the point of feeling that he actually looks out through all other eyes, becoming literally omniscient, but rather that his individual consciousness and existence is a point of view temporarily adopted by something immeasurably greater than himself.

The central core of the experience seems to be the conviction, or insight, that the immediate *now*, whatever its nature, is the goal and fulfillment of all living. Surrounding and flowing from this insight is an emotional ecstasy, a sense of intense relief, freedom, and lightness, and often of almost unbearable love for the world, which is, however, secondary. Often, the pleasure of the experience is confused with the experience and the insight lost in the ecstasy, so that in trying to retain the secondary effects of the experience the individual misses its point—that the immediate *now* is complete even when it is not ecstatic. For ecstasy is a necessarily impermanent contrast in the constant fluctuation of our feelings. But insight, when clear enough, persists; having once understood a particular skill, the facility tends to remain.

The terms in which a man interprets this experience are naturally drawn from the religious and philosophical ideas of his culture, and their differences often conceal its basic indentity. As water seeks the course of least resistance, so the emotions clothe themselves in the symbols that lie most readily to hand, and the association is so swift and automatic that the symbol may appear to be the very heart of the experience. Clarity—the disappearance of problems—suggests light, and in moments of such acute clarity there may be the physical sensation of light penetrating everything. To a theist this will naturally seem to be a glimpse of the presence of God, as in the celebrated testimony of Pascal:

> The year of grace 1654,
> Monday the 23rd of November, St. Clement's day. . . .
> From about half past ten in the evening
> until about half past twelve, midnight,
>   FIRE
> God of Abraham. God of Isaac. God of Jacob
>   not of the philosophers and the wise.
> Certainty, joy, certainty, feeling, joy, peace.

Or in a case quoted by William James:

> The very heavens seemed to open and pour down rays of light and glory. Not for a moment only, but all day and night, floods of light and glory seemed to pour through my soul, and oh, how I was changed, and everything became new. My horses and hogs and everybody seemed changed.

But clarity may also suggest transparency, or the sense that the world confronting us is no longer an obstacle and the body no longer a burden, and to a Buddhist this will just as naturally call to mind the doctrine of reality as the ungraspable, indefinable Void *(sunyata)*.

> I came back into the hall and was about to go to my seat when the whole outlook changed. A broad expanse opened, and the ground appeared as if all caved in. . . . As I looked around and up and down, the whole universe with its multitudinous sense-objects now appeared quite different; what was loathsome before, together with ignorance and passions, was now seen to be nothing else but the outflow of my own inmost nature which in itself remained bright, true, and transparent.[1]

As one and the same pain may be described either as a hot pang or as a cold sting, so the descriptions of this experience may take forms that seem to be completely opposed. One person may say that he has found the answer to the whole mystery of life, but somehow cannot put it into words. Another will say that there never was a mystery and thus no answer to it, for what the experience made clear to him was the irrelevance and artificiality of all our questions. One declares himself convinced that there is no death, his true self being as eternal as the universe. Another states that death has simply ceased to matter, because the present moment is so complete that it requires no future. One feels himself taken up and united with a life infinitely other

[1]Yüan-chou (*d.* 1287), quoted by Suzuki, *Essays in Zen Buddhism*, Vol. 2, p. 92.

than his own. But as the beating of the heart may be regarded as something that *happens* to you or something that you *do,* depending on the point of view, so another will feel that he has experienced, not a transcendent God, but his own inmost nature. One will get the sense that his ego or self has expanded to become the entire universe, whereas another will feel that he has lost himself altogether and that what he called his ego was never anything but an abstraction. One will describe himself as infinitely enriched, while another will speak of being brought to such absolute poverty that he owns not even his mind and body, and has not a care in the world.

Rarely is the experience described without metaphors that might be misleading if taken literally. But in reading Bernard Berenson's *Sketch for a Self-Portrait* I came across a passage which is one of the simplest and "cleanest" accounts of it I have ever seen.

> It was a morning in early summer. A silver haze shimmered and trembled over the lime trees. The air was laden with their fragrance. The temperature was like a caress. I remember—I need not recall—that I climbed up a tree stump and felt suddenly immersed in Itness. I did not call it by that name. I had no need for words. It and I were one.[2]

Just "It"—as when we use the word to denote the superlative, or the exact point, or intense reality, or what we were always looking for. Not the neuter sense of the mere object, but something still more alive and far wider than the personal, and for which we use this simplest of words because we have no word for it.

It is especially difficult to find the right means of expression for the experience in the cultural context of Christianity. For while this enlightenment comes just as much to Christians as to anyone else, the Christian mystic has always been in danger of conflict with the defenders of orthodoxy. Christian dogmatics insist firmly upon the radical difference between God and his created universe, as between God and the human soul. They insist upon God's eternal opposition to and abhorrence of evil and sin, and, since these are very present realities, upon the effective salvation of the world only at the end of time. Even then, hell will remain forever as the state of permanent imprisonment and torment for the forces of evil. Nevertheless, the doctrine of omnipotence—that nothing, not even sin, can happen without the permission of God's will—makes it possible even in this difficult framework for the Christian mystic to express the unspeakable doctrine that "sin is behovable, but all shall be well, and all shall be well, and all manner of thing shall be well."[3]

[2]Bernard Berenson, *Sketch for a Self-Portrait* (New York: Pantheon Books, 1949), p. 18.

Alan W. Watts

The Christian sense of the reality of evil and of time and history as the process of overcoming evil remains with us so strongly even in the post-Christian intellectual climate of today that we have difficulty in accepting the "cosmic consciousness" as more than an inspiring hallucination. Admissible it may be as the vision of some "far-off divine event" in the future, but with our progressive view of the world it seems impossible to accept it as a vision of the way things *are*. Even in the description which Bucke gives of his own experience there is a significant use of the future tense:

> All at once, without warning of any kind, I found myself wrapped in a flame-colored cloud. For an instant I thought of fire, an immense conflagration somewhere close by in the great city; the next, I knew that the fire was within myself. Directly afterward there came upon me a sense of exultation, of immense joyousness accompanied or immediately followed by an intellectual illumination impossible to describe. Among other things, I did not merely come to believe, but I saw that the universe is not composed of dead matter, but is, on the contrary, a living Presence; I became conscious in myself of eternal life. It was not a conviction that I would have eternal life, but a consciousness that I possessed eternal life then; I saw that all men are immortal; that the cosmic order is such that without any peradventure all things work together for the good of each and all; that the foundation principle of the world, of all the worlds, is what we call love, and that the happiness of each and all is *in the long run* absolutely certain. The vision lasted a few seconds and was gone; but the memory of it and the sense of the reality of what it taught has remained during the quarter of a century which has since elapsed.[4]

Nevertheless, the "consciousness that I possessed eternal life *then*" corresponds to the Buddhist realization that "all things are in Nirvana from the very beginning," and that the enlightenment or awakening is not the creation of a new state of affairs but the recognition of what always is.

Such experiences imply, then, that our normal perception and valuation of the world is a subjective but collective nightmare. They suggest that our ordinary sense of practical reality—of the world as seen on Monday morning—is a construct of socialized conditioning and repression, a system of selective inattention whereby we are taught to screen out aspects and relations within nature which do not accord with the rules of the game of civilized life. Yet the vision almost invariably includes the realization that

[3]Dame Julian of Norwich (c. 1342–1414), *Revelations of Divine Love*, xxvii. Ed. Grace Warrack. London, 1949. "Behovable" has the sense of "playing a necessary part." Compare the celebrated passage in the Roman liturgy of Holy Saturday, "O truly necessary sin of Adam, which the death of Christ has blotted out! O happy fault, that merited such and so great a redeemer!"

[4]Quoted from a privately printed account of the experience by William James, *Varieties of Religious Experience* (London, 1929), p. 399. Italics mine.

this very restriction of consciousness is also part of the eternal fitness of things. In the words of the Zen master Gensha:

> If you understand, things are such as they are;
> If you do not understand, things are such as they are—

this "such as they are" being the utterly unproblematic and self-sufficient character of this eternal now in which, as Chuang-tzu said,

> A duck's legs, though short, cannot be lengthened without discomfort to the duck; a crane's legs, though long, cannot be shortened without discomfort to the crane.

For in some way the vision seems to come about through accepting the rightness of the fact that one does not have it, through being willing to be as imperfect as one is—perfectly imperfect.

Now it is easy to see how this way of seeing things might be acceptable in cultures without the sense of hope and history, how, indeed, it might be the only basis for a philosophy that would make life tolerable. Indeed, it is very probable that the "historical dynamism" of the Christian West is a rather recent theological discovery, for we can no longer sing, without qualms of the social conscience, the *laissez-faire* hymn which says:

> *The rich man in his castle, the poor man at his gate,*
> *He made them high or lowly, and ordered their estate—*

and then go on to exclaim:

> *All things bright and beautiful, all creatures great and small,*
> *All things wise and wonderful, the Lord God made them all!*

But, even though it may be exploited for this purpose, the experience itself is in no sense a philosophy designed to justify or to desensitize oneself to the inequalities of life. Like falling in love, it has a minimal connection with any particular cultural background or economic position. It descends upon the rich and the poor, the moral and the immoral, the happy and the miserable without distinction. It carries with it the overwhelming conviction that the world is in every respect a miracle of glory, and though this might logically exclude the necessity to share the vision with others and awaken them from their nightmare, the usual reaction is a sense not of duty, but of sheer delight in communicating the experience by word or deed.

From this new perspective the crimes and follies of man's ordinary nightmare life seem neither evil nor stupid but simply pitiable. One has the extraordinarily odd sensation of seeing people in their mean or malicious pursuits looking, at the same time, like gods—as if they were supremely happy without knowing it. As Kirillov puts it in Dostoyevsky's *The Possessed,*

> "Man is unhappy because he doesn't know he's happy. It's only that. That's all, that's all! If anyone finds out he'll become happy at once, that minute. . . . It's all good. I discovered it all of a sudden."
>
> "And if anyone dies of hunger," [asks Stavrogin], "and if anyone insults and outrages the little girl, is that good?"
>
> "Yes! And if anyone blows his brains out for the baby, that's good too. And if anyone doesn't, that's good too. It's all good, all. It's good for all those who know that it's all good. If they knew that it was good for them, it would be good for them, but as long as they don't know it's good for them, it will be bad for them. That's the whole idea, the whole of it! . . . They're bad because they don't know they're good. When they find out, they won't outrage a little girl. They'll find out that they're good and they'll all become good, every one of them."[5]

Ordinarily one might feel that there is a shocking contrast between the marvelous structure of the human organism and its brain, on the one hand, and the uses to which most people put it, on the other. Yet there could perhaps be a point of view from which the natural wonder of the organism simply outshines the degrading performances of its superficial consciousness. In a somewhat similar way this strange opening of vision does not permit attention to remain focused narrowly upon the details of evil; they become subordinate to the all-pervading intelligence and beauty of the total design.

Such insight has not the slightest connection with "shallow optimism" nor with grasping the meaning of the universe in terms of some neat philosophical simplification. Beside it, *all* philosophical opinions and disputations sound like somewhat sophisticated versions of children yelling back and forth—"'Tis!" "'Tisn't!" "'Tis!" "'Tisn't!"—until (if only the philosophers would do likewise) they catch the nonsense of it and roll over backwards with hoots of laughter. Furthermore, so far from being the smug rationalization of a Mr. Pangloss, the experience has a tendency to arise in situations of total extremity or despair, when the individual finds himself without any alternative but to surrender himself entirely.

Something of this kind came to me in a dream when I was about eight years old. I was sick at the time and almost delirious with fever, and in the dream I found myself attached, face-downward and spread-eagled, to an

---

[5]Dostoyevsky, *The Possessed*, pp. 240–41. Trans. Constance Garnett (Modern Library, New York, 1936).

immense ball of steel which was spinning about the earth. I knew in this dream with complete certainty that I was doomed to be spun in this sickening and terrifying whirl forever and ever, and the conviction was so intense that there was nothing for it but to give up—for this was hell itself and nothing lay before me but a literal everlastingness of pain. But in the moment when I surrendered, the ball seemed to strike against a mountain and disintegrate, and the next thing I knew was that I was sitting on a stretch of warm sand with nothing left of the ball except crumpled fragments of sheet metal scattered around me. This was not, of course, the experience of "cosmic consciousness," but simply of the fact that release in extremity lies through and not away from the problem.

That other experience came much later, twice with intensity, and other times with what might be called more of a glow than a brilliant flash. Shortly after I had first begun to study Indian and Chinese philosophy, I was sitting one night by the fire, trying to make out what was the right attitude of mind of meditation as it is practiced in Hindu and Buddhist disciplines. It seemed to me that several attitudes were possible, but as they appeared mutually exclusive and contradictory I was trying to fit them into one—all to no purpose. Finally, in sheer disgust, I decided to reject them all and to have no special attitude of mind whatsoever. In the force of throwing them away it seemed that I threw myself away as well, for quite suddenly the weight of my own body disappeared. I felt that I owned nothing, not even a self, and that nothing owned me. The whole world became as transparent and unobstructed as my own mind; the "problem of life" simply ceased to exist, and for about eighteen hours I and everything around me felt like the wind blowing leaves across a field on an autumn day.

The second time, a few years later, came after a period when I had been attempting to practice what Buddhists call "recollection" *(smriti)* or constant awareness of the immediate present, as distinct from the usual distracted rambling of reminiscence and anticipation. But, in discussing it one evening, someone said to me, "But why *try* to live in the present? Surely we are always completely *in* the present even when we're thinking about the past or the future?" This, actually quite obvious, remark again brought on the sudden sensation of having no weight. At the same time, the present seemed to become a kind of moving stillness, an eternal stream from which neither I nor anything could deviate. I saw that everything, just as it is now, is IT—is the whole point of there being life and a universe. I saw that when the *Upanishads* said, "That art thou!" or "All this world is Brahman," they meant just exactly what they said. Each thing, each event, each experience in its inescapable nowness and in all its own particular individuality, was precisely what it should be, and so much so that it acquired a divine authority

21

and originality. It struck me with the fullest clarity that none of this depended on my seeing it to be so; that was the way things were, whether I understood it or not, and if I did not understand, that was IT too. Furthermore, I felt that I now understood what Christianity might mean by the love of God—namely, that despite the commonsensical imperfection of things, they were nonetheless loved by God just as they are, and that this loving of them was at the same time the godding of them. This time the vivid sensation of lightness and clarity lasted a full week.

These experiences, reinforced by others that have followed, have been the enlivening force of all my work in writing and in philosophy since that time, though I have come to realize that how I *feel*, whether the actual sensation of freedom and clarity is present or not, is not the point—for, again, to feel heavy or restricted is also IT. But with this point of departure a philosopher is faced with a strange problem of communication, especially to the degree that his philosophy seems to have some affinity with religion. People appear to be under the fixed impression that one speaks or writes of these things in order to improve them or do them some good, assuming, too, that the speaker has himself been improved and is able to speak with authority. In other words, the philosopher is forced into the role of preacher, and is in turn expected to practice what he preaches. Thereupon the truth of what he says is tested by his character and his morals—whether he shows anxiety or not, whether he depends upon "material crutches" such as wine or tobacco, whether he has stomach ulcers or likes money, whether he loses his temper, or gets depressed, or falls in love when he shouldn't, or sometimes looks a bit tired and frayed at the edges. All these criteria might be valid if the philosopher were preaching freedom from being human, or if he were trying to make himself and others radically better.

In the span of one lifetime it is, of course, possible for almost every human being to improve himself—within limits set by energy, time, temperament, and the level from which he begins. Obviously, then, there is a proper place for preachers and other technical advisers in the disciplines of human betterment. But the limits within which such improvements may be made are small in comparison with the vast aspects of our nature and our circumstances which remain the same, and which will be very difficult to improve even were it desirable to do so. I am saying, therefore, that while there is a place for bettering oneself and others, solving problems and coping with situations is by no means the only or even the chief business of life. Nor is it the principal work of philosophy.

Human purposes are pursued within an immense circling universe which does not seem to me to have purpose, in our sense, at all. Nature is much more playful than purposeful, and the probability that it has no special goals for the future need not strike one as a defect. On the contrary, the processes of nature as we see them both in the surrounding world and in the involuntary aspects of our own organisms are much more like art than like business, politics, or religion. They are especially like the arts of music and dancing, which unfold themselves without aiming at future destinations. No one imagines that a symphony is supposed to improve in quality as it goes along, or that the whole object of playing it is to reach the finale. The point of music is discovered in every moment of playing and listening to it. It is the same, I feel, with the greater part of our lives, and if we are unduly absorbed in improving them we may forget altogether to live them. The musician whose chief concern is to make every performance better than the last may so fail to participate and delight in his own music that he will impress his audience only with the anxious rigor of his technique.

Thus it is by no means the main work of a philosopher to be classed with the moralists and reformers. There is such a thing as philosophy, the love of wisdom, in the spirit of the artist. Such philosophy will not preach or advocate practices leading to improvement. As I understand it, the work of the philosopher as artist is to reveal and celebrate the eternal and purposeless background of human life. Out of simple exuberance or wonder he wants to tell others of the point of view from which the world is unimaginably good as it is, with people just as they are. No matter how difficult it may be to express this point of view without sounding smug or appearing to be a wishful dreamer, some hint of it may be suggested if the philosopher has had the good fortune to have experienced it himself.

This may sound like a purpose, like a desire to improve, to those who insist upon seeing all human activity in terms of goal-seeking. The trouble is that our Western common sense is firmly Aristotelian, and we therefore believe that the will never acts except for some good or pleasure. But upon analysis this turns out to say no more than that we do what we do, for if we *always* do what pleases us—even in committing suicide—there is no means of showing what pleases us apart from what we do. In using such logic I am only throwing a stone back to the glass house from which it came, for I am well aware that expressions of mystical experience will not stand the test of logic. But, unlike the Aristotelian, the mystic does not claim to be logical. His sphere of experience is the unspeakable. Yet this need mean no more than that it is the sphere of physical nature, of all that is not simply conceptions, numbers, or words.

If the experience of "cosmic consciousness" is unspeakable, it is true that in trying to utter it in words one is not "saying" anything in the sense of conveying information or making a proposition. The speech expressing such an experience is more like an exclamation. Or better, it is the speech of

23

poetry rather than logic, though not poetry in the impoverished sense of the logical positivist, the sense of decorative and beautiful nonsense. For there is a kind of speech that may be able to convey something without actually being able to say it. Korzybski ran into this difficulty in trying to express the apparently simple point that things are not what we *say* they are, that, for example, the word "water" is not itself drinkable. He formulated it in his "law of nonidentity," that "whatever you say a thing *is*, it *isn't*." But from this it will follow that it isn't a thing either, for if I say that a thing is a thing, it isn't. What, then, are we talking about? He was trying to show that we are talking about the unspeakable world of the physical universe, the world that is other than words. Words represent it, but if we want to *know* it directly we must do so by immediate sensory contact. What we call things, facts, or events are after all no more than convenient units of perception, recognizable pegs for names, selected from the infinite multitude of lines and surfaces, colors and textures, spaces and densities which surround us. There is no more a fixed and final way of dividing these variations into things than of grouping the stars in constellations.

From this example, however, it is certainly clear that we can point out the unspeakable world, and even convey the idea of its existence, without being able to say exactly *what* it is. We do not know what it is. We know only that it is. To be able to say what it is we must be able to classify it, but obviously the "all" in which the whole multiplicity of things is delineated cannot be classified.

The sphere of "cosmic consciousness" is, I believe, the same as the unspeakable world of Korzybski and the semanticists. It is nothing "spiritual" in the usual sense of abstract or ideational. It is concretely physical, yet for this very reason ineffable (or unspeakable) and indefinable. "Cosmic" consciousness is a release from self-consciousness, that is to say from the fixed belief and feeling that one's organism is an absolute and separate thing, as distinct from a convenient unit of perception. For if it becomes clear that our use of the lines and surfaces of nature to divide the world into units is only a matter of convenience, then all that I have called myself is actually inseparable from everything. This is exactly what one experiences in these extraordinary moments. It is not that the outlines and shapes which we *call* things and use to delineate things disappear into some sort of luminous void. It simply becomes obvious that though they may be used as divisions they do not really divide. However much I may be impressed by the difference between a star and the dark space around it, I must not forget that I can see the two only in relation to each other, and that this relation is inseparable.

The most astonishing feature of this experience is, however, the conviction that this entire unspeakable world is "right," so right that our normal anxieties become ludicrous, that if only men could see it they would go wild with joy.

> *And the king be cutting capers,*
> *And the priest be picking flowers.*

Quite apart from the difficulty of relating this sensation to the problem of evil and pain, there is the question of the very meaning of the assertion "All shall be well, and all shall be well, and all manner of thing shall be well." I can say only that the meaning of the assertion is the experience itself. Outside that state of consciousness it has no meaning, so much so that it would be difficult even to believe in it as a revelation without the actual experience. For the experience makes it perfectly clear that the whole universe is through and through the playing of love in every shade of the word's use, from animal lust to divine charity. Somehow this includes even the holocaust of the biological world, where every creature lives by feeding on others. Our usual picture of this world is reversed so that every victim is seen as offering itself in sacrifice.

If we are to ask whether this vision is true, we may first answer that there are no such things as truths by themselves: a truth is always in relation to a point of view. Fire is hot in relation to skin. The structure of the world appears as it does in relation to our organs of sense and our brains. Therefore, certain alterations in the human organism may turn it into the sort of percipient for which the world *is* as it is seen in this vision. But, in the same way, other alterations will give us the truth of the world as it appears to the schizophrenic, or to the mind in black depression.

There is, however, a possible argument for the superior truth of the "cosmic" experience. Its basis is simply that no energy system can be completely self-controlling without ceasing to move. Control is restraint upon movement, and because complete control would be complete restraint, control must always be subordinate to motion if there is to be motion at all. In human terms, total restraint of movement is the equivalent of total doubt, of refusal to trust one's senses or feelings in any respect, and perhaps its embodiment is the extreme catatonic who refuses every motion or communication. On the other hand, movement and the release of restraint are the equivalent of faith, of committing oneself to the uncontrolled and unknown. In an extreme form this would mean the abandonment of oneself to utter caprice, and at first sight a life of such indiscriminate faith might seem to correspond to a vision of the world in which "everything is right." Yet this point of view would exclude all control as wrong, and thus there would be no place in it for the rightness of restraint. An essential part of the "cosmic" experience is, however, that the normal restriction of consciousness to the ego-feeling is also right, but only and always because it is subordinate to absence of restriction, to movement and faith.

The point is simply that, if there is to be any life and movement at all, the attitude of faith must be basic—the final and fundamental attitude—and the attitude of doubt secondary and subordinate. This is another way of saying that toward the vast and all-encompassing background of human life, with which the philosopher as artist is concerned, there must be total affirmation and acceptance. Otherwise there is no basis at all for caution and control with respect to details in the foreground. But it is all too easy to become so absorbed in these details that all sense of proportion is lost, and for man to make himself mad by trying to bring everything under his control. We become insane, unsound, and without foundation when we lose consciousness of and faith in the uncontrolled and ungraspable background world which is ultimately what we ourselves are. And there is a very slight distinction, if any, between complete, conscious faith and love.

Such was the Buddha's impact that people sometimes felt he must be something more than human.

'Are you a God?' they wondered.
'No' replied the Buddha.
'Are you an angel?'
'No'
'Then what are you?' they asked
'I am awake'

HUSTON SMITH, *The Religions of Man*

It is you who must make the effort
The masters only point the way

THE BUDDHA

Those who . . . shall be a lamp unto themselves, relying upon themselves only and not relying upon any external help, but holding fast to the truth as their lamp, and seeking salvation in the truth alone, shall not look for assistance to anyone besides themselves, it is they . . who shall reach the very top most height! But they must be anxious to learn.

THE BUDDHA (*as he died*)

THE PERENNIAL PHILOSOPHY

A L D O U S   H U X L E Y

Aldous Huxley's prolific pen performed a wonderful service to humanity, yet if he had written nothing but *The Perennial Philosophy*, he would nevertheless be gratefully remembered. The immense learning and scholarship which Huxley brought to the task of surveying world religions and spiritual texts was under the direction of a mind highly illumined by the light of eternal truth. Published in 1944, *The Perennial Philosophy* was the first popular book to articulate enlightenment as the core truth of the world's sacred traditions. It showed the unity and universality of that core truth behind the multitude of names and forms it has taken throughout history. Moreover, because the human race was engaged in the bloodiest war of all history and thoughtful people were searching desperately for safety and sanity, Huxley's high standing as an intellectual commanded public attention for the subject of enlightenment and made the quest for it "respectable."

Huxley noted in his introduction that the book is an anthology of the Perennial Philosophy in the sense of his having brought together a number of selections from the writings of every religious tradition and in all the principle languages of Asia and Europe. The selections are arranged under various heads and, as he put it, embedded in a commentary of his own designed to illustrate, connect and elucidate the selections. The result is a work of exceptional usefulness to the spiritual seeker. The selections are significant, memorable and beautiful; the arrangement of chapters on topics such as self-knowledge, grace and free will, silence, prayer, faith and spiritual exercises is practical, and the commentary, like all of Huxley's writings, is marked by a graceful style that engages the reader on all levels. *The Perennial Philosophy* is, as book reviewers say, highly recommended.

PHILOSOPHIA PERENNIS—the phrase was coined by Leibniz; but the thing—the metaphysic that recognizes a divine Reality substantial to the world of things and lives and minds; the psychology that finds in the soul something similar to, or even identical with, divine Reality; the ethic that places man's final end in the knowledge of the immanent and transcendent Ground of all being—the thing is immemorial and universal. Rudiments of the Perennial Philosophy may be found among the traditionary lore of primitive peoples in every region of the world, and in its fully developed forms it has a place in every one of the higher religions. A version of this Highest Common Factor in all preceding and subsequent theologies was first committed to writing more than twenty-five centuries ago, and since that time the inexhaustible theme has been treated again and again, from the standpoint of every religious tradition and in all the principal languages of Asia and Europe. . . .

Knowledge is a function of being. When there is a change in the being of the knower, there is a corresponding change in the nature and amount of knowing. For example, the being of a child is transformed by growth and education into that of a man; among the results of this transformation is a revolutionary change in the way of knowing and the amount and character of the things known. As the individual grows up, his knowledge becomes more conceptual and systematic in form, and its factual, utilitarian content is enormously increased. But these gains are offset by a certain deterioration in the quality of immediate apprehension, a blunting and a loss of intuitive power. Or consider the change in his being which the scientist is able to induce mechanically by means of his instruments. Equipped with a spectro-scope and a sixty-inch reflector an astronomer becomes, so far as eyesight is concerned, a superhuman creature; and, as we should naturally expect, the knowledge possessed by this superhuman creature is very different, both in quantity and quality, from that which can be acquired by a star-gazer with unmodified, merely human eyes.

Nor are changes in the knower's physiological or intellectual being the only ones to affect his knowledge. What we know depends also on what, as moral beings, we choose to make ourselves. "Practice," in the words of William James, "may change our theoretical horizon, and this in a twofold way: it may lead into new worlds and secure new powers. Knowledge we could never attain, remaining what we are, may be attainable in consequen-ces of higher powers and a higher life, which we may morally achieve." To put the matter more succinctly, "Blessed are the pure in heart, for they shall see God." And the same idea has been expressed by the Sufi poet, Jalal-uddin Rumi, in terms of a scientific metaphor: "The astrolabe of the mysteries of God is love."

. . . The Perennial Philosophy is primarily concerned with the one, divine Reality substantial to the manifold world of things and lives and minds. But the nature of this one Reality is such that it cannot be directly and immediately apprehended except by those who have chosen to fulfill certain conditions, making themselves loving, pure in heart, and poor in spirit. Why should this be so? We do not know. It is just one of those facts which we have to accept, whether we like them or not and however implausible and unlikely they may seem. Nothing in our everyday experience gives us any reason for supposing that water is made up of hydrogen and oxygen; and yet when we subject water to certain rather drastic treatments, the nature of its constituent elements becomes manifest. Similarly, nothing in our everyday experience gives us much reason for supposing that the mind of the average sensual man has, as one of its constituents, something resembling, or identical with, the Reality substantial to the manifold world; and yet, when that mind is subjected to certain rather drastic treatments, the divine element, of which it is in part at least composed, becomes manifest, not only to the mind itself, but also, by its reflection in external behavior, to other minds. It is only by making physical experiments that we can discover the intimate nature of matter and its potentialities. And it is only by making psychological and moral experiments that we can discover the intimate nature of mind and its potentialities. In the ordinary circumstances of average sensual life these potentialities of the mind remain latent and unmanifested. If we would realize them, we must fulfill certain conditions and obey certain rules, which experience has shown empirically to be valid.

In regard to few professional philosophers and men of letters is there any evidence that they did very much in the way of fulfilling the necessary conditions of direct spiritual knowledge. When poets or metaphysicians talk about the subject matter of the Perennial Philosophy, it is generally at second hand. But in every age there have been some men and women who chose to fulfill the conditions upon which alone, as a matter of brute empirical fact, such immediate knowledge can be had; and of these a few have left accounts of the Reality they were thus enabled to apprehend and have tried to relate, in one comprehensive system of thought, the given facts of this experience with the given facts of their other experiences. To such first-hand exponents of the Perennial Philosophy those who knew them have generally given the name of "saint" or "prophet," "sage," or "enlightened one." . . .

[We] shall here confine our attention to but a single feature of this traditional psychology—the most important, the most emphatically insisted upon by all exponents of the Perennial Philosophy and, we may add, the least psychological. For the doctrine that is to be illustrated in this section belongs to autology rather than psychology—to the science, not of the personal ego, but of that eternal Self in the depth of particular, individualized selves, and identical with, or at least akin to, the divine Ground. Based upon the direct experience of those who have fulfilled the necessary conditions of such knowledge, this teaching is expressed most succinctly in the Sanskrit formula, *tat tvam asi* ("That are thou"); the Atman, or immanent eternal Self, is one with Brahman, the Absolute Principle of all existence; and the last end of every human being is to discover the fact for himself, to find out Who he really is.

Aldous Huxley

The more God is in all things, the more He is outside them. The more He is within, the more without.

ECKHART

Only the transcendent, the completely other, can be immanent without being modified by the becoming of that in which it dwells. The Perennial Philosophy teaches that it is desirable and indeed necessary to know the spiritual Ground of things, not only within the soul, but also outside in the world and, beyond world and soul, in its transcendent otherness—"in heaven."

> Though GOD is everywhere present, yet He is only present to thee in the deepest and most central part of thy soul. The natural senses cannot possess God or unite thee to Him; nay, thy inward faculties of understanding, will and memory can only reach after God, but cannot be the place of his habitation in thee. But there is a root or depth of thee from whence all these faculties come forth, as lines from a centre, or as branches from the body of the tree. This depth is called the centre, the fund or bottom of the soul. This depth is the unity, the eternity—I had almost said the infinity—of thy soul; for it is so infinite that nothing can satisfy it or give it rest but the infinity of God.
>
> WILLIAM LAW

This extract seems to contradict what was said above; but the contradiction is not a real one. God within and God without—these are two abstract notions which can be entertained by the understanding and expressed in words. But the facts to which these notions refer cannot be realized and experienced except in "the deepest and most central part of the soul." And this is true no less of God without than of God within. But though the two abstract notions have to be realized (to use a spatial metaphor) in the same place, the intrinsic nature of the realization of God within is qualitatively different from that of the realization of God without, and each in turn is different from that of the realization of the Ground as simultaneously within and without—as the Self of the perceiver and at the same time (in the words of the Bhagavad-Gita) as "That by which all this world is pervaded." . . .

The man who wishes to know the "That" which is "thou" may set to work in any one of three ways. He may begin by looking inwards into his own particular *thou* and, by a process of "dying to self"—self in reasoning, self in willing, self in feeling—come at last to a knowledge of the Self, the Kingdom of God that is within. Or else he may begin with the *thous* existing outside himself, and may try to realize their essential unity with God and, through God, with one another and with his own being. Or, finally (and this is doubtless the best way), he may seek to approach the ultimate That both from within and from without, so that he comes to realize God experimentally as at once the principle of his own *thou* and of all other *thous,* animate and inanimate. The completely illuminated human being knows, with Law, that God "is present in the deepest and most central part of his own soul"; but he is also and at the same time one of those who, in the words of Plotinus,

> see all things, not in process of becoming, but in Being, and see themselves in the other. Each being contains in itself the whole intelligible world. Therefore All is everywhere. Each is there All, and All is each. Man as he now is has ceased to be the All. But when he ceases to be an individual, he raises himself again and penetrates the whole world.

It is from the more or less obscure intuition of the oneness that is the ground and principle of all multiplicity that philosophy takes its source. And not alone philosophy, but natural science as well. All science, in Meyerson's phrase, is the reduction of multiplicities to identities. Divining the One within and beyond the many, we find an intrinsic plausibility in any explanation of the diverse in terms of a single principle.

The philosophy of the *Upanishads* reappears, developed and enriched, in the *Bhagavad-Gita* and was finally systematized, in the ninth century of our era, by Shankara. Shankara's teaching (simultaneously theoretical and practical, as is that of all true exponents of the Perennial Philosophy) is summarized in his versified treaties, *Viveka-Chudamani* ("The Crest-Jewel of Wisdom"). All the following passages are taken from this conveniently brief and untechnical work.

> The Atman is that by which the universe is pervaded, but which nothing pervades; which causes all things to shine, but which all things cannot make to shine. . . .

> The nature of the one Reality must be known by one's own clear spiritual perception; it cannot be known through a pandit (learned man). Similarly the form of the moon can only be known through one's own eyes. How can it be known through others? . . .

> Liberation cannot be achieved except by the perception of the identity of the individual spirit with the universal Spirit. It can be achieved neither by Yoga (physical training), nor by Sankhya (speculative philosophy), nor by the practice of religious ceremonies, nor by mere learning. . . .

> Disease is not cured by pronouncing the name of medicine, but by taking medicine. Deliverance is not achieved by repeating the word "Brahman," but by directly experiencing Brahman. . . .

> The wise man is one who understands that the essence of Brahman and of Atman is Pure Consciousness, and who realizes their absolute identity. The identity of Brahman and Atman is affirmed in hundreds of sacred texts. . . .

Caste, creed, family and lineage do not exist in Brahman. Brahman has neither name nor form, transcends merit and demerit, is beyond time, space and the objects of sense-experience. Such is Brahman, and "thou art That." Meditate upon this truth within your consciousness.

Supreme, beyond the power of speech to express, Brahman may yet be apprehended by the eye of pure illumination. Pure, absolute and eternal Reality—such is Brahman, and "thou art That." Meditate upon this truth within your consciousness. . . .

Though One, Brahman is the cause of the many. There is no other cause. And yet Brahman is independent of the law of causation. Such is Brahman, and "thou art That." Meditate upon this truth within your consciousness. . . .

It is ignorance that causes us to identify ourselves with the body, the ego, the senses, or anything that is not the Atman. He is a wise man who overcomes this ignorance by devotion to the Atman. . . .

SHANKARA

In the Taoist formulations of the Perennial Philosophy there is an insistence, no less forcible than in the *Upanishads,* the *Gita* and the writings of Shankara, upon the universal immanence of the transcendent spiritual Ground of all existence. What follows is an extract from one of the great classics of Taoist literature, the Book of Chuang Tzu, most of which seems to have been written around the turn of the fourth and third centuries B.C.

Do not ask whether the Principle is in this or in that; it is in all beings. It is on this account that we apply to it the epithets of supreme, universal, total. . . . It has ordained that all things should be limited, but is Itself unlimited, infinite. As to what pertains to manifestation, the Principle causes the succession of its phases, but is not this succession. It is the author of causes and effects, but is not the causes and effects. It is the author of condensations and dissipations (birth and death, changes of state), but is not itself condensations and dissipations. All proceeds from It and is under its influence. It is in all things, but is not identical with beings, for it is neither differentiated nor limited.

CHUANG TZU

From Taoism we pass to that Mahayana Buddhism which, in the Far East, came to be so closely associated with Taoism, borrowing and bestowing until the two came at last to be fused in what is known as Zen. The Lankavatara Sutra, from which the following extract is taken, was the scripture which the founder of Zen Buddhism expressly recommended to his first disciples.

Those who vainly reason without understanding the truth are lost in the jungle of the Vijnanas (the various forms of relative knowledge), running about here and

32

there and trying to justify their view of ego-substance.

The self realized in your inmost consciousness appears in its purity; this is the Tathagata-garbha (literally, Buddha-womb), which is not the realm of those given over to mere reasoning. . . .

Pure in its own nature and free from the category of finite and infinite, Universal Mind is the undefiled Buddha-womb, which is wrongly apprehended by sentient beings.

LANKAVATARA SUTRA

One Nature, perfect and pervading, circulates in all natures,
One Reality, all-comprehensive, contains within itself all realities.
The one Moon reflects itself wherever there is a sheet of water,
And all the moons in the waters are embraced within the one Moon
The Dharma-body (the Absolute) of all the Buddhas enters into my own being.
And my own being is found in union with theirs. . . .
The Inner Light is beyond praise and blame;
Like space it knows no boundaries,
Yet it is even here, within us, ever retaining its serenity and fullness.
It is only when you hunt for it that you lose it;
You cannot take hold of it, but equally you cannot get rid of it,
And while you can do neither, it goes on its own way.
You remain silent and it speaks; you speak, and it is dumb;
The great gate of charity is wide open, with no obstacles before it.

YUNG-CHIA TA-SHIH

I am not competent . . . to discuss the doctrinal differences between Buddhism and Hinduism. Let it suffice to point out that, when he insisted that human beings are by nature "non-Atman," the Buddha was evidently speaking about the personal self and not the universal Self. The Brahman controversialists, who appear in certain of the Pali scriptures, never so much as mention the Vedanta doctrine of the identity of Atman and Godhead and the non-identity of ego and Atman. What they maintain and Gautama [Buddha] denies is the substantial nature and eternal persistence of the individual psyche. "As an unintelligent man seeks for the abode of music in the body of the lute, so does he look for a soul within the *skandhas* (the material and psychic aggregates, of which the individual mind-body is composed.)" About the existence of the Atman that is Brahman, as about most other metaphysical matters, the Buddha declines to speak, on the ground that such discussions do not tend to edification or spiritual progress among the members of a monastic order, such as he had founded. But though it has its dangers, though it may become the most absorbing, because the most serious and noblest, of distractions, metaphysical thinking is unavoidable and finally necessary. Even the Hinayanists found this, and the later Mahayanists were to develop, in connection with the practice of their religion, a splendid and imposing system of cosmological, ethical, and psychological thought. This system was based upon the postulates of a strict idealism and professed to dispense with the idea of God. But moral and spiritual experience was too strong for philosophical theory, and under the inspiration of direct experience, the writers of the Mahayana sutras found themselves using all their ingenuity to explain why the Tathagata and the Bodhisattvas display an infinite charity towards beings that do not really exist. At the same time they stretched the framework of subjective idealism so as to make room for Universal Mind; qualified the idea of soullessness with the doctrine that, if purified, the individual mind can identify itself with the Universal Mind or Buddha-womb; and, while maintaining godlessness, asserted that this realizable Universal Mind is the inner consciousness of the eternal Buddha and that the Buddha-mind is associated with "a great compassionate heart" which desires the liberation of every sentient being and bestows divine grace on all who make a serious effort to achieve man's final end. In a word, despite their inauspicious vocabulary, the best of the Mahayana sutras contain an authentic formulation of the Perennial Philosophy—a formulation which in some respects (as we shall see when we come to the section, "God in the World") is more complete than any other.

In India, as in Persia, Mohammedan thought came to be enriched by the doctrine that God is immanent as well as transcendent, while to Mohammedan practice were added the moral disciplines and "spiritual exercises," by means of which the soul is prepared for contemplation or the unitive knowledge of the Godhead. It is a significant historical fact that the poet-saint Kabir is claimed as a co-religionist both by Moslems and Hindus. The politics of those whose goal is beyond time are always pacific; it is the idolaters of past and future, of reactionary memory and Utopian dream, who do the persecuting and make the wars.

Behold but One in all things; it is the second that leads you astray.

KABIR

That this insight into the nature of things and the origin of good and evil is not confined exclusively to the saint, but is recognized obscurely by every human being, is proved by the very structure of our language. For language, as Richard Trench pointed out long ago, is often "wiser, not merely than the vulgar, but even than the wisest of those who speak it. Sometimes it locks up truths which were once well known, but have been forgotten. In other cases it holds the germs of truths which, though they were never plainly discerned, the genius of its framers caught a glimpse of in a happy moment of divination." For example, how significant it is that in the Indo-European languages, as Darmsteter has pointed out, the root meaning "two" should connote badness. The Greek prefix dys- (as dyspepsia) and the Latin dis- (as in dishonorable) are both derived from "duo." The cognate bis- gives a

34

pejorative sense to such modern French words as *bévue* ("blunder," literally "two-sight"). Traces of that "second which leads you astray" can be found in "dubious," "doubt" and *Zweifel*—for to doubt is to be double-minded. Bunyan has his Mr. Facing-both-ways, and modern American slang its "two-timers." Obscurely and unconsciously wise, our language confirms the findings of the mystics and proclaims the essential badness of division— a word, incidentally, in which our old enemy "two" makes another decisive appearance.

Here it may be remarked that the cult of unity on the political level is only an idolatrous *ersatz* for the genuine religion of unity on the personal and spiritual levels. Totalitarian regimes justify their existence by means of a philosophy of political monism, according to which the state is God on earth, unification under the heel of the divine state is salvation, and all means to such unification, however intrinsically wicked, are right and may be used without scruple. This political monism leads in practice to excessive privilege and power for the few and oppression for the many, to discontent at home and war abroad. But excessive privilege and power are standing temptations to pride, greed, vanity and cruelty; oppression results in fear and envy; war breeds hatred, misery and despair. All such negative emotions are fatal to the spiritual life. Only the pure in heart and poor in spirit can come to the unitive knowledge of God. Hence, the attempt to impose more unity upon societies than their individual members are ready for makes it psychologically almost impossible for those individuals to realize their unity with the divine Ground and with one another.

Among the Christians and the Sufis, to whose writings we now return, the concern is primarily with the human mind and its divine essence.

My Me is God, nor do I recognize any other Me except my God Himself.
ST. CATHERINE OF GENOA

In those respects in which the soul is unlike God, it is also unlike itself.
ST. BERNARD

I went from God to God, until they cried from me in me, "O thou I!"
BAYAZID OF BISTUN

Two of the recorded anecdotes about this Sufi saint deserve to be quoted here. "When Bayazid was asked how old he was, he replied, 'Four years.' They said, 'How can that be?' He answered, 'I have been veiled from God by the world for seventy years, but I have seen Him during the last four years. The period during which one is veiled does not belong to one's life.' " On another occasion someone knocked at the saint's door and cried, "Is Bayazid here?" Bayazid answered, "Is anybody here except God?"

> To gauge the soul we must gauge it with God, for the Ground of God and the Ground of the Soul are one and the same.
>
> ECKHART

> The spirit possesses God essentially in naked nature, and God the spirit.
>
> RUYSBROECK

> The knower and the known are one. Simple people imagine that they should see God, as if He stood there and they here. This is not so. God and I, we are one in knowledge.
>
> ECKHART

"I live, yet not I, but Christ in me." Or perhaps it might be more accurate to use the verb transitively and say, "I live, yet not I; for it is the Logos who *lives me*"—lives me as an actor lives his part. In such a case, of course, the actor is always infinitely superior to the role. Where real life is concerned, there are no Shakespearean characters, there are only Addisonian Catos or, more often, grotesque Monsieur Perrichons and Charlie's Aunts mistaking themselves for Julius Caesar or the Prince of Denmark. But by a merciful dispensation it is always in the power of every *dramatis persona* to get his low, stupid lines pronounced and supernaturally transfigured by the divine equivalent of a Garrick.

> O my God, how does it happen in this poor old world that Thou art so great and yet nobody finds Thee, that Thou callest so loudly and nobody hears Thee, that Thou art so near and nobody feels Thee, that Thou givest Thyself to everybody and nobody knows Thy name? Men flee from Thee and say they cannot find Thee; they turn their backs and say they cannot see Thee; they stop their ears and say they cannot hear Thee.
>
> HANS DENK

Between the Catholic mystics of the fourteenth and fifteenth centuries and the Quakers of the seventeenth there yawns a wide gap of time made hideous, so far as religion is concerned, with interdenominational wars and persecutions. But the gulf was bridged by a succession of men, whom Rufus Jones, in the only accessible English work devoted to their lives and teachings, has called the "Spiritual Reformers." Denk, Franck, Castellio, Weigel, Everard, the Cambridge Platonists—in spite of the murdering and the madness, the apostolic succession remains unbroken. The truths that had been spoken in the *Theologia Germanica*—that book which Luther professed to love so much and from which, if we may judge from his career, he learned so singularly little—were being uttered once again by Englishmen during the Civil War and under the Cromwellian dictatorship. The mystical tradition, perpetuated by the Protestant Spiritual Reformers, had become diffused, as it were, in the religious atmosphere of the time when George Fox had his first great "opening" and knew by direct experience

> that Every Man was enlightened by the Divine Light of Christ, and I saw it shine through all; And that they that believed in it came out of Condemnation and came to the Light of Life, and became the Children of it; And that they that hated it and did not believe in it, were condemned by it, though they made a profession of Christ. This I saw in the pure Openings of Light, without the help of any Man, neither did I then know where to find it in the Scriptures, though afterwards, searching the Scriptures, I found it.
>
> From *Fox's Journal*

The doctrine of the Inner Light achieved a clearer formulation in the writings of the second generation of Quakers. "There is," wrote William Penn, "something nearer to us than Scriptures, to wit, the Word in the heart from which all Scriptures come." And a little later Robert Barclay sought to explain the direct experience of *tat tvam asi* in terms of an Augustinian theology that had, of course, to be considerably stretched and trimmed before it could fit the facts. Man, he declared in his famous theses, is a fallen being, incapable of good, unless united to the Divine Light. This Divine Light is Christ within the human soul, and is as universal as the seed of sin. All men, heathen as well as Christian, are endowed with the Inward Light, even though they may know nothing of the outward history of Christ's life. Justification is for those who do not resist the Inner Light and so permit of a new birth of holiness within them.

> Goodness needeth not to enter into the soul, for it is there already, only it is unperceived.
>
> THEOLOGIA GERMANICA

> When the Ten Thousand things are viewed in their oneness, we return to the Origin and remain where we have always been.
>
> SEN T'SEN

It is because we don't know Who we are, because we are unaware that the Kingdom of Heaven is within us, that we behave in the generally silly, the often insane, the sometimes criminal ways that are so characteristically human. We are saved, we are liberated and enlightened, by perceiving the hitherto unperceived good that is already within us, by returning to our eternal Ground and remaining where, without knowing it, we have always been. Plato speaks in the same sense when he says, in the *Republic,* that "the virtue of wisdom more than anything else contains a divine element which always remains." And in the *Theaetetus* he makes the point, so frequently

37

insisted upon by those who have practiced spiritual religion, that it is only by becoming Godlike that we can know God—and to become Godlike is to identify ourselves with the divine element which in fact constitutes our essential nature, but of which, in our mainly voluntary ignorance, we choose to remain unaware.

> They are on the way to truth who apprehend God by means of the divine, Light by the light.
>
> PHILO

Philo was the exponent of the Hellenistic Mystery Religion which grew up, as Professor Goodenough has shown, among the Jews of the Dispersion, between about 200 B.C. and A.D. 100. Reinterpreting the Pentateuch in terms of a metaphysical system derived from Platonism, Neo-Pythagoreanism, and Stoicism, Philo transformed the wholly transcendental and almost anthropomorphically personal God of the Old Testament into the immanent-transcendent Absolute Mind of the Perennial Philosophy. But even from the orthodox scribes and Pharisees of that momentous century which witnessed, along with the dissemination of Philo's doctrines, the first beginnings of Christianity and the destruction of the Temple at Jerusalem, even from the guardians of the Law we hear significantly mystical utterances. Hillel, the great rabbi whose teachings on humility and the love of God and man read like an earlier, cruder version of some of the Gospel sermons, is reported to have spoken these words to an assemblage in the courts of the Temple. "If I am here," (it is Jehovah who is speaking through the mouth of his prophet) "everyone is here. If I am not here, no one is here."

> The Beloved is all in all; the lover merely veils Him; The Beloved is all that lives, the lover a dead thing.
>
> JALAL-UDDIN RUMI

> There is a spirit in the soul, untouched by time and flesh, flowing from the Spirit, remaining in the Spirit, itself wholly spiritual. In this principle is God, ever verdant, ever flowering in all the joy and glory of His actual Self. Sometimes I have called this principle the Tabernacle of the soul, sometimes a spiritual Light, anon I say it is a Spark. But now I say that it is more exalted over this and that than the heavens are exalted above the earth. So now I name it in a nobler fashion. . . . It is free of all names and void of all forms. It is one and simple, as God is one and simple, and no man can in any wise behold it.
>
> ECKHART

Crude formulations of some of the doctrines of the Perennial Philosophy are to be found in the thought-systems of the uncivilized and so-called primitive peoples of the world. Among the Maoris, for example, every human being is regarded as a compound of four elements—a divine eternal principle, known as the *toiora;* an ego, which disappears at death; a ghost-shadow, or psyche, which survives death; and finally a body. Among the Oglala Indians the divine element is called the *sican,* and this is regarded as identical with the *ton,* or divine essence of the world. Other elements of the self are the *nagi,* or personality, and *niya,* or vital soul. After death the *sican* is reunited with the divine Ground of all things, the *nagi* survives in the ghost world of psychic phenomena and the *niya* disappears into the material universe.

In regard to no twentieth-century "primitive" society can we rule out the possibility of influence by, or borrowing from, some higher culture. Consequently, we have no right to argue from the present to the past. Because many contemporary savages have an esoteric philosophy that is monotheistic with a monotheism that is sometimes of the "That art thou" variety, we are not entitled to infer offhand that neolithic or palaeolithic men held similar views.

More legitimate and more intrinsically plausible are the inferences that may be drawn from what we know about our own physiology and psychology. We know that human minds have proved themselves capable of everything from imbecility to Quantum Theory, from *Mein Kampf* and sadism to the sanctity of Philip Neri, from metaphysics to crossword puzzles, power politics, and the *Missa Solemnis.* We also know that human minds are in some way associated with human brains, and we have fairly good reasons for supposing that there have been no considerable changes in the size and conformation of human brains for a good many thousands of years. Consequently, it seems justifiable to infer that human minds in the remote past were capable of as many and as various kinds and degrees of activity as are minds at the present time.

It is, however, certain that many activities undertaken by some minds at the present time were not, in the remote past, undertaken by any minds at all. For this there are several obvious reasons. Certain thoughts are practically unthinkable except in terms of an appropriate language and within the framework of an appropriate system of classification. Where these necessary instruments do not exist, the thoughts in question are not expressed and not even conceived. Nor is this all: the incentive to develop the instruments of certain kinds of thinking is not always present. For long periods of history and prehistory it would seem that men and women, though perfectly capable of doing so, did not wish to pay attention to problems which their descendants found absorbingly interesting. For example, there is no reason to suppose that, between the thirteenth century and the twentieth, the human mind underwent any kind of evolutionary change comparable to the change, let us say, in the physical structure of the horse's foot during an incomparably longer span of geological time. What happened was that men turned their attention from certain aspects of reality to certain other aspects. The result, among other things, was the development of the natural sciences. Our perceptions and our understanding are directed, in large measure, by our will. We are aware of, and we think about, the things which, for one reason or another, we want to see and understand. Where there's a will there is always an intellectual way. The capacities of the human mind are almost indefinitely great. Whatever we will to do, whether it be to come to the unitive knowledge of the Godhead, or to manufacture self-propelled flame-throwers—that we are able to do, provided always that the willing be sufficiently intense and sustained. It is clear that many of the things to which modern men have chosen to pay attention were ignored by their predecessors. Consequently, the very means for thinking clearly and fruitfully about those things remained uninvented, not merely during prehistoric times, but even to the opening of the modern era.

The lack of a suitable vocabulary and an adequate frame of reference, and the absence of any strong and sustained desire to invent these necessary instruments of thought—here are two sufficient reasons why so many of the almost endless potentialities of the human mind remained for so long unactualized. Another and, on its own level, equally cogent reason is this: much of the world's most original and fruitful thinking is done by people of poor physique and of a thoroughly unpractical turn of mind. Because this is so, and because the value of pure thought, whether analytical or integral, has everywhere been more or less clearly recognized, provision was and still is made by every civilized society for giving thinkers a measure of protection from the ordinary strains and stresses of social life. The hermitage, the monastery, the college, the academy, and the research laboratory; the begging bowl, the endowment, patronage and the grant of taxpayers' money—such are the principal devices that have been used by actives to conserve that rare bird, the religious, philosophical, artistic, or scientific contemplative. In many primitive societies conditions are hard and there is no surplus wealth. The born contemplative has to face the struggle for existence and social predominance without protection. The result, in most cases, is that he either dies young or is too desperately busy merely keeping alive to be able to devote his attention to anything else. When this happens the prevailing philosophy will be that of the hardy, extroverted man of action.

All this sheds some light—dim, it is true, and merely inferential—on the problem of the perennialness of the Perennial Philosophy. In India the scriptures were regarded, not as revelations made at some given moment of history, but as eternal gospels, existent from everlasting to everlasting, inasmuch as coeval with man, or for that matter with any other kind of corporeal or incorporeal being possessed of reason. A similar point of view is expressed by Aristotle, who regards the fundamental truths of religion as everlasting and indestructible. There have been ascents and falls, periods (literally "roads around" or cycles) of progress and regress; but the great fact of God as the First Mover of a universe which partakes of His divinity has always been recognized. In the light of what we know about prehistoric man (and what we know amounts to nothing more than a few chipped stones, some paintings, drawings and sculptures) and of what we may legitimately infer from other, better documented fields of knowledge, what are we to think of these traditional doctrines? My own view is that they may be true. We know that born contemplatives in the realm both of analytic and of integral thought have turned up in fair numbers and at frequent intervals during recorded history. There is therefore every reason to suppose that they turned up before history was recorded. That many of these people died young or were unable to exercise their talents is certain. But a few of them must have survived. In this context it is highly significant that, among many contemporary primitives, two thought patterns are found—an exoteric pattern for the unphilosophic many and an esoteric pattern (often monotheistic, with a belief in a God not merely of power, but of goodness and wisdom) for the initiated few. There is no reason to suppose that circumstances were any harder for prehistoric men than they are for many contemporary savages. But if an esoteric monotheism of the kind that seems to come natural to the born thinker is possible in modern savage societies, the majority of whose members accept the sort of polytheistic philosophy that seems to come natural to men of action, a similar esoteric doctrine might have been current in prehistoric societies. True, the modern esoteric doctrines may have been derived from higher cultures. But the significant fact remains that, if so derived, they yet had a meaning for certain members of the primitive society and were considered valuable enough to be carefully preserved. We have seen that many thoughts are unthinkable apart from an appropriate vocabulary and frame of reference. But the fundamental ideas of the Perennial Philosophy can be formulated in a very simple vocabulary, and the experiences to which the ideas refer can and indeed must be had immediately and apart from any vocabulary whatsoever. Strange openings and theophanies are granted to quite small children who are often profoundly and permanently affected by these experiences. We have no reason to suppose that what happens now to persons with small vocabularies did not happen in remote antiquity. In the modern world (as Vaughan and Traherne and Wordsworth, among others, have told us) the child tends to grow out of his direct awareness of the one Ground of things; for the habit of analytical thought is fatal to the intuitions of integral thinking, whether on the "psychic" or the spiritual level. Psychic preoccupations may be and often are a major obstacle in the way of genuine spirituality. In primitive societies now (and, presumably, in the remote past) there is much preoccupation with, and a widespread talent for, psychic thinking. But a few people may have worked their way through psychic into genuinely spiritual experience—just as, even in modern industrialized societies, a few people work their way out of the prevailing preoccupation with matter and through the prevailing habits of analytical thought into the direct experience of the spiritual Ground of things.

Such, then, very briefly are the reasons for supposing that the historical traditions of oriental and our own classical antiquity may be true. It is interesting to find that at least one distinguished contemporary ethnologist is in agreement with Aristotle and the Vedantists. "Orthodox ethnology," writes Dr. Paul Radin in his *Primitive Man as Philosopher*, "has been nothing but an enthusiastic and quite uncritical attempt to apply the Darwinian theory of evolution to the facts of social experience." And he adds that "no progress in ethnology will be achieved until scholars rid themselves once and for all of the curious notion that everything possesses a history; until they realize that certain ideas and certain concepts are as ultimate for man, as a social being, as specific physiological reactions are ultimate for him, as a biological being." Among these ultimate concepts, in Dr. Radin's view, is that of monotheism. Such monotheism is often no more than the recognition of a single dark and numinous Power ruling the world. But it may sometimes be genuinely ethical and spiritual.

The nineteenth century's mania for history and prophetic Utopianism tended to blind the eyes of even its acutest thinkers to the timeless facts of eternity. Thus we find T. H. Green writing of mystical union as though it were an evolutionary process and not, as all the evidence seems to show, a state which man, as man, has always had it in his power to realize. "An animal organism, which has its history in time, gradually becomes the vehicle of an eternally complete consciousness, which in itself can have no history, but a history of the process by which the animal organism becomes its vehicle." But in actual fact it is only in regard to peripheral knowledge that there has been a genuine historical development. Without much lapse of time and much accumulation of skills and information, there can be but an imperfect knowledge of the material world. But direct awareness of the "eternally complete consciousness," which is the ground of the material world, is a possibility occasionally actualized by some human beings at almost any stage of their own personal development, from childhood to old age, and at any period of the race's history.

> The one who practices a scalpel self-dissection will know an expansion of universal pity. Release is given him from the deafening demands of ego. The love of God flowers on such soil.
>
> PARAMHANSA YOGANANDA, *Autobiography of a Yogi*

> It is of no value to discuss whether one Way is better than another: each man who treads a Way suited to his temperament with diligence and complete sincerity is fulfilling the purpose of his incarnation.
>
> RAYNOR JOHNSON, *The Imprisoned Splendor*

> It may perhaps be an easier step to leap from the plane of the quiescent Mind through contemplation into realization of God, but it is a still greater achievement on the plane of matter and action. Indeed, there can never be full enlightenment until it is found and retained on every level of consciousness.
>
> RAYNOR JOHNSON, *The Imprisoned Splendor*

THE UNITIVE LIFE

E V E L Y N   U N D E R H I L L

"Ignorance of spiritual laws is bondage; knowledge of spiritual laws is freedom; application of spiritual laws is wisdom." The full fruition of spirituality—wise, dedicated, and loving service that aims to elevate human consciousness—is described in Evelyn Underhill's 1911 classic, *Mysticism,* as "the unitive life." It is characteristic of the mystical ascent to godhead that inner experience is translated more and more into outer behavior because the mystic sees that in reality there is no such division as "inner" and "outer." They are simply differing aspects of the One Great Truth of Existence. The God-realized person sees the "seamless garment" of Being and, seeing it, quite naturally brings his or her activities more and more in alignment with that awareness. Amid the diversity of activities they may pursue, there is unity because they see that all is God and there is *only* God.

In her study of the mystic way, Underhill distinguishes five stages in the process of self-transcendence and return to the Source: awakening or conversion, self-knowledge or purgation, illumination, the dark night of the soul, and union or the unitive life. In that final state, which is the true goal of the mystic quest, she says, "the Absolute life is not merely perceived and enjoyed by the self, as in illumination" but is *one* with it." And that inevitably impels them to activity which is *in* the world but not *of* the world. That is, if they engage in worldly activities, they do so in such a manner as to purify and sanctify those activities, offering them selflessly to the glory of God and the liberation of humanity. Our lives are blessed by that. In this selection, Underhill artfully describes how "inner" and "outer" work together in the unitive life, and what the "rewards" of the mystic quest are for the one who rests enlightened at the summit of self-transcedence.

WHAT IS the unitive life? . . . Since the normal man knows little about his own true personality, and nothing at all about that of Deity, the orthodox description of it as "the life in which man's will is united with God," does but echo the question in an ampler form; and conveys no real meaning to the student's mind.

That we should know, by instinct, its character from within—as we know, if we cannot express, the character of our own normal human lives—is of course impossible. We deal here with the final triumph of the

44

spirit, the flower of mysticism, humanity's top note: the consummation towards which the contemplative life, with its long slow growth and costly training, has moved from the first. We look at a small but ever-growing group of heroic figures, living at transcendent levels of reality which we, immersed in the poor life of illusion, cannot attain: breathing an atmosphere whose true quality we cannot even conceive. Here, then, as at so many other points in our study of the spiritual consciousness, we must rely for the greater part of our knowledge upon the direct testimony of the mystics who alone can tell the character of that "more abundant life" which they enjoy.

Yet we are not wholly dependent on this source of information. It is the peculiarity of the unitive life that it is often lived, in its highest and most perfect forms, in the world; and exhibits its works before the eyes of men. As the law of our bodies is "earth to earth" so, strangely enough, is the law of our souls. The spirit of man having at last come to full consciousness of reality, completes the circle of being; and returns to fertilize those levels of existence from which it sprang. Hence, the enemies of mysticism, who have easily drawn a congenial moral from the "morbid and solitary" lives of contemplatives in the earlier and educative stages of the mystic way, are here confronted very often by the disagreeable spectacle of the mystic as a pioneer of humanity, a sharply intuitive and painfully practical person: an artist, a discoverer, a religious or social reformer, a national hero, a "great active" amongst the saints. By the superhuman nature of that which these persons accomplish, we can gauge something of the supernormal vitality of which they partake. The things done, the victories gained over circumstances by St. Bernard or St. Joan of Arc, by St. Catherine of Siena, St. Ignatius Loyola, St. Teresa, George Fox, are hardly to be explained unless these great spirits had indeed a closer, more intimate, more bracing contact than their fellows with that life "which is the light of men."

We have, then, these two lines of investigation open to us: first, the comparison and elucidation of that which the mystics tell us concerning their transcendent experience; secondly, the testimony which is borne by their lives to the existence within them of supernal springs of action, contact set up with deep levels of vital power. In the third place, we have such critical machinery as psychology has placed at our disposal; but this, in dealing with these giants of the spirit, must be used with peculiar caution and humility.

The unitive life, though so often lived in the world, is never of it. It belongs to another plane of being, moves securely upon levels unrelated to our speech, and hence eludes the measuring powers of humanity. We, from the valley, can only catch a glimpse of the true life of these elect spirits, transfigured upon the mountain. They are far away, breathing another air: we cannot reach them. Yet it is impossible to overestimate their importance for the race. They are our ambassadors to the "absolute." They vindicate humanity's claim to the possible and permanent attainment of reality; bear witness to the practical qualities of the transcendental life. In Eucken's words, they testify to "the advent of a triumphing Spiritual Power, as distinguished from a spirituality which merely lays the foundations of life or struggles to maintain them":[1] to the actually life-enhancing power of the love of God, once the human soul is freely opened to receive it.

Coming first to the evidence of the mystics themselves, we find that in their attempts toward describing the unitive life they have recourse to two main forms of symbolic expression: both very dangerous, and liable to be misunderstood, both offering ample opportunity for harsh criticism to hostile investigators of the mystic type. We find also, as we might expect from our previous encounters with the symbols used by contemplatives and ecstatics, that these two forms of expression belong respectively to mystics of the transcendent-metaphysical and of the intimate-personal type; and that their formulæ, if taken alone, appear to contradict one another.

(1) The metaphysical mystic, for whom the absolute is impersonal and transcendent, describes his final attainment of that absolute as *deification,* or the utter transmutation of the self in God. (2) The mystic for whom intimate and personal communion has been the mode under which he best apprehended reality, speaks of the consummation of this communion, its perfect and permanent form, as the *spiritual marriage* of his soul with God. Obviously, both these terms are but the self's guesses concerning the intrinsic character of a state which it has felt in its wholeness rather than analyzed; and bear the same relation to the ineffable realities of that state, as our clever theories concerning the nature and meaning of life bear to the vital processes of men. It is worthwhile to examine them, but we shall not understand them till we have also examined the life which they profess to explain.

The language of "deification" and of "spiritual marriage," then, is temperamental language, and is related to subjective experience rather than to objective fact. It describes on the one hand the mystic's astonished recognition of a profound change effected in his own personality[2]—the transmutation of his salt, sulphur, and mercury into spiritual gold—on the

---

[1] *Der Sinn und Wert des Lebens,* p. 140.
[2] Compare Dante's sense of a transmuted personality when he first breathed the air of Paradise:

> "S' io era sol di me quel che creasti
> novellamente, Amor che il ciel governi,
> tu il sai, che col tuo lume mi levasti" (Par. i. 73).

("If I were only that of me which thou didst new create, oh Love who rulest heaven, thou knowest who with thy light didst lift me up.")

other, the rapturous consummation of his love. Hence, by a comparison of these symbolic reconstructions, by the discovery and isolation of the common factor latent in each, we may perhaps learn something of the fundamental fact which each is trying to portray.

Again, the mystics describe certain symptoms either as the necessary preliminaries or as the marks and fruits of the unitive state; and these too may help us to fix its character.

The chief, in fact the one essential, preliminary is that pure surrender of selfhood, or "self-naughting," which the trials of the "dark night" tended to produce. "This," says Julian of Norwich, "is the cause why that no soul is rested till it is naughted of all things that are made. When it is willingly made naught for love to have Him that is all, then is it able to receive spiritual rest."[3] Only the thoroughly detached, "naughted soul" is "free," says "the mirror of simple souls," and the unitive state is essentially a state of free and filial participation in eternal life. The capital marks of the state itself are (1) a complete absorption in the interests of the Infinite, under whatever mode It is apprehended by the self; (2) a consciousness of sharing Its strength, acting by Its authority, which results in a complete sense of freedom, an invulnerable serenity, and usually urges the self to some form of heroic effort or creative activity; (3) the establishment of the self as a "power for life," a center of energy, an actual parent of spiritual vitality in other men. By assembling these symptoms and examining them, and the lives of those who exhibit them, in the light of psychology, we can surely get some news— however fragmentary—concerning the transcendent condition of being which involves these characteristic states and acts. . . .

We will then consider the unitive life (1) as it appears from the standpoint of the psychologist; (2) as it is described to us by those mystics who use (*a*) the language of deification, and (*b*) that of Spiritual Marriage; (3) finally, we will turn to those who have lived it; and try, if we can, to realize it as an organic whole.

(1) From the point of view of the pure psychologist, what do the varied phenomena of the unitive life, taken together, seem to represent? He would probably say that they indicate the final and successful establishment of that higher form of consciousness which has been struggling for supremacy during the whole of the mystic way. The deepest, richest levels of human personality have now attained to light and freedom. The self is remade, transformed, has at last unified itself; and with the cessation of stress, power has been liberated for new purposes.

"The beginning of the mystic life," says Delacroix, "introduced into

---

[3]*Revelations of Divine Love*, cap. v.

the personal life of the subject a group of states which are distinguished by certain characteristics, and which form, so to speak, a special psychological system. At its term, it has, as it were, suppressed the ordinary self, and by the development of this system has established a new personality, with a new method of feeling and of action. Its growth results in the transformation of personality: it abolishes the primitive consciousness of selfhood, and substitutes for it a wider consciousness; the total disappearance of selfhood in the divine, the substitution of a Divine Self for the primitive self."[4] We give a philosophic content to this conception if we say further that man, in this unitive state, by this substitution of the divine for the "primitive" self, has at last risen to true freedom; "entered on the fruition of reality."[5] Hence, he has opened up new paths for the inflow of that triumphing power which is the very substance of the real; has remade his consciousness, and in virtue of this total regeneration is "transplanted into that Universal Life, which is yet not alien but our own."[6] From contact set up with this universal life, this "energetic word of God, which nothing can contain"—from those deep levels of being to which his shifting, growing personality is fully adapted at last—he draws the amazing strength, that immovable peace, that power of dealing with circumstances, which is one of the most marked characteristics of the unitive life. "That secret and permanent personality of a superior type"[7] which gave to the surface-self constant and ever more insistent intimations of its existence at every stage of the mystic's growth—his real, eternal self—has now consciously realized its destiny, and begins at last fully to *be*. In the travail of the dark night it has conquered and invaded the last recalcitrant elements of character. It is no more limited to acts of profound perception, overpowering intuitions of the absolute; no more dependent for its emergence on the psychic states of contemplation and ecstasy. *Anima* and *animus* are united. The mystic has at last resolved the Stevensonian paradox and is not truly two, but truly *one*.

(2) The mystic, I think, would acquiesce in these descriptions, so far as they go; but he would probably translate them into his own words and gloss them with an explanation which is beyond the power and province of psychology. He would say that his long-sought correspondence with transcendental reality, his union with God, has now been finally established; that his self, though intact, is wholly penetrated—as a sponge by the sea—by the ocean of life and love to which he has attained. "I live, yet not I but God in me." He is conscious that he is now at length cleansed of the last

---

[4]Delacroix, *Etudes sur le Mysticisme*, p. 197
[5]Eucken, *Der Sinn und Wert des Lebens*, p. 12.
[6]*Ibid.*, p. 96
[7]Delacroix, *op. cit.*, p. 114 (*vide supra*, p. 273).

stains of separation, and has become, in a mysterious manner, "that which he beholds."

In the words of the Sūfi poet, the mystic's journey is now prosecuted not only *to* God but *in* God. He has entered the eternal order; attained here and now the state to which the magnet of the universe draws every living thing. Moving through periods of alternate joy and anguish, as his spiritual self awoke, stretched, and was tested in the complementary fires of love and pain, he was inwardly conscious that he moved toward a definite objective. Insofar as he was a great mystic, he was also conscious that this objective was no mere act of knowing, however intense, exultant, and sublime; but a condition of being, fulfilment of that love which impelled him, steadily and inexorably, to his own place. In the image of the alchemists, the fire of love has done its work: the mystic mercury of the wise—that little hidden treasure, that scrap of reality within him—has utterly transmuted the salt and sulphur of his mind and his sense. Even the white stone of illumination, once so dearly cherished, has been resigned to the crucible. Now, the great work is accomplished, the last imperfection is gone, and he finds within himself the "noble tincture"—the gold of spiritual humanity.

(*a*) We have said that the mystic of the impersonal type—the seeker of a transcendent absolute—tends to describe the consummation of his quest in the language of *deification*. The unitive Life necessarily means for him, as for all who attain it, something which infinitely transcends the sum total of its symptoms; something which normal men cannot hope to understand. In it he declares that he "partakes directly of the Divine Nature," enjoys the fruition of reality. Since we "only behold that which we are," the doctrine of deification results naturally and logically from this claim.

"Some may ask," says the author of the *Theologia Germanica*, "what is it to be a partaker of the Divine Nature, or a Godlike [*vergottet*, literally deified] man? Answer: he who is imbued with or illuminated by the Eternal or Divine Light and inflamed or consumed with Eternal or Divine Love, he is a deified man and a partaker of the Divine Nature."[8]

Such a word as "deification" is not, of course, a scientific term. It is a metaphor, an artistic expression which tries to hint at a transcendent fact utterly beyond the powers of human understanding, and therefore without equivalent in human speech: that fact of which Dante perceived the "shadowy preface" when he saw the saints as petals of the sempiternal rose.[9] Since we know not the being of God, the mere statement that a soul is transformed in Him may convey to us an ecstatic suggestion, but will never

---

[8]*Theologia Germanica*, cap. xli.
[9]Par. xxx. 115–130 and xxxi. 1–12.

give exact information, except of course to those rare selves who have experienced these supernal states. Such selves, however—or a large proportion of them—accept this statement as approximately true. Whilst the more clear-sighted are careful to qualify it in a sense which excludes pantheistic interpretations, and rebuts the accusation that extreme mystics preach the annihilation of the self and regard themselves as coequal with the Deity, they leave us in no doubt that it answers to a definite and normal experience of many souls who attain high levels of spiritual vitality. Its terms are chiefly used by those mystics by whom reality is apprehended as a state or place rather than a person;[10] and who have adopted, in describing the earlier stages of their journey to God, such symbols as rebirth or transmutation.

The blunt and positive language of these contemplatives concerning deification has aroused more enmity amongst the unmystical than any other of their doctrines or practices. It is of course easy, by confining oneself to its surface sense, to call such language blasphemous, and the temptation to do so has seldom been resisted. Yet, rightly understood, this doctrine lies at the heart, not only of all mysticism, but also of much philosophy and most religion. It pushes their first principles to a logical end. Christian mysticism, says Delacroix with justice, springs from "that spontaneous and half-savage longing for deification which all religions contain."[11] Eastern Christianity has always accepted it and expressed it in its rites. "The Body of God deifies me and feeds me," says Simeon Metaphrastes; "it deifies my spirit and it feeds my soul in an incomprehensible manner."[12]

The Christian mystics justify this dogma of the deifying of man by exhibiting it as the necessary corollary of the incarnation—the humanizing of God. They can quote the authority of the fathers in support of this argument. "He became man that we might be made God," says St. Athanasius.[13] "I heard," says St. Augustine, speaking of his pre-converted period, "Thy voice from on high crying unto me, 'I am the Food of the fullgrown: grow, and then thou shalt feed on Me. Nor shalt thou change Me into thy substance as thou changest the food of thy flesh, but thou shalt be changed into Mine.' "[14] Eckhart therefore did no more than expand the patristic view when he wrote, "Our Lord says to every living soul, 'I became man for you. If you do not become God for me, you do me wrong.' "[15]

If we are to allow that the mystics have ever attained the object of their

[10]Compare, p. 128.
[11]*Op. cit.*, ix. But it is difficult to see why we need stigmatize as "half-savage" man's primordial instinct for his destiny.
[12]Divine Liturgy of the Orthodox Eastern Church. Prayers before Communion.
[13]Athanasius, De Incarn, Verbi, i. 108.
[14]Aug. Conf., bk. vii, cap. x.
[15]Pred. lvii.

quest, I think we must also allow that such attainment involves the transmutation of the self to that state which they call, for want of exact language, "deified." The necessity of such transmutation is an implicit of their first position: the law that "we behold that which we are, and are that which we behold." Eckhart, in whom the language of deification assumes its most extreme form, justifies it upon this necessity. "If," he says, "I am to know God directly, I must become completely He and He I: so that this He and this I become and are one I."[16]

God, said St. Augustine, is the Country of the soul: its Home, says Ruysbroeck. The mystic in the unitive state is living in and of his native land; no exploring alien, but a returned exile, now wholly identified with it, part of it, yet retaining his personality intact. As none know the spirit of England but the English; and they know it by intuitive participation, by mergence, not by thought; so none but the "deified" know the secret life of God. This, too, is a knowledge conferred only by participation; by living a life, breathing an atmosphere, "union with that same Light by which they see, and which they see."[17] It is one of those rights of citizenship which cannot be artificially conferred. Thus, it becomes important to ask the mystics what they have to tell us of their life lived upon the bosom of reality; and to receive their reports without prejudice, however hard the sayings they contain.

The first thing which emerges from these reports, and from the choice of symbols which we find in them, is that the great mystics are anxious above all things to establish and force on us the truth that by *deification* they intend no arrogant claim to identification with God, but as it were a transfusion of their selves by His self; an entrance upon a new order of life, so high and so harmonious with reality that it can only be called divine. Over and over again they assure us that personality is not lost, but made more real. "When," says St. Augustine, "I shall cleave to Thee with all my being, then shall I in nothing have pain and labour; and *my life shall be a real life,* being wholly full of Thee."[18] "My life shall be a real life" because it is "full of Thee." The achievement of reality and deification are then one and the same thing; necessarily so, since we know that only the divine is the real.[19]

Mechthild of Magdeburg, and after her Dante, saw Deity as a flame or river of fire that filled the universe; and the "deified" souls of the saints as ardent sparks therein, ablaze with that fire, one thing with it, yet distinct.[20] Ruysbroeck, too, saw "Every soul like a live coal, burned up by God on the

[16]Pred. xcix. (*Mystische Schriften*, p. 122).

[17]Ruysbroeck, *De Ornatu Spiritalium Nuptiarum*, 1. iii. cap. iii.

[18]Aug. Conf., bk. x. cap. xxviii.

[19]Cf. Coventry Patmore, *The Rod, the Root, and the Flower, Magna Moralia,* xxii.

[20]Par. xxx. 64.

heart of His Infinite Love."[21] Such fire imagery has seemed to many of the mystics a peculiarly exact and suggestive symbol of the transcendent state which they are struggling to describe. No longer confused by the dim cloud of unknowing, they have pierced to its heart, and there found their goal: that uncreated and energizing fire which guided the children of Israel through the night. By a deliberate appeal to the parallel of such great impersonal forces—to fire and heat, light, water, air—mystic writers seem able to bring out a perceived aspect of the Godhead, and of the transfigured soul's participation therein, which no merely personal language, taken alone, can touch. Thus Boehme, trying to describe the union between the word and the soul, says, "I give you an earthly similitude of this. Behold a bright flaming piece of iron, which of itself is dark and black, and the fire so penetrateth and shineth through the iron, that it giveth light. Now, the iron doth not *cease to be*; it is iron still. And the source (or property) of the fire retaineth its own propriety; it doth not take the iron into it, but it penetrateth (and shineth) through the iron. It is iron then as well as before, *free* in itself, and so also is the source or property of the *fire*. In such a manner is the soul set in the Deity; the Deity penetrateth through the soul, and dwelleth in the soul, yet the soul doth not comprehend the Deity, but the Deity comprehendeth the soul, but doth not alter it (from being a soul) but only giveth it the divine source (or property) of the Majesty."[22]

Almost exactly the same image of deification was used five hundred years before Boehme's day, by Richard of St. Victor, a mystic whom he is hardly likely to have read. "When the soul is plunged in the fire of divine love," he says, "like iron, it first loses its blackness, and then growing to white heat, it becomes like unto the fire itself. And lastly, it grows liquid, and losing its nature is transmuted into an utterly different quality of being." "As the difference between iron that is cold and iron that is hot," he says again, "so is the difference between soul and soul, between the tepid soul and the soul made incandescent by divine love."[23] Other contemplatives say that the deified soul is transfigured by the inundations of the uncreated light; that it is like a brand blazing in the furnace, transformed to the likeness of the fire. "These souls," says the divine voice to St. Catherine of Siena, "thrown into the furnace of My charity, no part of their will remaining outside but the whole of them being inflamed in Me, are like a brand, wholly consumed in the furnace, so that no one can take hold of it to extinguish it, because it has become fire. In the same way no one can seize these souls, or draw them outside of Me, because they are made *one thing* with Me through grace, and I never withdraw Myself from them by sentiment, as in the case of those

[21]*De Septem Gradibus Amoris*, cap. xiv.
[22]*The Threefold Life of Man*, cap. vi. 88.
[23]*De Quatuor Gradibus Violentae Charitatis* (Migne, Patrologia Latina cxcvi.)

52

whom I am leading on to perfection."[24]

For the most subtle and delicate descriptions of the unitive or deified state, understood as self-loss in the "Ocean Pacific" of God, we must go to the great genius of Ruysbroeck. He alone, whilst avoiding all its pitfalls, has conveyed the suggestion of its ineffable joys in a measure which seems, as we read, to be beyond all that we had supposed possible to human utterance. Awe and rapture, theological profundity, keen psychological insight, are here tempered by a touching simplicity. We listen to the report of one who has indeed heard "the invitation of love" which "draws interior souls toward the One" and says "Come home." A humble receptivity, a meek self-naughting is with Ruysbroeck, as with all great mystics, the gate of the City of God. "Because they have abandoned themselves to God in doing, in leaving undone, and in suffering," he says of the deified souls, "they have steadfast peace and inward joy, consolation and savour, of which the world cannot partake; neither any dissembler, nor the man who seeks and means himself more than the glory of God. Moreover, those same inward and enlightened men have before them in their inward seeing, whenever they will, the Love of God as something drawing or urging them into the Unity; for they see and feel that the Father with the Son through the Holy Ghost, embrace Each Other and all the chosen, and draw themselves back with eternal love into the unity of Their Nature. Thus the Unity is ever drawing to itself and inviting to itself everything that has been born of It, either by nature or by grace. And therefore, too, such enlightened men are, with a free spirit, lifted up above reason into a bare and imageless vision, wherein lives the eternal indrawing summons of the Divine Unity; and, with an imageless and bare understanding, they pass through all works, and all exercises, and all things, until they reach the summit of their spirits. There, their bare understanding is drenched through by the Eternal Brightness, even as the air is drenched through by the sunshine. And the bare, upifted will is transformed and drenched through by abysmal love, even as iron is by fire. And the bare, uplifted memory feels itself enwrapped and established in an abysmal Absence of Image. And thereby the created image is united above reason in a threefold way with its Eternal Image, which is the origin of its being and its life. . . . Yet the creature does not become God, for the union takes place in God through grace and our homeward-turning love: and therefore the creature in its inward contemplation feels a distinction and an otherness between itself and God. And though the union is without means, yet the manifold works which God works in heaven and on earth are nevertheless hidden from the spirit. For though God gives Himself as He is,

[24]Dialogo, cap. lxxviii.

with clear discernment, He gives Himself in the essence of the soul, where the powers of the soul are simplified above reason, and where, in simplicity, they suffer the transformation of God. There all is full and overflowing, for the spirit feels itself to be one truth and one richness and one unity with God. Yet even here there is an essential tending forward, and therein is an essential distinction between the being of the soul and the Being of God; and this is the highest and finest distinction which we are able to feel."[25]

"When love has carried us above and beyond all things," he says in another place, "above the light, into the Divine Dark, there we are wrought and transformed by the Eternal Word Who is the image of the Father; and as the air is penetrated by the sun, thus we receive in idleness of spirit the Incomprehensible Light, enfolding us and penetrating us. And this Light is nothing else but an infinite gazing and seeing. We behold that which we are, and we are that which be behold; because our thought, life and being are uplifted in simplicity and made one with the Truth which is God."[26]

Here the personal aspect of the absolute seems to be reduced to a minimum, yet all that we value in personality—love, action, will—remains unimpaired. We seem caught up to a plane of vision beyond the categories of the human mind, to the contemplation of a something other: our home, our hope, and our passion, the completion of our personality, and the substance of all that is. Such an endless contemplation, such a dwelling within the substance of goodness, truth and, beauty, is the essence of that beatific vision, that participation of eternity, "of all things most delightful and desired, of all things most loved by them who have it,"[27] which theology presents to us as the objective of the soul.

Those mystics of the metaphysical type who tend to use these impersonal symbols of place and thing often see in the unitive life a foretaste of the beatific vision: an entrance here and now into that absolute life within the Divine Being, which shall be lived by all perfect spirits when they have cast off the limitations of the flesh and reentered the eternal order for which they were made. For them, in fact, the "deified man," in virtue of his genius for transcendental reality, has run ahead of human history and attained a form of consciousness which other men will only know when earthly life is past.

In the *Book of Truth*, Suso has a beautiful and poetic comparison between the life of the blessed spirits dwelling within the ocean of divine love, and that approximate life which is lived on earth by the mystic who has renounced all selfhood and merged his will in that of the eternal truth. Here

---

[25]Ruysbroeck, *Samuel*, cap. xi. (English translation: *The Book of Truth*.)
[26]*Ibid.*, *De Calculo*, cap. ix.
[27]St. Thomas Aquinas, *Summa Contra Gentiles*, bk. iii. cap. lxii.

we find one of the best of many answers to the ancient but apparently immortal accusation that the mystics teach the total annihilation of personality as the end and object of their quest. "Lord, tell me," says the Servitor, "what remains to a blessed soul which has wholly renounced itself." Truth says, "When the good and faithful servant enters into the joy of his Lord, he is inebriated by the riches of the house of God; for he feels, in an ineffable degree, that which is felt by an inebriated man. He forgets himself, he is no longer conscious of his selfhood; he disappears and loses himself in God, and becomes one spirit with Him, as a drop of water which is drowned in a great quantity of wine. For even as such a drop disappears, taking the colour and the taste of wine, so it is with those who are in full possession of blessedness. All human desires are taken from them in an indescribable manner, they are rapt from themselves, and are immersed in the divine will. If it were otherwise, if there remained in the man some human thing that was not absorbed, those words of Scripture which say that God must be all in all would be false. *His being remains, but in another form, in another glory, and in another power.* And all this is the result of entire and complete renunciation. . . . Herein thou shalt find an answer to thy question; for the true renunciation and veritable abandonment of a man to the divine will in the temporal world is an imitation and reduction of that self-abandonment of the blessed, of which Scripture speaks; and this imitation approaches its model more or less, according as men are more or less united with God and become more or less one with God. Remark well that which is said of the blessed: they are stripped of their personal initiative, and changed into another form, another glory, another power. What then is this other form if it be not the divine nature and the divine being whereinto they pour themselves, and which pours itself into them, and becomes one thing with them? And what is that other glory if it be not to be illuminated and made shining in the inaccessible light? What is that other power if it be not that by means of his union with the divine personality, there is given to man a divine strength and a divine power that he may accomplish all which pertains to his blessedness and omit all which is contrary thereto? And thus it is that, as has been said, a man comes forth from his selfhood."[28]

All the mystics agree that the stripping off of the I, the me, the mine, utter renouncement, or "self-naughting"—self-abandonment to the direction of a larger will—is an imperative condition of the attainment of the unitive life. The temporary denudation of the mind, whereby the contemplative made space for the vision of God, must now be applied to the whole life. Here, they say, there is a final swallowing up of that willful I-hood, that

[28]Suso, *Buchlein von der Wahrheit*, cap. iv.

surface individuality which we ordinarily recognize as ourselves. It goes forever, and something new is established in its room. The self is made part of the mystical body of God; and, humbly taking its place in the corporate life of reality, would "fain be to the Eternal Goodness what his own hand is to a man."[29] That strange "hunger and thirst of God for the soul," "at once avid and generous," of which they speak in their most profound passages, here makes its final demand and receives its satisfaction. "All that He has, all that He is, He gives; all that we have, all that we are, He takes."[30] The self, they declare, is devoured, immersed in the abyss; "sinks into God, Who is the deep of deeps." In their efforts toward describing to us this, the supreme mystic act, and the new life to which it gives birth, they are often driven to the use of images which must seem to us grotesque were it not for the flame which burns behind: as when Ruysbroeck cries, "To eat and be eaten! this is Union! . . . Since His desire is without measure, to be devoured of Him does not greatly amaze me."[31]

(*b*) At this point we begin to see that the language of deification, taken alone, will not suffice to describe the soul's final experience of reality. The personal and emotional aspect of man's relation with his source is also needed if that which he means by "union with God" is to be even partially expressed. Hence, even the most "transcendental" mystic is constantly compelled to fall back on the language of love in the endeavor to express the content of his metaphysical raptures, and forced in the end to acknowledge that the perfect union of lover and beloved cannot be suggested in the precise and arid terms of religious philosophy. Such arid language eludes the most dangerous aspects of "divine union," the pantheistic on one hand, the "amoristic" on the other; but it also fails to express the most splendid side of that amazing experience. It needs some other, more personal and intimate vision to complete it, and this we shall find in the reports of those mystics of the "intimate" type to whom the unitive life has meant not self-loss in an essence, but self-fulfillment in the union of heart and will.

The extreme form of this kind of apprehension of course finds expression in the well-known and heartily abused symbolism of the spiritual marriage between God and the soul: a symbolism which goes back to the Orphic Mysteries, and thence descended via the Neoplatonists into the stream of Christian tradition. But there are other, less concrete embodiments of it, wholly free from the dangers which are supposed to lurk in "erotic" imagery of this kind. Thus Jalalu'd Din, by the use of metaphors which are hardly human yet charged with passionate feeling, tells, no less successfully

[29]*Theologia Germanica*, cap. x.
[30]Ruysbroeck, *Speculum Æternæ Salutis*, cap. vii.
[31]*Regnum Deum Amantium*, cap. xxii.

than the writer of the *Song of Songs*, the secret of "his union in which 'heart speaks to heart.' "

> With Thy Sweet Soul, this soul of mine
>   Hath mixed as Water doth with Wine.
> Who can the Wine and Water part,
>   Or me and Thee when we combine?
> Thou art become my greater self;
>   Small bounds no more can me confine.
> Thou hast my being taken on,
>   And shall not I now take on Thine?
> Me Thou for ever hast affirmed,
>   That I may ever know Thee mine.
> Thy Love has pierced me through and through,
>   Its thrill with Bone and Nerve entwine.
> I rest a Flute laid on Thy lips;
>   A lute, I on Thy breast recline
> Breathe deep in me that I may sigh;
>   Yet strike my strings, and tears shall shine."[32]

What the mystic here desires to tell us is that his new life is not only a free and conscious participation in the life of eternity—a fully-established existence on real and transcendental levels—but also the conscious sharing of an inflowing *personal life* greater than his own; a tightening of the bonds of that companionship which has been growing in intimacy and splendor during the course of the mystic way. This companionship, at once the most actual and most elusive fact of human experience, is utterly beyond the resources of speech. So, too, are those mysteries of the communion of love whereby the soul's humble, active and ever-renewed self-donation becomes the occasion of her glory: and "by her love she is made the equal of Love"—the beggar maid sharing Cophetua's throne.

Thus, the anonymous author of the *Mirror* writes in one of his most daring passages, " 'I am God,' says Love, 'for Love is God, and God is Love. And this soul is God by condition of love: but I am God by Nature Divine. And this [state] is hers by righteousness of love, so that this precious beloved of me, is learned, and led of Me without her [working]. . . . This [soul] is the eagle that flies high, so right high and yet more high than doth any other bird; for she is feathered with fine love.' "[33]

The simplest expression of the unitive life, the simplest interpretation which we can put on its declarations, is that it is the complete and conscious fulfillment here and now of this perfect love. In it certain elect spirits, still in

---

[32]Jalalu 'd Din, *The Festival of Spring* (Hastie's translation, p. 10).
[33]*The Mirror of Simple Souls*, Div. iv. cap. i.

the flesh, "fly high and yet more high," till "taught and led out of themselves," they become, in the exaggerated language of the *Mirror*, "God by condition of love." Homegrown English mysticism tried as a rule to express the inexpressible in homelier, more temperate terms. "I would that thou knew," says the unknown author of the *Epistle of Prayer*, "what manner of working it is that knitteth man's soul to God, and that maketh it one with Him in love and accordance of will after the word of St. Paul, saying thus: *'Qui adhaeret Deo, unus spiritus est cum illo';* that is to say: 'Whoso draweth near to God as it is by such a reverent affection touched before, he is one spirit with God.' That is, though all that God and he be two and sere in kind, nevertheless yet in grace they are so knit together that they are but one in spirit; and all this is one for onehead of love and accordance of will; and in this onehead is the marriage made between God and the soul which shall never be broken, though all that the heat and the fervor of this work cease for a time, but by a deadly sin. In the ghostly feeling of this onehead may a loving soul both say and sing (if it list) this holy word that is written in the Book of Songs in the Bible, *'Dilectus meus mihi et ego illi,'* that is, My loved unto me, and I unto Him; understanding that God shall be knitted with the ghostly glue of grace on His party, and the lovely consent in gladness of spirit on thy party."[34]

I think no one can deny that the comparison of the bond between the soul and the absolute to "ghostly glue," though crude, is wholly innocent. Its appearance in this passage as an alternative to the symbol of wedlock may well check the uncritical enthusiasm of those who hurry to condemn at sight all "sexual" imagery. That it has seemed to the mystics appropriate and exact is proved by its reappearance in the next century in the work of a greater contemplative. "Thou givest me," says Petersen, "Thy whole Self to be mine whole and undivided, if at least I shall be Thine whole and undivided. And when I shall be thus all Thine, even as from everlasting Thou hast loved Thyself, so from everlasting Thou hast loved me; for this means nothing more than that Thou enjoyest Thyself in me, and that I by Thy grace enjoy Thee in myself and myself in Thee. And when in Thee I shall love myself, nothing else but Thee do I love, because *Thou art in me and I in Thee, glued together as one and the selfsame thing,* which henceforth and forever cannot be divided."[35]

From this kind of language to that of the spiritual marriage, as understood by the pure minds of the mystics, is but a step.[36] They mean by it no

---

[34]*The Epistle of Prayer*. Printed from Pepwell's edition in "The Cell of Self-knowledge," edited by Edmund Gardner, p. 88.

[35]Gerlac Petersen, *Ignitum cum Deo Soliloqium*, cap. xv.

[36]Compare Pt. i. Cap. vi. It seems needless to repeat here the examples there given.

rapturous satisfactions, no dubious spiritualizing of earthly ecstasies, but a life-long bond "that shall never be lost or broken," a close personal union of will and of heart between the free self and that "Fairest in Beauty" whom it has known in the act of contemplation.

The mystic way has been a progress, a growth, in love; a deliberate fostering of the inward tendency of the soul toward its source, an eradication of its disorderly tendencies to "temporal goods." But the only proper end of love is union: "a perfect uniting and coupling together of the lover and the loved into one."[37] It is "a unifying principle," the philosophers say:[38] life's mightiest agent upon every plane. Moreover, just as earthly marriage is understood by the moral sense less as a satisfaction of personal desire than as a part of the great process of life—the fusion of two selves for new purposes—so such spiritual marriage brings with it duties and obligations. With the attainment of a new order, the new infusion of vitality, comes a new responsibility, the call to effort and endurance on a new and mighty scale. It is not an act but a state. Fresh life is imparted by which our lives are made complete; new creative powers are conferred. The self, lifted to the divine order, is to be an agent of the divine fecundity; an energizing center, a parent of transcendental life. "The last perfection," says Aquinas, "to supervene upon a thing, is its becoming the cause of other things. While then a creature tends by many ways to the likeness of God, the last way left open to it is to seek the divine likeness by being the cause of other things, according to what the Apostle says, *Dei enim sumus adjutores*."[39]

We find as a matter of fact, when we come to study the history of the mystics, that the permanent unitive state, or spiritual marriage, does mean for those who attain to it, such an access of creative vitality. It means man's small derivative life invaded and enhanced by the absolute life; the appearance in human history of personalities and careers which seem superhuman when judged by the surface mind. Such activity, such a bringing forth of "the fruits of the spirit," may take many forms. But where it is absent, where we meet with personal satisfactions, personal visions or raptures—however sublime and spiritualized—presented as marks of the unitive way, ends or objects of the quest of reality, we may be sure that we have wandered from the "strait and narrow road" which leads not to eternal rest but to eternal life. "The fourth degree of love is spiritually fruitful,"[40] said Richard of St.

---

[37]Hilton, *The Treatise Written to a Devout Man*, cap. viii.
[38]Cf. Ormond, *Foundations of Knowledge*, p. 442. "When we love any being, we desire either the unification of its life with our own, or our own unification with its life. Love in its innermost motive is a unifying principle."
[39]*Summa Contra Gentiles*, bk. ii. cap. xxi.
[40]*De Quatuor Gradibus Violentæ Charitatis* (Migne, Patrologia Latina cxcvi. col. 1216 D).

Victor. Wherever we find a sterile love, a "holy passivity," we are in the presence of quietistic heresy, not of the unitive life. "I hold it for a certain truth," says St. Teresa, "that in giving these graces our Lord intends, as I have often told you, to strengthen our weakness so that we may imitate Him by suffering much. . . . Whence did St. Paul draw strength to support his immense labors? We see clearly in him the effects of visions and contemplations which come indeed from our Lord, and not from our own imagination or the devil's fraud. Do you suppose St. Paul hid himself in order to enjoy in peace these spiritual consolations, and did nothing else? You know that on the contrary he never took a day's rest so far as we can learn, and worked at night in order to earn his bread. . . . Oh my sisters! how forgetful of her own ease, how careless of honors, should she be whose soul God thus chooses for His special dwelling place! For if her mind is fixed on Him, as it ought to be, she must needs forget herself; all her thoughts are bent on how to please Him better, and when and how she may show Him her love. *This* is the end and aim of prayer, my daughters; *this* is the object of that spiritual marriage whose children are always good works. *Works* are the best proof that the favors which we receive have come from God."[41] "To give our Lord a perfect hospitality" she says in the same chapter, "Mary and Martha must combine."

When we look at the lives of the great theopathetic mystics, the true initiates of eternity—inarticulate as these mystics often are—we find ourselves in the presence of an amazing, a superabundant vitality, of a "triumphing force" over which circumstance has no power. The incessant production of good works seems indeed to be the object of that spirit, by whose presence their interior castle is now filled.

We see St. Paul, abruptly enslaved by the first and only fair, not hiding himself to enjoy the vision of reality, but going out single-handed to organize the Catholic Church. We ask how it was possible for an obscure Roman citizen, without money, influence, or good health, to lay these colossal foundations, and he answers "Not I, but Christ in me."

We see St. Joan of Arc, a child of the peasant class, leaving the sheepfold to lead the armies of France. We ask how this incredible thing can be and are told "Her Voices bade her." A message, an overpowering impulse, came from the suprasensible, vitality flowed in on her and she knew not how or why. She was united with the infinite life, and became its agent, the medium of its strength, "what his own hand is to a man."

We see St. Francis, "God's troubadour," marked with His wounds, inflamed with His joy—obverse and reverse of the earnest-money of eterni-

---

[41]*El Castillo Interior*, Moradas Sétimas, cap. iv.

ty—or St. Ignatius Loyola, our Lady's knight, a figure at once militant and romantic, go out to change the spiritual history of Europe. Where did they find—born and bred to the most ordinary of careers, in the least spiritual of atmospheres—that superabundant energy, that genius for success which triumphed best in the most hopeless situations? Francis found it before the crucifix in St. Damiano and renewed it in the ineffable experience of La Verna when "by mental possession and rapture he was transfigured of God." Ignatius found it in the long contemplations and hard discipline of the cave of Manresa, after the act of surrender in which he dedicated his knighthood to the service of the Mother of God.

We see St. Teresa, another born romantic, pass to the unitive state after long and bitter struggles between her lower and higher personality. A chronic invalid over fifty years of age, weakened by long ill-health and the mortifications of the purgative way, she deliberately broke with her old career in obedience to the inward voice, left her convent, and started a new life, coursing through Spain, and reforming a great religious order in the teeth of the ecclesiastical world. Yet more amazing, St. Catherine of Siena, an illiterate daughter of the people, after a three years' retreat consummated the mystic marriage, and emerged from the cell of self-knowledge to dominate the politics of Italy. How was it that these apparently unsuitable men and women, checked on every side by inimical environment, ill-health, custom, or poverty, achieved these stupendous destinies? The explanation can only lie in the fact that all these persons were great mystics, living upon high levels the theopathetic life. In each a character of the heroic type, of great vitality, deep enthusiasms, unconquerable will, was raised to the spiritual plane, remade on higher levels of consciousness. Each by surrender of selfhood, by acquiescence in the large destinies of life, had so furthered that self's natural genius for the infinite that their human limitations were overcome. Hence they rose to freedom and attained to the one ambition of the "naughted soul," "I would fain be to the Eternal Goodness what his own hand is to a man."

Even Madame Guyon's natural tendency to passive states breaks down with her entrance on the unitive way. Though she cannot be classed amongst the greatest of its initiates, she too felt its fertilizing power, was stung from her "holy indifference" to become, as it were, involuntarily true to type.

"The soul," she says of the self entering upon union—and we cannot doubt that as usual she is describing her own carefully docketed "states"— "feels a secret vigor taking more and more strongly possession of all her being; and little by little she receives a new life, never again to be lost, at least so far as one can be assured of anything in this life. . . . This new life is not like that which she had before. It is a life in God. It is a perfect life. She no longer lives or works of herself. But God lives, acts, and works in her, and this grows little by little till she becomes perfect with God's perfection, is rich with His riches, and loves with His love." . . .[42]

This new, intense, and veritable life has other and even more vital characteristics than those which lead to "the performance of acts" or "the incessant production of good works." It is in an actual sense, as Richard of St. Victor reminded us, fertile, creative, as well as merely active. In the fourth degree of love, the soul brings forth its children. It is the agent of a fresh outbirth of spiritual vitality into the world; the helpmate of the transcendent order, the mother of a spiritual progeny. The great unitive mystics are each of them the founders of spiritual families, centers wherefrom radiates new transcendental life. The "flowing light of the Godhead" is focused in them as in a lens, only that it may pass through them to spread out on every side. So, too, the great creative seers and artists are the parents, not merely of their own immediate works, but also of whole schools of art; whole groups of persons who acquire or inherit their vision of beauty or truth. Thus within the area of influence of a Paul, a Francis, an Ignatius, a Teresa, an atmosphere of reality is created, and new and vital spiritual personalities gradually appear and meet for the work which these great founders set in hand. The real witness to St. Paul's ecstatic life in God is the train of Christian churches by which his journeyings are marked. Wherever Francis passed, he left Franciscans, "fragrant with a wondrous aspect," where none had been before.[43] The Friends of God spring up, individual mystics, here and there through the Rhineland and Bavaria. Each becomes the center of an ever-widening circle of transcendent life, the parent of a spiritual family. They are come like their master, that men may have life more abundantly: from them new mystic energy is actually born into the world. Again, Ignatius leaves Manresa a solitary: maimed, ignorant, and poor. He comes to Rome with his company already formed and ablaze with his spirit; veritably his children, begotten of him, part and parcel of his life.

Teresa finds the order of Mount Carmel hopelessly corrupt; its friars and nuns blind to reality, indifferent to the obligations of the cloistered life. She is moved by the spirit to leave her convent and begin, in abject poverty, the foundation of new houses where the most austere and exalted life of contemplation shall be led. She enters upon this task to the accompaniment of an almost universal mockery. Mysteriously, as she proceeds, novices of the spiritual life appear and cluster around her. They come into existence, one knows not how, in the least favorable of atmospheres; but one and all are

---

[42]*Les Torrents*, pt. i. cap. ix.
[43]Thomas of Celano, *Legenda Secunda*, cap. xii.

salted with the Teresian salt. They receive the infection of her abundant vitality; embrace eagerly and joyously the heroic life of the Reform. In the end, every city in Spain has within it Teresa's spiritual children: a whole order of contemplatives as truly born of her as if they were indeed her sons and daughters in the flesh. Well might the spiritual alchemists say that the true "Lapis Philosophorum" is a *tinging stone* which imparts its goldness to the base metals brought within its sphere of influence.

This reproductive power is one of the greatest marks of the theopathetic life, the true "mystic marriage" of the individual soul with its source. Those rare personalities in whom it is found are the *media* through which that triumphing spiritual life which is the essence of reality forces an entrance into the temporal order and begets children; heirs of the superabundant vitality of the transcendental universe.

But the unitive life is more than the sum total of its symptoms; more than the heroic and apostolic life of the "great active"; more than the divine motherhood of new "sons and daughters of the absolute." These are only its outward signs, its expression in time and space. I have first laid stress upon that expression, because it is the side which all critics and some friends of the mystics persistently ignore. The contemplative's power of living this intense and creative life within the temporal order, however, is tightly bound up with that other life in which he attains to complete communion with the absolute order, and submits to the inflow of its supernal vitality. In discussing the relation of the mystical experience to philosophy,[44] we saw that the complete mystic consciousness, and therefore, of course, the complete mystic world, had a twofold character which could hardly be reconciled with the requirements of monism. It embraced a reality which seems from the human standpoint at once static and dynamic, transcendent and immanent, eternal and temporal; accepted both the absolute world of pure being and the unresting world of becoming as integral parts of its vision of truth, demanding on its side a dual response. All through the mystic way we caught glimpses of the growth and exercise of this dual intuition of the real. Now, the mature mystic, having come to his full stature, passed through the purifications of sense and of spirit and entered on his heritage, must and does take up as a part of that heritage not merely (*a*) a fruition of the divine goodness, truth, and beauty, his place within the sempiternal rose, nor (*b*) the creative activity of an agent of the eternal wisdom, still immersed in the river of life, but both together—the twofold destiny of the spiritual man, called to "incarnate the eternal in time." To use the old scholastic language,

---

[44]*Supra*, Pt. I. Cap. II.

he is at once patient and agent: patient as regards God, agent as regards the world.

In a deep sense it may be said of him that he now participates according to his measure in that divine human life which mediates between man and the eternal, and constitutes the "salvation of the world." Therefore, though his outward heroic life of action, his divine fecundity, may seem to us the best evidence of his state, it is the inner knowledge of his mystical sonship whereby "we feel eternal life in us above all other thing,"[45] which is for him the guarantee of absolute life. He has many ways of describing this central fact, this peculiar consciousness of his own transcendence which coexists with, and depends on, a complete humility. Sometimes he says that whereas in the best moments of his natural life he was but the "faithful servant" of the eternal order, and in the illuminated way became its "secret friend," he is now advanced to the final, most mysterious state of "hidden child." "How great," says Ruysbroeck, "is the difference between the secret friend and the hidden child! For the friend makes only loving, living, but measured ascents towards God. But the child presses on to lose his own life upon the summits, in that simplicity which knoweth not itself. . . . When we transcend ourselves and become in our ascent toward God so simple that the bare supreme love can lay hold of us, then we cease, and we and all our selfhood die in God. And in this death we become the hidden children of God, and find a new life within us."[46]

Though the outer career of the great mystic, then, is one of superhuman industry, a long fight with evil and adversity, his real and inner life dwells securely upon the heights in the perfect fruition which he can only suggest to us by the paradoxical symbols of ignorance and emptiness. He dominates existence because he transcends it, is a son of God, a member of the eternal order, shares its substantial life. "Tranquility according to His essence, activity according to His Nature: absolute repose, absolute fecundity." This, says Ruysbroeck again, is the twofold property of Godhead, and the secret child of the absolute participates in this dual character of reality—"for this dignity has man been made."[47]

Those two aspects of truth which he has so clumsily classified as static and dynamic, as being and becoming, now find their final reconciliation within his own nature, for that nature has become conscious in all its parts, has unified itself about its highest elements. That strange, tormenting vision of a perfect peace, a joyous self-loss, annihilation in some mighty life that

[45]Ruysbroeck, *De Calculo*, cap. ix.
[46]*Op. cit.*, cap. viii, and ix. (condensed).
[47]*Vide supra*, p. 35.

overpassed his own, which haunts man throughout the whole course of his history, and finds a more or less distorted expression in all his creeds, a justification in all his ecstasies, is now traced to its source and found to be the inevitable expression of an instinct by which he recognized, though he could not attain, the noblest part of his inheritance. This recognition of his has of necessity been imperfect and oblique. It has taken in many temperaments an exaggerated form, and has been further disguised by the symbolic language used to describe it. The tendency of Indian mysticism to regard the unitive life wholly in its passive aspect, as a total self-annihilation, a disappearance into the substance of the Godhead, results, I believe, from such a distortion of truth. The Oriental mystic "presses on to lose his life upon the heights"; but he does not come back and bring to his fellowmen the life-giving news that he has transcended mortality in the interests of the race. The temperamental bias of Western mystics toward activity has saved them as a rule from such one-sided achievement as this; and hence it is in them that the unitive life, with its "dual character of activity and rest," has assumed its richest and noblest forms.

Of these Western mystics none has expressed more lucidly or splendidly than Ruysbroeck the double nature of man's reaction to reality. It is the heart of his vision of truth. In all his books he returns to it again and again, speaking, as none familiar with his writings can doubt, the ardent, joyous, vital language of firsthand experience, not the platitudes of philosophy. . . .

It is then from Ruysbroeck that I shall make my quotations; and if they be found somewhat long and difficult of comprehension, their unique importance for the study of man's spiritual abilities must be my excuse.

First, his vision of God:—

"The Divine Persons," he says, "Who form one sole God, are in the fecundity of their nature ever active, and in the simplicity of their essence they form the Godhead and eternal blessedness. Thus God according to the Persons is Eternal Work; but according to the essence and Its perpetual stillness, He is Eternal Rest. Now love and fruition live between this activity and this rest. Love would ever be active, for its nature is eternal working with God. Fruition is ever at rest, for it consists above all will and all desire, in the embrace of the well-beloved by the well-beloved in a simple and imageless love; wherein the Father, together with the Son, enfolds His beloved ones in the fruitive unity of His Spirit, above the fecundity of nature. And that same Father says to each soul in His infinite loving kindness, 'Thou art Mine and I am thine: I am thine and thou art Mine, for I have chosen thee from all eternity.' "[48]

[48]*De Septem Gradibus Amoris*, cap. xiv.

Next the vision of the self's destiny: "Our activity consists in loving God and our fruition in enduring God and being penetrated by His love. There is a distinction between love and fruition, as there is between God and His Grace. When we unite ourselves to God by love, then we are spirit: but when we are caught up and transformed by His Spirit, then we are led into fruition. And the spirit of God Himself breathes us out from Himself that we may love, and may do good works; and again He draws us into Himself that we may rest in fruition. And this is Eternal Life, even as our mortal life subsists in the indrawing and outgoing of our breath."[49]

"Understand," he says again, "God comes to us incessantly, both with means and without means; and He demands of us both action and fruition, in such a way that the action never hinders the fruition, nor the fruition the action, but they strengthen one another. And this is why the interior man [*i.e.*, the contemplative] lives his life according to these two ways; that is to say, in rest and in work. And in each of them he is wholly and undividedly, for he dwells wholly in God in virtue of his restful fruition and wholly in himself in virtue of his active love. And God, in His communications, perpetually calls and urges him to renew both this rest and this work. And because the soul is just, it desires to pay at every instant that which God demands of it; and this is why each time it is irradiated of Him, the soul turns inward in a manner that is both active and fruitive, and thus it is renewed in all virtues and ever more profoundly immersed in fruitive rest. . . . It is active in all loving work, for it sees its rest. It is a pilgrim, for it sees its country. For love's sake it strives for victory, for it sees its crown. Consolation, peace, joy, beauty and riches, all that can give delight, all this is shown to the mind illuminated in God, in spiritual similitudes and without measure. And through this vision and touch of God, love continues active. For such a just man has built up in his own soul, in rest and in work, a veritable life which shall endure for ever; but which shall be transformed after this present life to a state still more sublime. Thus this man is just, and he *goes toward* God by inward love, in eternal work, and he goes *in* God by his fruitive inclination in eternal rest. And he dwells in God; and yet he goes out toward all creatures, in a spirit of love toward all things, in virtue and in works of righteousness. *And this is the supreme summit of the inner life.*"[50]

Compare this description with the careers of the theopathic mystics in whom, indeed, "action has not injured fruition, nor fruition action," who have by some secret adjustment contrived to "possess their lives in rest and in work" without detriment to inward joy or outward industry. Bear in mind

---

[49]*Ibid., loc. cit.*
[50]Ruysbroeck, *De Ornatu Spiritalium Nuptiarum*, 1. ii. cap. lxv.

as you read these words—Ruysbroeck's supreme effort to tell the true relation between man's created spirit and his God—the great public ministry of St. Catherine of Siena, which ranged from the tending of the plague-stricken to the reforming of the Papacy, and was accompanied by the inward fruitive consciousness of the companionship of Christ. Remember the humbler but not less beautiful and significant achievement of her Genoese namesake: the strenuous lives of St. Francis of Assisi, St. Ignatius, St. Teresa, outwardly encumbered with much serving, observant of an infinitude of tiresome details, composing rules, setting up foundations, neglecting no aspect of their business which could conduce to its practical success, yet "altogether dwelling in God in restful fruition." Are not all these supreme examples of the state in which the self, at last fully conscious, knowing reality because she is wholly real, pays her debt? Unable to rest entirely either in work or in fruition, she seizes on this twofold expression of the superabundant life by which she is possessed, and, on the double wings of eagerness and effort, takes flight toward her home.

In dwelling as we have done on the ways in which the great mystic makes actual to himself the circumstances of the unitive state, we must not forget that this state is, in essence, a fulfillment of love; the attainment of a "heart's desire." By this attainment, this lifting of the self to free union with the real—as by the earthly marriage which dimly prefigures it—a new life is entered upon; new powers, new responsibilities are conferred. But this is not all. The three prime activities of the normal self—feeling, intellect, and will—though they seem to be fused, are really carried up to a higher term. They are unified, it is true, but still present in their integrity; and each demands and receives full satisfaction in the attainment of this final "honor for which man has been made." The intellect is immersed in that mighty vision of truth, known now not as a vision but as a home; where St. Paul saw things which might not be uttered, St. Teresa found the "perpetual companionship of the Blessed Trinity," and Dante, caught to its heart for one brief moment, his mind smitten by the blinding flash of the uncreated light, knew that he had resolved reality's last paradox: the unity of *cerchio* and *imago*—the infinite and personal aspects of God.[51] The enhanced will, made over to the interests of the transcendent, receives new worlds to conquer, new strength to match its exalted destiny. But the heart here too enters on a new order and begins to live upon high levels of joy. "This soul, says Love, swims in the sea of joy: that is, in the sea of delight, the stream of divine influences."[52]

[51]Par. xxxiii. 137.
[52]*The Mirror of Simple Souls*, f. 161.

"Amans volat, currit et laetatur: liber est et non tenetur,"[53] said à Kempis: classic words, which put before us once and forever the inward joyousness and liberty of the saints. They "fly, run, and rejoice," those great, laborious souls, often spent with amazing mortifications, vowed to hard and never-ending tasks. They are "free, and nothing can hold them," though they seem to the world fenced in by absurd renunciations and restrictions, deprived of that cheap license which it knows as liberty.

That fruition of joy which Ruysbroeck speaks of in majestic phrases, as constituting the interior life of mystic souls immersed in the absolute—the translation of the beatific vision into the terms of a supernal feeling-state—is often realized in the secret experience of those same mystics as the perennial possession of a childlike gaiety, an inextinguishable gladness of heart. The transfigured souls move to the measures of a "love dance" which persists in mirth without comparison, through every outward hardship and tribulation. They enjoy the high spirits peculiar to high spirituality, and shock the world by a delicate playfulness, instead of exhibiting the morose resignation which it feels to be proper to the "spiritual life." Thus St. Catherine of Siena, though constantly suffering, "was always jocund and of a happy spirit." When prostrate with illness she overflowed with gaiety and gladness, and "was full of laughter in the Lord, exultant and rejoicing."[54]

Moreover, the most clear-sighted among the mystics declare such joy to be an implicit of reality. Thus Dante, initiated into Paradise, sees the whole universe laugh with delight as it glorifies God,[55] and the awful countenance of perfect love adorned with smiles.[56] Thus the souls of the great theologians dance to music and laughter in the heaven of the sun;[57] the loving seraphs, in their ecstatic joy, whirl about the being of God.[58] *"O luce eterna che . . . ami ed arridi,"* exclaims the pilgrim, as the divine essence is at last revealed to him,[59] and he perceives love and joy as the final attributes of the triune God. Thus Beatrice with *"suoi occhi ridenti"*—so different from the world's idea of a suitable demeanour for the soul's supreme instructress—laughs as she mounts with him the ladder to the stars. So, if the deified soul has indeed run ahead of humanity and "according to his fruition dwells in heaven," he too, like Francis, will run, rejoice and make merry, join the eager dance of the universe about the One. "If," says Patmore, "we

[53]*De Imitatione Christi*, 1. iii. cap. v.
[54]Contestatio Fr. Thomae Caffarina, Processus, col. 1258 (E. Gardner, *St. Catherine of Siena*, p. 48).
[55]Par. xxvii. 4.
[56]*Ibid.*, xx. 13.
[57]*Ibid.*, x. 76. 118.
[58]*Ibid.*, xxviii. 100.
[59]*Ibid.*, xxxiii. 124–26.

may credit certain hints contained in the lives of the saints, love raises the spirit above the sphere of reverence and worship into one of laughter and dalliance; a sphere in which the soul says:

" *'Shall I, a gnat which dances in Thy ray,*
    Dare *to be reverent?' "*[60]

Richard Rolle has expressed this exultant "spirit of dalliance" with peculiar insight and delicacy. "Among the delights which he tastes in so sweet love burning," he says of the true lover who "in the bond of the lovers' will stably is confirmed," "a heavenly privity inshed he feels, that no man can know but he that has received it, and in himself bears the electuary that anoints and makes happy all joyful lovers in Jesu; so that they cease not to hie in heavenly seats to sit, endlessly their Maker to enjoy. Hereto truly they yearn in heavenly sights abiding; and inwardly set afire, all their inward parts are glad with pleasant shining in light. And themselves they feel gladdened with merriest love, and in joyful song wonderfully melted. . . . But this grace generally and to all is not given, but to the holy soul imbued with the holiest is taught; in whom the excellence of love shines, and songs of lovely loving, Christ inspiring, commonly burst up, and being made as it were a pipe of love, in sight of God more goodly than can be said, joying sounds. The which (soul) the mystery of love knowing, with great cry to its Love ascends, in wit sharpest, and in knowledge and in feeling subtle; not spread in things of this world but into God all gathered and set, that in cleanness of conscience and shining of soul to Him it may serve Whom it has purposed to love, and itself to Him to give. Surely the clearer the love of the lover is, the nearer to him and the more present God is. And thereby more clearly in God he joys, and of the sweet Goodness the more he feels, that to lovers is wont Itself to inshed, and to mirth without comparison the hearts of the meek to turn."[61]

The state of burning love, said Rolle, which he could conceive no closer reaction to reality, was the state of sweetness and song, the welling up of glad music in the simple soul, man's natural expression of a joy which overpasses the descriptive powers of our untuneful speech. In the gay rhythms of that primordial art he may say something of the secret which the more decorous periods of religion and philosophy will never let him tell; something, too, which in its very childishness, its freedom from the taint of solemnity and self-importance, expresses the quality of that inward life, that perpetual youth, which the "secret child" of the transcendent order enjoys:

[60]Coventry Patmore, *The Rod, the Root, and the Flower, Aurea Dicta,*
[61]Richard Rolle, *The Fire of Love,* bk. ii. cap. vii.

"As it were a pipe of love" in the sight of God he "joying sounds." The music of the spheres is all about him: he is a part of the great melody of the divine. "Sweetest forsooth," says Rolle again, "is the rest which the spirit takes whilst sweet goodly sound comes down, in which it is delighted; and in most sweet song and playful the mind is ravished, to sing likings of love everlasting."[62]

When we come to look at the lives of the mystics, we find it literally true that such "songs of lovely loving commonly burst up" whenever we can catch them unawares; see behind the formidable and heroic activities of reformer, teacher, or leader of men, the *vie intime* which is lived at the hearth of love. "What are the servants of the Lord but His minstrels?" said St. Francis,[63] who saw nothing inconsistent between the celestial melodies and the Stigmata of Christ. Moreover, the songs of such troubadours, as the hermit of Hampole learned in his wilderness, are not only sweet but playful. Dwelling always in a light of which we hardly dare to think, save in the extreme terms of reverence and awe, they are not afraid with any amazement: they are at home.

The whole life of St. Francis of Assisi, that spirit transfigured in God, who "loved above all other birds a certain little bird which is called the lark,"[64] was one long march to music through the world. To sing seemed to him a primary spiritual function; he taught his friars in their preaching to urge. all men to this.[65] It appeared to him appropriate and just to use the romantic language of the troubadours in praise of the perfect love which had marked him as its own. "Drunken with the love and compassion of Christ, blessed Francis on a time did things such as these. For the most sweet melody of spirit boiling up within him, frequently broke out in French speech, and the veins of murmuring which he heard secretly with his ears broke forth into French-like rejoicing. And sometimes he picked up a branch from the earth, and laying it on his left arm, he drew in his right hand another stick like a bow over it, as if on a viol or other instrument, and, making fitting gestures, sang with it in French unto the Lord Jesus Christ."[66]

Many a time has the romantic quality of the unitive life—its gaiety, freedom, assurance, and joy—broken out in "French-like rejoicings"; which have a terribly frivolous sound for worldly ears, and seem the more preposterous as coming from people whose outward circumstances are of the most uncomfortable kind. St. John of the Cross wrote love songs to his love. St. Rose of Lima sang duets with the birds. St. Teresa, in the austere and

---

[62]*Op. cit.*, bk. i. cap. xi.
[63]*Speculum Perfectionis*, cap. c. (Steele's translation).
[64]*Speculum*, cap. cxiii.
[65]*Ibid.*, cap. c.
[66]*Ibid.*, cap. xciii., also Thomas of Celano, Vita Secunda, cap. xc.

poverty-stricken seclusion of her first foundation, did not disdain to make rustic hymns and carols for her daughters' use in the dialect of Old Castile. Like St. Francis, she had a horror of solemnity. It was only fit for hypocrites, thought these rejuvenators of the church. The hard life of prayer and penance on Mount Carmel was undertaken in a joyous spirit to the sound of many songs. Its great reformer was quick to snub the too-spiritual sister who "thought it better to contemplate than to sing," and was herself heard, as she swept the convent corridor, to sing a little ditty about the most exalted of her own mystical experiences: that ineffable transverberation in which the fiery arrow of the seraph pierced her heart.[67]

But the most lovely and real, most human and near to us, of all these descriptions of the celestial exhilaration which mystic surrender brings in its train, is the artless, unintentional self-revelation of St. Catherine of Genoa, whose inner and outer lives in their balanced wholeness provide us with one of our best standards by which to judge the right proportions of the mystic way. Here the whole essence of the unitive life is summed up and presented to us by one who lived it upon heroic levels and who was, in fruition and activity, in rest and in work, not only a great active and a great ecstatic, but one of the deepest gazers into the secrets of eternal love that the history of Christian mysticism contains. Yet perhaps there is no passage in the works of these same mystics which comes to so unexpected, so startling a conclusion as this, in which St. Catherine, with a fearless simplicity, shows to her fellowmen the nature of the path that she has trodden and the place that she has reached.

"When," she says, in one of her reported dialogues—and though the tone be impersonal it is clearly personal experience which speaks—"the loving kindness of God calls a soul from the world, He finds it full of vices and sins; and first He gives it an instinct for virtue, and then urges it to perfection, and then by infused grace leads it to true self-naughting, and at last to true transformation. And this noteworthy order serves God to lead the soul along the way. But when the soul is naughted and transformed, then of herself she neither works nor speaks nor wills, nor feels nor hears nor understands; neither has she of herself the feeling of outward or inward, where she may move. And in all things it is God who rules and guides her, without the mediation of any creature. And the state of this soul is then a feeling of such utter peace and tranquility that it seems to her that her heart and her bodily being, and all both within and without, is immersed in an ocean of utmost peace from where she shall never come forth for anything that can befall her in this life. And she stays immovable, imperturbable,

[67]*Cf.* G. Cunninghame Graham, *Santa Teresa,* vol. i. pp. 180, 300, 304.

impassible. So much so that it seems to her in her human and her spiritual nature, both within and without, she can feel no other thing than sweetest peace. And she is so full of peace that though she press her flesh, her nerves, her bones, no other thing comes forth from them than peace. Then says she all day for joy such rhymes as these, making them according to her manner:—

" *'Vuoi tu che tu mostr'io*
Presto che cosa è Dio?
Pace non trova chi da lui si partiò.' "[68]

"Then says she all day for joy such rhymes as these"—nursery rhymes, one might almost call them; so infantile, so naïve is their rhythm. Who would have suspected this to be the secret manner of communion between the exalted soul of Catherine and her love? How many of those who actually saw that great and able woman laboring in the administration of her hospital—who heard that profound and instinctive Christian Platonist instructing her disciples, and declaring the law of universal and heroic love—how many of these divined that *questa santa benedetta* who seemed to them already something more than earthly, a matter of solemn congratulation and reverential approach, went about her work with a heart engaged in no lofty speculations on eternity, no outpourings of mystic passion for the absolute; but "saying all day for joy," in a spirit of childlike happiness, gay and foolish little songs about her love?

Standing at the highest point of the mystic ladder which can be reached by human spirits in this world of time and space, looking back upon the course of that slow interior alchemy, that "noteworthy order" of organic transformation, by which her selfhood had been purged of imperfection, raised to higher levels, compelled at last to surrender itself to the all-embracing, all-demanding life of the real: this is St. Catherine's deliberate judgment on the relative and absolute aspects of the mystic life. The "noteworthy order" which we have patiently followed, the psychic growth and rearrangement of character, the visions and ecstasies, the joyous illu-

[68]"Dost thou wish that I should show
All God's Being thou mayst know?
Peace is not found of those who do not with Him go."

(*Vita e Dottrina*, cap. xviii.)
    Here, in spite of the many revisions to which the Vita has been subjected, I cannot but see an authentic report of St. Catherine's inner mind; highly characteristic of the personality which "came joyous and rosy-faced" from its ecstatic encounters with Love. The very unexpectedness of its conclusion, so unlike the expressions supposed to be proper to the saints, is a guarantee of its authenticity. On the text of the *Vita* see Von Hügel, *The Mystical Element of Religion*, vol. i., Appendix.

mination and bitter pain—these but "served to lead the soul along the way." In the mighty transvaluation of values which takes place when that way has at last been trod, these "abnormal events" sink to insignificance. For us, looking out wistfully along the pathway to reality, they stand out, it is true, as supreme landmarks by which we may trace the homeward course of pilgrim man. Their importance cannot be overrated for those who would study the way to that world from this. But the mystic, safe in that silence where lovers lose themselves, "his cheek on Him Who for his coming came," remembers them no more. In the midst of his active work, his incessant spiritual creation, joy and peace enfold him. He needs no stretched and sharpened intuition now for he dwells in that "most perfect form of contemplation" which "consists in simple and perceived contact of the substance of the soul with that of the divine."[69]

The wheel of life has made its circle. Here, at the last point of its revolution, the extremes of sublimity and simplicity are seen to meet. It has swept the soul of the mystic through periods of alternate stress and glory; tending ever to greater transcendence, greater freedom, closer contact with "the supplier of true life." He emerges from that long and wondrous journey to find himself, in rest and in work, a little child upon the bosom of the Father. In that most dear relation all feeling, will, and thought attain their end. Here, all the teasing complications of our separated selfhood are transcended. Hence the eager striving, the sharp vision, are not wanted anymore. In that mysterious death of selfhood on the summit which is the medium of eternal life, heights meet the deeps: supreme achievement and complete humility are one.

In a last brief vision, a glimpse as overpowering to our common minds as Dante's final intuition of reality to his exalted and courageous soul, we see the triumphing spirit sent out before us, the best that earth can offer, stoop and strip herself of the insignia of wisdom and power. Achieving the highest, she takes the lowest place. Initiated into the atmosphere of eternity, united with the absolute, possessed at last of the fullness of its life, the soul, selfnaughted becomes as a little child. Such is the kingdom of heaven.

---

[69]Coventry Patmore, *The Rod, the Root, and the Flower, Magna Moralia*, xv.

Evelyn Underhill

I died a mineral and became a plant.
I died a plant and rose an animal.
I died an animal and I was man.
Why should I fear. When was I less than dying?
Yet once more I shall die as man, to soar with the blessed angels;
But even from angelhood I must pass on.
All except God perishes.
When I have sacrificed my angel soul,
I shall become that which no mind ever concieved.
O, let me not exist! for Non-Existence proclaims
'To Him we shall return'

YOGI AMRIT DESAI

Pain exists only in resistance.
Joy exists only in acceptance.
Painful situations which you accept heartily become joyful.
Joyful situations which you do not accept become painful.
There is no such thing as a bad experience.
Bad experiences are simply the creations of your resistance to what is.

JALAL-UDDIN RUMI

THE SACRED UNCONSCIOUS

H U S T O N   S M I T H

The term "the sacred unconscious" was coined by Huston Smith to denote the substratum of human consciousness. If we move from surface levels of self identity, the individual and the social unconscious, through intermediate structures and the collective unconscious, to that divine state of selfhood in which we ultimately have our being, Smith asks, what would we experience? What would a person be like if he or she were to live out of the sacred unconscious? His answer is a description of the *jivanmukta*, the self-realized human.

This selection is an abbreviated study of the psychology of the fully enlightened being. The later selection by Roger Walsh, "Exceptional Mental Health," can be read as a kind of extension or amplification of Smith's psychological study of the spiritually liberated person. Both make the point that altered *states* of consciousness lead to altered *traits* of consciousness. As you expand awareness, as you move to deeper levels of self, your life-understanding, your values, your sense of relationships change—and, consequently, your behavior. More and more you seek to live a seamless life aligned to truth and love.

In a public lecture, Smith once described the self-realized person in terms given him by his Zen roshi. The enlightened being, the roshi told Smith, is infinitely grateful to those who have gone before, infinitely compassionate to those who are now present, and infinitely responsible for those who are to come. That is a mighty message for so few words—and the basis for a lifetime's study and practice.

IN *THE NEXT MILLION YEARS*, a book published around the time of Darwin's Centennial, his grandson, Charles Galton Darwin, considered the prospects for genetic engineering. Writing as a geneticist, he concluded that the difficulties were formidable but solvable. What was not solvable, he thought, was the goal of such engineering—agreement as to the kind of person we would like it to produce. Nietzsche and van Gogh were geniuses but went mad—would we want their genes in our gene pool? It's a good question. It makes us see the nerve of a book—the present one—that tries to define the highest good for man.

As a philosopher and historian of religions, let me venture my perception of this "human best" as follows: if Marx unmasked our social unconscious and Freud our personal unconscious, both piercing through super-structures, or rather substructures, that hide true causes and motives, the supreme human opportunity is to strike deeper still and become aware of the "sacred unconscious" that forms the bottom line of our selfhood.

I shall not go into reasons for assuming that this final unconscious exists; I have discussed some of them in my book *Forgotten Truth: The Primordial Tradition,* where I use the word "spirit" for what I am here calling the sacred unconscious. Nor will I here map our human consciousness to show the relation of this deepest level to ones that are more proximate; that I attempted in the chapter on "The Levels of Selfhood" in the book just mentioned. Instead I shall try to surmise what our lives would be like if our deepest unconscious were directly available to us. What would a supremely realized human being, human here conceived as one who is consciously aware of his or her sacred unconscious, be like? How would such beings look to others and feel to themselves?

It is easier to say what such a person would *not* be like than to picture him or her positively, as the "tragic flaw" theory of art reminds us. No writer would dream of trying to create a perfect hero; he would sense instinctively that such a figure would seem completely fictitious—a cardboard cut-out. However, let the author endow an otherwise strong character with a tragic weakness—Hamlet's indecision is the standard example—and our imaginations will correct that weakness on their own; convincingly, moreover, for we graft the missing virtue onto a character whose imperfection makes him believable. The same principles apply when we try (as here) to describe human wholeness not concretely as the artist does, but abstractly: we are on firmest ground when we state the case negatively. To cite a historical instance, the Buddha's characterization of enlightenment as the absence of hatred, greed, and ignorance draws its force from being solidly anchored in real life: its key terms refer to traits we live with all the time. Yet if we try to restate his formula in positive terms and say that to be enlightened is to be filled with love, wisdom, and an impartial acceptance of everything, our description becomes abstract. Obviously we have some acquaintance with these virtues, but acquaintance is not what is at stake. The goal is to be *suffused* with these virtues: to be filled by them completely. That we have only the faintest notion of what these positive terms mean when they are raised to their maximum goes without saying.

So we now have two wise caveats before us: Darwin's, that we don't know what the summum bonum is; and Buddha's, that we do best to approach it negatively. In keeping with what I take to be the presumptuous spirit of this book as a whole, I propose to throw these warnings to the wind and attempt a positive depiction of a *jivanmukta,* as the Indians would refer to a fully realized person: a *jiva* (soul) that is *mukti* (liberated, enlightened) in this very life. The project must fail, of course, but that doesn't keep it from being interesting. Perhaps, in keeping with the tragic flaw theory I just alluded to, its very failure may induce the reader to round out in his own imaging the picture which words can never adequately portray.

An enlightened being, I am proposing, is one who is in touch with his deepest unconscious, an unconscious which (for reasons I shall be introducing) deserves to be considered sacred. Our century has acquainted us with regions of our minds that are hidden from us and the powerful ways they control our perceptions. My thesis is that underlying these proximate layers of our unconscious minds is a final substrate that opens mysteriously onto the world as it actually is. To have access to this final substrate is to be objective in the best sense of the word and to possess the virtues and benefits that go with this objectivity.

Normally we are, not in touch with this objective component of ourselves—which paradoxically is also our deepest subjective component—because intermediate layers of our unconscious screen it from us, while at the same time screening the bulk of the *world* from us. Our interests, drives, and concerns, their roots largely hidden from our gaze, cause us to see what we *want* to see and *need* to see; most of the rest of reality simply passes us by. The Tibetans make this point by saying that when a pickpocket meets a saint, what he sees are his pockets. Moreover, the things we *do* see, we see through lenses that are "prescription ground," so to speak: our interests and conditionings distort the way they appear to us. When poor children are asked to draw a penny, they draw it larger than do children for whom pennies are commonplace; it looms larger in their mind's eye. In many such ways, what we take to be objective facts are largely psychological constructs, as the Latin *factum,* "that which is made," reminds us.

This much is now psychological truism. We enter more interesting terrain when we note that at a deeper level the thoughts and feelings that control what we see are themselves shaped by what the Buddha called the Three Poisons: desire (lust, greed, grasping), aversion (fear, hatred, anger), and ignorance*—and the greatest of these is ignorance. For it is ignorance—most pointedly ignorance concerning our true identity, who we really are—that causes us to divide the world into what we like and dislike.

---

*I could get where I want to go through any of the great traditions, but having started with a Buddhist allusion several paragraphs back, I shall continue mainly with Buddhism where historical pointers seem helpful. This also makes sense because the primary orientation of this book [*Beyond Health and Normality*] is psychological, and of the great traditions it is Buddhism that puts its message most psychologically.

Thinking that we are separate selves,[1] we seek what augments these selves and shun what threatens them. What we call our "self" is the amalgam of desires and aversions that we have wrapped tightly, like the elastic of a golf ball, around the core of separate identity that is its center.

This tight, constricted, golf-ball self is inevitably in for hard knocks, but what concerns us here is that on the average it doesn't feel very good. Anxiety hovers round its edges. It can feel victimized and grow embittered. It is easily disappointed and can become unstrung. To others, it often seems no prettier than it feels to itself: petty, self-centered, drab, and bored.

I am deliberately putting down this golf-ball self—hurling it to the ground, as it were—because we want to see how high our total self can bounce: how far toward heaven it can rise. In order *to* rise, it must break out of the hard rubber strings that are normally stretched so tightly around it, encasing it in what Alan Watts called "the skin-encapsulated ego." If we change our image from rubber to glass and picture the Three Poisons as a lens that refracts light waves in keeping with our private, importunate demands, then release from such egocentric distortions will come through progressively decreasing our lens' curve—reducing its bulge. The logical terminus of this would then be clear glass. Through this glass we would be able to see things objectively, as they are in themselves in their own right.

This clear glass, which for purposes of vision is equivalent to no glass at all, is our sacred unconscious. It is helpful to think of it as an absence because, like window glass, it functions best when it calls no attention to itself. Yet it is precisely its absence that makes the world available to us: "the less there is of self, the more there is of Self," as Eckhart put the matter. From clear glass we have moved to no glass—the removal of everything that might separate subject from object, self from world. Zen uses the image of the Great Round Mirror. When the Three Poisons are removed from it, it reflects the world just as it is.

To claim that human consciousness can move permanently into this condition may be going too far, but advances along the asymptotic curve that slopes in its direction are clearly perceptible. When our aversion lens is powerful, bulging toward the limits of a semicircle, we like very little that comes our way. The same holds, of course, for our desire lens which is only the convex side of our aversion's concave: the more these bend our evaluations toward our own self-interests, the less we are able to appreciate things in their own right. Blake's formulation of the alternative to this self-centered outlook has become classic: "If the doors of perception were cleansed every thing would appear to man as it is, infinite."

The fully realized human being is one whose doors of perception have been cleansed. These doors, which up to this point I have referred to as windows, I am here envisioning as successive layers of our unconscious minds.[2] Those that are near the surface vary from person to person, for they are deposited by our idiosyncratic childhood experiences. At some level, though, we encounter the Three Poisons (once again: desire, aversion, and ignorance) that are common to mankind, and perhaps in some degree essential for our human functioning. However, the deepest layer, we have seen, is really a no-layer, for being a glass door ajar or a mirror that discloses other things rather than itself, it isn't there. Even if it were there, in what sense could we call it ours? For when we look toward it we see simply—world.

This opening out onto the world's infinity is one good reason for calling this deepest stratum of the human unconscious sacred, for surely holiness has something to do with the Whole, but the concreteness of Blake's formulation is instructive. He doesn't tell us that a cleansed perception discloses the infinite per se. It finds it in the things at hand, in keeping with those Buddhist stories which tell that the most sacred scriptures are its unwritten pages—an old pine tree gnarled by wind and weather, or a skein of geese flying across the autumn sky.

Thus far I have defined a jivanmukta; it remains to describe him or her. What does life feel like to such a person, and how does he appear to others.

Basically he lives in the unvarying presence of the numinous. This does not mean that such a person is excited or "hyped"; his or her condition has nothing to do with adrenaline flow, or with manic states that call for depressive ones to balance the emotional account. It's more like what Kipling had in mind when he said of one of his characters, "He believed that all things were one big miracle, and when a man knows that much he knows something to go upon." The opposite of the sense of the sacred is not serenity or sobriety. It is drabness, taken-for-grantedness, lack of interest, the humdrum and prosaic.

All other attributes of a jivanmukta must be relativized against this one absolute: a honed sense of the astounding mystery of everything.[3] All else we say of such a person must have a yes/no quality. Is he or she always happy? Well, yes and no. On one level he emphatically is not; if he were he couldn't "weep with those who mourn"—he would be an unfeeling monster, a callous brute. If anything, a realized soul is more in touch with the grief and sorrow that is part and parcel of the human condition, knowing that it too needs to be accepted and lived as all life needs to be lived. To reject the shadow side of life, to pass it by with averted eyes—refusing our share of common sorrow while expecting our share of common joy—would cause the unlived, rejected shadows to deepen in us as fear, including the fear of death. A story that is told of the recent Zen master Shaku Soen points up the dialectical stance of the realized soul toward happiness that we have been noting. When he was able to do so he liked to take an evening stroll through a nearby village. One evening he heard wailing in a house he was passing and, on entering quietly, found that the householder had died and his family and neighbors were crying. Immediately he sat down and began crying too. An elderly gentleman, shaken by this display of emotion in a famous master, remarked, "I would have thought that you at least were beyond such things." "But it is this which puts me beyond it," the master replied through his sobs.[4]

The master's tears we can understand; the sense in which he was "beyond" them is more difficult to fathom, like the peace that passeth understanding. The peace that comes when a man is hungry and finds food, is sick and recovers, or is lonely and finds a friend—peace of this sort is readily intelligible; but the peace that *passeth* understanding comes when the pain of life is not relieved. It shimmers on the crest of a wave of pain; it is the spear of frustration transformed into a shaft of light. The master's sobs were real, yet paradoxically they did not erode the yes-experience of the East's "it is as it should be" and the West's "Thy will be done."

In our efforts to conceive the human best, everything turns on an affirmation that steers between cynicism on the one hand and sentimentality on the other. A realized self isn't incessantly, and thereby oppresively, cheerful—oppressively, not only because we suspect some pretense in an unvarying smile, but also because it underscores our moodiness by contrast. Not every room a jivanmukta enters floods with sunlight; he can flash indignation and upset money changers' tables. Not invariance but appropriateness is his hallmark, an appropriateness that has the whole repertoire of emotions at its command. The Catholic church is right in linking radiance with sanctity, but the paradoxical, "in spite of" character of this radiance must again be stressed. Along with being a gift to be received, life is a task to be performed. The adept performs it: whatever his hand finds to do, he does with all his might. Even if it proves his lot to walk stretches of life as a desert waste, he walks it rather than pining for an alternative. Happiness enters as by-product. What matters focally, as the Zen master Dogen never tired of noting, is resolve.

If a jivanmukta isn't forever radiating sweetness and light, neither does he constantly emit blasts of energy. He can be forceful when need be; we find it restoring rather than draining to be in his presence, and he has reserves to draw on, as when Socrates stood all night in a trance and outpaced the militia with bare feet on ice. In general, though, we sense him as relaxed and composed rather than charged—the model of the dynamic and magnetic personality tends to have a lot of ego in it; it demands attention. Remember, everything save the adept's access to inner vistas, the realms of gold I am calling the sacred unconscious, must be relativized. If leadership is called for, the adept steps forward; otherwise, he is just as happy to follow. He isn't debarred from being a guru, but equally he does not need to be one—he doesn't need disciples to prop up his ego. Focus or periphery, limelight or shadow—it doesn't really matter. Both have their opportunities; both, their limitations.

All these relativities I have mentioned—happiness, energy, prominence, impact—pertain to the jivamukti's finite self which he progressively pushes aside as he makes his way toward his final, sacred unconscious. As his goal is an impersonal, impartial one, his identification with it involves a dying to his finite selfhood. That part of his being is engaged in a vanishing act, as Coomaraswamy suggested when he wrote, "Blessed is the man on whose tomb can be written, *'Hic jacet nemo,'*" here lies no one.[5]

However, having insisted above that there is only one absolute or constant in the journey toward this self-naughting, namely, the sense of the sacred, that luminous mystery in which all things are bathed, I must now admit that there is another: the realization of how far we all are from the goal that beckons, how many ranges of hills remain to be crossed. "Why callest thou me good? . . ." As human beings we are made to surpass ourselves and are truly ourselves only when transcending ourselves. Only the slightest of barriers separates us from our sacred unconscious; it is infinitely close to us. Yet we are infinitely far from it, so for us the barrier looms as a mountain that we must remove with our own hands. We scrape away at the earth, but in vain; the mountain remains. Still we go on digging at the mountain, in the name of God or whatever. Of the final truth, we for the most part only hear; very rarely do we actually see it. The mountain isn't there. It never was there.

References

1. One of the most interesting and original recent analyses of this most universal (yet ultimately questionable) assumption is to be found in Comfort, A. *I and That*. New York: Crown Publishers, 1979. Many studies now approach this subject in terms of both Asian and Western thought, but few also draw recent science as ably into the discussion as does this one.
2. Daniel Brown has uncovered something here that is interesting and probably important—I am indebted to Kendra Smith for pointing this out to me as well as for other helpful suggestions in this chapter. Writing in the *International Journal of Clinical and Experimental Hypnosis* (October 1977, *24,* 4), he notes that the steps in Tantric Buddhist medi-

tation reverse the stages of perceptive and cognitive development as these have been discovered by the constructivist school in child psychology: Piaget, Gesell, Kagan, Lois Murphy, Brunner, et al. Whereas the infant successively acquires (constructs), first a sense of self around which to organize his experience and then structures for organizing his perceptions and after that his thoughts, Tantric meditation throws this process into reverse. After an initial stage that trains the lama to introspect intently, a second state disrupts his thought structures, regressing him to the world of pure perception. Step three takes over from there and disrupts the perception-patterning processes he developed in infancy. The fourth and final stage breaks through the organizing mechanisms that constructed the infant's sense of ego and enables the lama to experience a world in which there is no obstructing sense of self. In the vocabulary we are using here, such meditation peels back intermediate layers of our unconscious minds and allows us to be in direct touch with our sacred unconscious.

3. Isaac Newton provides a lovely instance of the quality I am thinking of. What could be more everyday or obvious than gravity, enabling and ruling (as it does) our every action. Yet Newton pierced through our habituation with the force to see that it is incomprehensible. "That one body may act upon another at a distance through a vacuum without the mediation of anything else," he wrote to a friend, "is to me so great an absurdity that . . . no man who has in philosophic matters a competent faculty of thinking could ever fall into it." Quoted in Zukav, G. *The Dancing Wu Li Masters*. New York: Morrow, 1979, p. 49.

4. Schloegl, I. *The Wisdom of the Zen Masters*. New York: New Directions, 1975, p. 21.

5. *Hinduism and Buddhism*. Westport, Conn.: Greenwood Press, 1943, p. 30.

MEHER BABA AND THE QUEST OF CONSCIOUSNESS

ALLAN Y. COHEN

"Who am I?" has been one of the perennial questions begetting the personal quest. That quest—for self-understanding, for the ultimate meaning of personhood—has been answered throughout history in various ways that all point to an experience in which the seeker and the sought merge in the realization, "I am God; there is no other."

Meher Baba, like all sages, asserts this as the truth of life. You are the eternal condition behind all conditions—the Ancient One, as Meher Baba says—which was never born and which never dies and from which all creation springs. The essence of all creation—God—is as much within us as it is within trees, mountains, stars, and the cosmic void.

More properly speaking, you are within it. Enlightenment is simply waking up from the dream of conventional life generated by the ego-based sense of a separate self. And in the enlightened state, all apparently separate forms of life and conditions of existence are seen to be masks of God—things in which the divine source of all worlds and beings chooses to hide a part of itself. When you realize that, you see, as both ancient tradition and Meher Baba put it, that God is One without a second. Some religions say there are many gods, some say there is one god. The enlightened, however, know that in reality, there is *only* God, the Great Being, the Ancient One, the Cosmic Person—and "thou art that."

It is not so much that you are within the cosmos as that the cosmos is within you.

MEHER BABA, *Life at Its Best*

CERTAIN EVENTS in Meher Baba's life raise obvious questions that are explored later in [*The Mastery of Consciousness*]. For now, it might be most helpful to examine Baba's ideas about the need for methods of spiritual development. Methods make no sense without goals, goals imply values, and the existence of values implies motivation.

To Meher Baba, the real desire of human beings consists in the "quest," that urge of consciousness to grow in wisdom and experience through many life forms. This most basic drive operates unconsciously for most, consciously for the occasional seeker. Baba sees the quest and its goal in at least two facets—the human and the cosmic.

83

Allan Y. Cohen

SEEDS OF THE SEARCH

Meher Baba comments on the human experience of the quest, man's *longing for happiness and searching desperately for some means of breaking out of the trap which his life has become. It is not his fault if he assumes that the solution to his deep dissatisfaction lies in a sensual life, or in achievement in business or the social world, or in a life of exciting experiences. Neither is it his fault if life is not usually long enough to teach him factually that he would find even more profound disillusionment if these goals were to be fulfilled to the hilt.*[1]

God either exists or does not exist. If He exists, search for Him is amply justified. And if He does not exist, there is nothing to lose by seeking Him. But man does not usually turn to a real search for God as a matter of voluntary and joyous enterprise. He has to be driven to this search by disillusionment with those worldly things which allure him and from which he cannot deflect his mind. . . . He tries as best he can to have pleasures of the senses and to avoid different kinds of suffering. . . . While he thus goes through the daily round of varied experiences, there often arises some occasion when he begins to ask himself, "What is the end of all this?" . . . He can no longer be content with the fleeting things of this life and he is thoroughly skeptical about the ordinary values which he had so far accepted without doubt. . . . In the moment of such divine desperateness *a man makes the important decision to discover and realize the aim of life. There thus comes into existence a true search for lasting values.*[2]

In Baba's view, the masking effect of limited experience is a necessary contrast for the appreciation of perfect consciousness. *One has to experience being caged if one is to appreciate freedom. If in the entire span of its life the fish has not come out of the water even once, it has no chance of appreciating the value of water. . . . In the same way, if life had been constantly free and manifested no bondage man would have missed the real significance of freedom. To experience spiritual bondage and know intense desire to be free from it are both a preparation for the full enjoyment of the freedom which is to come.*

As the fish which is taken out of water longs to go back in the water, the aspirant who has perceived the goal longs to be united with God. In fact, the longing to go back to the source is present in each being from the very time that it is separated from the source by the veil of ignorance. . . .[3]

Even as the individual can be wrong in his convictions regarding his own nature, so he is often quite wrong about the nature of the world around him. In reality, it is a world of illusion that separates him from his true birthright of freedom and happiness in oneness with the One. . . . If this illusion can be shattered, the shackles which bind happiness are automatically shattered as well. But how to shatter the illusion?[4]

The first step for anyone, Baba hints, is to act on that divine itch in moments of existential desperation, to break up old life patterns and plunge into the drama of Self-discovery. The true hero of this cosmic drama is God disguised as every individual soul, striving to comprehend its real nature.

THE JOURNEY OF THE SOUL TO THE OVERSOUL

For many spiritual teachers and aspirants, it is enough to presume the existence of the inherent drive of consciousness to perfect itself. The *why* of it all remains a mystery. But Meher Baba lays it all out. Although he points out that intellectual knowledge of metaphysics guarantees no particular inner advancement, his explanation of the creation, purpose, and evolution of the universe may be the most explicit and comprehensive ever written.[5]

Meher Baba's metaphysics depends upon only one basic assumption and its corollary: infinite existence exists, and it is capable of consciousness. In elaborate detail he explains how the universe is an arena where infinite existence, identifying with the apparently limited soul, becomes more and more conscious of its oneness with itself as the Oversoul. Thus, *The sole purpose of creation is that the soul should be able to enjoy the infinite state of the Oversoul consciously. Although the soul eternally exists in and with the Oversoul in an inviolable unity, it cannot be conscious of this unity independently of the creation, which is within the limitations of time. It must therefore evolve consciousness before it can realize its true status and nature as being identical with the Infinite Oversoul, which is* One without a second.[6] For Baba, "God" is infinite existence—simultaneously infinitely aware when identifying with creation and semiconscious when identifying with the apparently limited soul.

The implications of Baba's metaphysics are literally mindboggling, but Baba uses a helpful analogy to our own ordinary states of consciousness: unconscious sleep, the dream state, and the awake state. When we sleep deeply, we have no idea who we really are, yet we have an inherent urge to wake up. Because of our very nature, sooner or later we move toward full consciousness, most often through the dream state. While dreaming, we are quite thoroughly convinced of false and limiting identity; we are quite sure that we are a character in the dream and that the dream environment is fully real, replete with physical, emotional, and mental experience. If another dream character told us we were dreaming, that everything we perceived was not separate but truly one, that we had semiconsciously created the whole experienced world, we might think them out of touch with reality. But we realize the truth of it when we awake in the morning and remember the dream.

According to Meher Baba, a similar condition extends to a higher sphere of consciousness, one which experiences ordinary waking life as an advanced dream: *Here you are all sitting in this hall thinking that your being here is real—but I assure you, you are only dreaming it. Say, tonight, when you go to sleep, you are dreaming that you are sitting here, and someone comes in your dream and tells you you are only dreaming. You will reply, "I am not dreaming, I am actually experiencing sitting here listening to Baba's discourse with all the others around me!" But in the morning you will awake and remember it as a dream. So I tell you that one day you will really awaken and know for certain that everything you have done was only a dreaming. I am the Ancient One—so is each one of you. But whereas I have awakened, you are still held in your dreams.[7]* Waking from the dream of separateness and self-imposed limitation *is* the mystic path.

THE JOURNEY SUMMARIZED

In his discourses, Meher Baba has explained fully how the individualized soul gets caught up in the dream of illusion, why it starts with very finite consciousness, and how it goes through a systematic evolution. Essentially, consciousness identifies with various impressions *(sanskaras)*, experiencing the world through more and more complex physical forms, eventually reaching the human form. The soul then reincarnates systematically to gain necessary experience. Finally, it begins to shed false impressions and false identity in order to tread the inner path toward full Self-realization.

In the beginning, because it had not evolved consciousness, the soul was unconscious of its identity with the Oversoul, and hence, though part and parcel of the Oversoul, it could not realize its own identity with it or experience infinite peace, bliss, power, and knowledge. Even after the evolution of consciousness it could not realize the state of the Oversoul (although it is all the time in and with the Oversoul) because its consciousness is confined to the phenomenal world owing to the sanskaras *connected with the evolution of consciousness. Even on the Path, the soul is not conscious of itself, but is conscious only of the gross, subtle, and mental worlds which are its own illusory shadows. At the end of the Path, however, the soul frees itself from all* sanskaras *and desires connected with the gross, subtle, and mental worlds, and it becomes possible for it to free itself from the illusion of being finite, which came into existence owing to its identification with the gross, subtle, and mental bodies. At this stage the soul completely transcends the phenomenal world and becomes* Self-conscious *and* Self-realized. *For attaining this goal, the soul must retain its full consciousness and at the same time know itself to be different from the* Sharira *(gross body),* Prana *(subtle body, which is the vehicle of desires and vital forces), and* Manas *(mental body, which is the seat of the mind), and also as being beyond the gross, subtle, and mental worlds.*

The soul has to emancipate itself gradually from the illusion of being finite by (1) liberating itself from the bondage of sanskaras; *and (2) knowing itself to be different from its bodies—gross, subtle, and mental. It thus annihilates the false ego (i.e., the illusion that "I am the gross body, I am the subtle body, or I am the mental body"). While the soul thus frees itself from its illusion, it still retains full consciousness, which now results in Self-knowledge and realization of the Truth. Escaping through the cosmic illusion and realizing with full consciousness its identity with the Infinite Oversoul, is the goal of the long journey of the soul.[8]*

UNDERSTANDING THE JOURNEY

For Meher Baba all life, whether highly conscious or not, is moving toward one ultimate goal, an adventure seeking an eternal answer to the question of existence: *There is only one question. And once you know the answer to that question there are no more to ask. . . . Out of the depths of unbroken Infinity arose the Question, Who am I? and to that Question there is only one Answer—I am God![9]* The problem is that people do not know who they really are: *You are infinite. You are really everywhere; but you think you are the body, and therefore consider yourself limited. If you look within and experience your own soul in its true nature, you will realize that you are infinite and beyond all creation.[10]*

The notion of God as one's real Self is the very foundation of true spirituality and mysticism. It can be found in the teachings of the greatest spiritual Masters of history and is consistent with the essence of all world religion. It seems mysterious because of the paradox that God has to be, not *reached,* only *discovered: The spiritual journey does not consist of gaining what a person does not have, but in the dissipation of ignorance concerning himself and life, and the growth of understanding which begins with spiritual awakening. To find God is to come to one's own self.[11]*

According to Baba, the task of realization is immense, since it *boils down to the fact that the* Atma [soul] *has to go through one hell of a thing, one after the other, in order to become Self-conscious. To become Self-conscious is to experience the "I-Am-God" State consciously.[12]* But the gargantuan difficulties of the journey are overshadowed by its ultimate reward, where: *The shackles of limited individuality are broken; the world of shadows is at an end; the curtain of illusion is forever drawn. The feverishness and the agonizing distress of the pursuits of limited consciousness are replaced by the tranquility and bliss of Truth-consciousness. The restlessness and fury of temporal existence are swallowed up in the peace and stillness of Eternity.[13]* Thus, as sketched by Meher Baba, the universe is a cosmic and just playground where infinite existence, or God, in the form of innumerable souls, evolves from ignorance to full awareness, from suffering to bliss.

ORIENTATION FOR THE SEEKER

Even though Meher Baba's explanation of the nature of reality is focused on the ultimate, his message and method is aimed at the ordinary seeker. True, the path illuminated by Meher Baba is unquestionably a mystic path. Yet his orientation is neither irrational nor impractical.

Spiritual experience involves more than can be grasped by mere intellect. This is often emphasized by calling it a mystical experience. Mysticism is often regarded as something anti-intellectual, obscure and confused, or impractical and unconnected with experience. In fact, true mysticism is none of these. There is nothing irrational in true mysticism when it is, as it should be, a vision of Reality. It is a form of perception which is absolutely unclouded, and so practical that it can be lived every moment of life and expressed in everyday duties. Its connection with experience is so deep that, in one sense, it is the final understanding of all experience. . . . Real spiritual experience involves not only realization of the soul on higher planes, but also a right attitude towards worldly duties. If it loses its connection with the different phases of life, what we have is a neurotic reaction that is far from being a spiritual experience.[14]

A seeker may rightfully demand *personal* experience of the emerging truth, but *he is conscious of the limitations of his own individual experience and refrains from making it the measure of all possibilities. He has an open mind towards all things which are beyond the scope of his experience.[15]*

The serious seeker may have to experience ambiguity, and must be courageous: *In spiritual life it is not necessary to have a complete map of the Path in order to begin traveling. On the contrary, insistence upon having such complete knowledge may actually hinder rather than help the onward* march. *The deeper secrets of spiritual life are unraveled to those who take risks and who make bold experiments with it. They are not meant for the idler who seeks guarantees for every step. He who speculates from the shore about the ocean shall know only its surface, but he who would know the depths of the ocean must be willing to plunge into it.*[16]

If Meher Baba's description of existence is correct, every soul, in one lifetime or another, will reach a point where it can advance its spiritual development consciously. From Baba's perspective, that time cannot come too quickly.

Sooner or later, man must look within, ponder deeply, and search within his own heart for those factors which hold him down in spiritual thraldom; and sooner or later, he must break asunder the gnawing chains of separative thinking which keeps him away from the immense and limitless life of the spirit to which he is the rightful heir.

Then why not sooner, rather than later? Now is the time to cast off the veil of imagined duality and unreservedly surrender to the life of open and undisguised love which is pure and selfless and which knows no fear and needs no apology.[17]

References

1. *Listen, Humanity*, p. 151.
2. Meher Baba, *Discourses*, 3 vols. (San Francisco, 1967), 2:13–15.
3. Ibid., pp. 18–19.
4. *Listen, Humanity*, p. 152.
5. Meher Baba's definitive work on this subject is *God Speaks*, 2nd ed. (New York, 1973). A simpler introduction is given in Ivy O. Duce, *What Am I Doing Here?* (New York, 1972).
6. *Discourses*, 2:139.
7. Quoted in Francis Brabazon, *Stay with God* (Sydney, 1959), p. 107.
8. *Discourses*, 2:144–145.
9. Meher Baba, *The Everything and the Nothing* (Berkeley, California, 1971), p. 78.
10. Meher Baba, *Sparks from Meher Baba* (Myrtle Beach, South Carolina, 1962), pp. 9–10.
11. Ibid., p. 13.
12. *The Awakener*, vol. 10, no. 1 (1964), p. 29.
13. *Discourses*, 2:41.
14. Ibid., 1:20–21.
15. Ibid., 2:12.
16. Ibid., p. 191.
17. *Divya Vani*, vol. 1, no. 11 (1966), p. 10.

Allan Y. Cohen

The difference between Enlightenment and ordinary existence is the capacity to recognize the ordinariness, to understand ordinary existence as it is, to realize its purity, its Ultimate or Transcendental Condition, to recognize it. States of mind, states of body and the body's relations are just a very subtle transformation of your consciousness, the very energy of being. Isn't it obvious? Because of a transformation of consciousness everything has jelled, everything has become fixed in visibility, contact, difference. And on the basis of contact and difference, you develop the philosophy of otherness and concepts of God and impulses toward phenomena, but you must understand the most fundamental state or origin of all the things to which you respond, with which you become involved, with which you identify, on the basis of which you establish your drama of life.

What is the reality of this moment? Nothing but conscious energy. Everything is a modification of it. Isn't it obvious?

To become established in that most tacit understanding is Enlightenment. That is it!

DA FREE JOHN, *The Bodily Sacrifice of Attention*

LOVE, FREEDOM AND ENLIGHTENMENT

An Interview with J. Krishnamurti

J O H N   W H I T E

There are few, if any, contemporary spiritual figures who have had greater influence on modern man's search for meaning than Krishnamurti. He has been in the public eye for sixty years. His travels have often taken him around the world; his writings and published discourses have been translated into many languages.

Krishnamurti's message is both simple and complex. His justly famous 1929 statement, made when he dissolved the Order of the Star in the East that sought to "enthrone" him as the world teacher of our age (see his biography in Appendix 4) was this: "Truth is a pathless land." There is no need to seek it through any occult hierarchy, any guru, any doctrine, he said. "The important thing is to free your mind of envy, hate, and violence; and for that you don't need an organization."

I interviewed Krishnamurti—or Krishnaji, as he is more familiarly called—in April 1984. The interview shows he has not departed from his stance taken nearly six decades ago. He still fiercely calls people to examine their own hearts and minds to see the egotism and self-ignorance at the root of all suffering and troubles; precisely *that* is what prevents enlightenment. But he makes the call in a most polished and urbane manner, with grace and good humor, even as he puts his questioners or discussants "through the wringer" with his searing but totally impersonal dialogue. It is both exhausting and invigorating to experience direct contact with him. One does not leave his sphere of influence by leaving his presence.

WHITE: You use the word "mind" in what seems to be several different senses. Does your view of mind correspond to the Zen concept of Big Mind and Little Mind, meaning Buddha-mind and ego?

Krishnamurti: Sir, I don't read books, except for occasional detective stories, so I don't know what you mean when you say Big Mind and Little Mind. First of all there is the brain . . .

White: . . . which is different from the mind.

Krishnamurti: Yes. The mind is outside the brain. It's not related to the brain in any way. The brain has enormous capacity, but it's limited.

White: Enormous capacity for what?

Krishnamurti: For technological matters. But the brain is limited by thought, by sensory responses, by biological and psychological conditioning. It is conditioned by religion. It is conditioned by education. It is conditioned by society. Now, society is created by human beings who employ thought, which is limited, and so society, being psychological activity and external activity, is shaped by thought. Thought is limited because thought is born of memory, knowledge, and experience. Without experience, there is no knowledge. The whole scientific field is based on knowledge and experience, right?

White: If that is so, how does novelty occur, especially in the scientific world?

Krishnamurti: That's innovation, which has nothing to do with creation.

White: That's an interesting distinction. I'd like to hear more.

Krishnamurti: Knowledge is limited because it is based on experience. We have accumulated knowledge and therefore it will always be limited.

White: The perimeter of knowledge is constantly expanding, but every new answer raises a dozen new questions.

Krishnamurti: Yes. Knowledge is limited. Thought is limited. Thought is contained in the cells of the brain as memory. Memory is knowledge. Thought is always limited, either in the past, present, or future. There is no complete knowledge. There can never be. And even the traditional attribution to God of omniscience is still the derivation of thought.

White: Thought conceives the concept of infinity but does not itself encompass it.

Krishnamurti: Of course. I can *imagine* anything. I can conceive a god with ten arms and one eye. Or I can conceive God as being compassionate. I can conceive God as being most unjust.

White: And wrathful . . .

Krishnamurti: Anything you want!

White: So how do we distinguish among knowledge, imagination, and fantasy?

Krishnamurti: That's very simple. Most painters imagine. Poetry, novels, literature is based essentially on imagination and thought, romance and thought, sensation and thought.

White: But creative artists bring into reality the products of their imagination.

Krishnamurti: Yes, but they are themselves limited. Anything that is manifested on canvas or paper is limited—anything.

White: Granted, but the artists haven't claimed to be infinite or omniscient—only creative.

Krishnamurti: Yes. If they did otherwise they would be laughed at.

White: But if they are creative . . .

Krishnamurti: Let's question what is "creation" and what is "innovation." All the sciences are based on knowledge and therefore are inventive: computers, airplanes, electric lights, atom bombs, missiles. The whole field of technology is based on thought.

White: But you say that is not creative or innovative.

Krishnamurti: It is invention.

White: Then you're saying that inventing is not the same thing as creating or innovating. I'm interested to know what the distinction is.

Krishnamurti: We'll come to that in a minute. Now, if you see that thought is limited—never complete, never whole, never holistic—then thought begins to imagine there is God, angels, and so on and so on, with all the rituals that religion has put together.

White: Why do you attribute that to mere thought rather than to an expression of one's personal experience?

Krishnamurti: Experience is limited.

White: Granted that our conception or knowledge of God may be limited, that doesn't mean that it's strictly a product of the imagination.

Krishnamurti: No, I didn't say that. I said: First comes experience; then experience breeds knowledge; and that knowledge is limited, whether it is in the past, present, or future. Even so-called divine knowledge of religious people is still limited. And so without complete knowledge, thought is always limited. Now, from thought is created the most marvelous technological things, the most destructive technological things, and also all the things in the churches, the mosques, and the temples—all from thought. You may say, "No, it's a divine revelation . . ."

White: But it is nevertheless filtered through thought.

Krishnamurti: Yes. So thought cannot actually understand what is creation. It can speculate about it. . . .

White: But can there be different modes of thought?

Krishnamurti: Yes, but it's still thought!

White: Are there any modes of knowing beyond thought?

Krishnamurti: Ah! That's a good question—a different one altogether. *Insight* has nothing to do with thought. If insight is the product of thought, then that insight is partial.

White: Granted. That is the case by definition if we do not have omniscience . . .

Krishnamurti: We can never have it. Thought can never capture it. We might be an astrophysicist and investigate the universe, but the understanding will be always within the field of thought. So the universe can often be captured by thought. We can understand it logically, we can understand what the universe is made of—gases and so on. But that's not *universe.*

93

White: You're saying that we understand to some degree the constituents of the universe but we cannot comprehend the universe in its entirety.

Krishnamurti: Yes. We cannot comprehend the immensity and beauty of it. We can speculate, we can imagine. I can imagine a beautiful mountain and paint what I imagine, but the mountain is different from my imagination. So there can be partial insight or total insight. But total insight is not based on knowledge. It's not arrived at through thought. Insight is not the product of time.

White: Is this total insight another way of naming enlightenment?

Krishnamurti: Let me understand what you mean by enlightenment. And you're asking, "What is enlightenment?" I don't know exactly what you mean by that word.

White: I mean radical insight into the ultimate nature of oneself and creation—beyond all thought, beyond all logical, discursive, intellectual reasoning. It is direct and immediate perception of reality.

Krishnamurti: Immediate perception of *truth*—not reality.

White: How is truth different from reality?

Krishnamurti: I'll show you in a minute. Reality is that table. We can touch it and see it. But that table has been created by thought. That's also reality. Thought has created many illusions; that's also reality. I may think I'm Napoleon, and that's reality too. Anything that thought has created is reality. But nature is not created by thought. A tiger is not put together by thought.

White: Some would argue that the tiger is a thought of God.

Krishnamurti: No, no. You and I and others have named that animal of extraordinary beauty and strength "tiger." We could call it anything else if we agree on it. But nature—the trees, the flowers, the fields—is not put together by thought. Yet it is a reality. So physical objects are realities. Illusions are realities. And I may say, for example, "I believe in Jesus."

White: So belief is also reality.

Krishnamurti: Yes. Anything that thought creates is reality, but nature is not the product of thought. So reality is all that, but truth is not all that. So what are we talking about? You're asking, "What is enlightenment?" and you say "Immediate perception of truth—that which is eternal." Now, what do we mean by perception? Either we are logical, rational, sane—psychologically healthy—and then we go beyond that—or else we play all kinds of tricks on ourselves.

White: We get lost in fantasy and illusion.

Krishnamurti: Yes, romance and all that. So, you say enlightenment is instant perception of truth. What do you mean by "perception?" Is there a perceiver who perceives truth instantly?

White: If you're asking for my response, I would say it's a paradoxical yes-and-no situation.

Krishnamurti: No! It's not that at all. Who is the perceiver?

White: Let's take me for an example. I am the perceiver.

Krishnamurti: You are the perceiver perceiving truth.

White: Right.

Krishnamurti: What are you? Who is the perceiver?

White: There is the biological-organism aspect of myself. There is the genetic heritage. There is the social enculturation and conditioning . . .

Krishnamurti: Go on. There is fear, pleasure, pain.

White: All the emotional dimensions. Then there is the capacity for rational, logical, analytical thought.

Krishnamurti: There may not be. You may be deranged.

White: Yes, that's possible also.

Krishnamurti: Sir, is not the perceiver the past?

White: Not entirely.

Krishnamurti: What do you mean?

White: Because we have the capacity to be aware, we also have the capacity to disengage ourselves to take a mental stance over and against that which is perceived.

Krishnamurti: But, sir, you're not answering my question. Who is the perceiver?

White: Ultimately, the perceiver is the cosmic process operating through me.

Krishnamurti: Ah! Now we're on. "Cosmic process operating through me"—do you follow what you have said? The "me" is very limited! It is selfish, egotistic, suffering. The perceiver is that in which all this is included. It includes his biological responses, his illusions, his pet theories—right?—his conclusions and ideals by which he lives, and so on and so on. This whole bundle is basically memory. Without memory you couldn't think, you couldn't say all this.

White: Granted.

Krishnamurti: So memories invented all this.

White: If you equate thought with perception, yes. But I don't.

Krishnamurti: But you have said there is a perceiver who is all that.

White: But not only that.

Krishnamurti: How do you know? You like to think it is not only that.

White: My direct experience tells me it is not only that.

Krishnamurti: Experience is the most dangerous thing as an evaluator.

White: No, because even though the knowledge is ultimately subjective, it is tested in the shared community . . .

Krishnamurti: Yes, which is always limited.

White: Granted it's limited, but that doesn't mean it's false.

Krishnamurti: No, whether it's false knowledge or true knowledge, they're both knowledge. It's *knowledge* we're talking about, not whether it is good knowledge or bad knowledge.

White: Well, you just said that my knowledge or my experience might not be true.

Krishnamurti: No, I said the perceiver is the past operating in the present.

White: What follows from that?

Krishnamurti: As long as the past is observing, is perceiving, then it's not true. As long as the perceiver is the past, which we agree is true, he perceives what he considers true but which is really not true, because he is evaluating, judging truth according to his past, which is memory.

White: Let me test your perspective with a simple example. If I observe a beautiful sunset and just become immersed in it, there is no thought, no memory, no mental comparisons. It is just the direct appreciation . . .

Krishnamurti: No, no, not even appreciation. The experience is so great that there is nothing but that—immersion in the experience of the sunset. Then what happens? You don't leave it there. Thought takes over and says, "How marvelous! How beautiful! I must come back and see it again tomorrow."

White: Is that wrong?

Krishnamurti: Then you've already made a picture in your mind. It's been recorded in the brain. The moment that's manifested, it's limited. When you were simply watching, there was neither pleasure nor any memories, but a second later thought comes along and says, "Look, I'll go tell my friend about the sunset." Gone! The experience of simple watching is gone. So you paint it, write a poem, or whatever.

White: What is your response?

Krishnamurti: As long as there is the perceiver, what he perceives will be limited, and therefore it's not true.

White: It's real but not necessarily true.

Krishnamurti: I don't say necessarily it is not true. But you can perceive all kinds of things. As long as the perceiver remains, the perceiver is deception.

White: Is there a self that is unlimited which can perceive?

Krishnamurti: Ah! You see, the moment you say that you have already invented a superself.

White: No, I'm only asking at this point.

Krishnamurti: There is no such thing as superself. There is only self.

Superconscious—they have played with this idea long before now—centuries before. But whether you call it superself, superconsciousness, atman, or whatever, it is still within the field of thought. You may say there is a superior self, or you may say your guru says there is, but there is no authority in these matters. Authority must be totally denied. This idea can only happen when there is a great deal of skepticism, doubt. This is not allowed in the world, except for science. The religious world is total authoritarianism.

White: But in moving beyond that authoritarianism that so conditions the mind and perceptions and knowledge . . .

Krishnamurti: You cannot unless you actually do it.

White: Yes. Let's say a person dares, risks, whatever. In the process, does one totally disregard authority, or only test authority?

Krishnamurti: The authority of policemen, or of the so-called elected government, or the authority of the totalitarian governments—they're all authority. We are forced to obey, whether we like it or not.

White: I mean authority in the field of knowledge.

Krishnamurti: In the field of knowledge, you may know much more than I do. But why should there be authority at all? You may use the authority to control me.

White: The true teacher does not use knowledge that way.

Krishnamurti: Therefore there is the authority of the policeman, law, government. But in the field of—you use the word "spiritual"—there is no authority.

White: Except oneself?

Krishnamurti: No. Oneself is also put together by thought.

White: Including you?

Krishnamurti: Oh, everything! For those who go beyond the self, there is no authority.

White: You mean they do not have a sense of themselves as being an authority for others.

Krishnamurti: Yes. There is no authority in themselves.

White: There's a true sense of humility.

Krishnamurti: No. Now wait a minute. Humility is not the opposite of authority or pride.

White: Explain that, please.

Krishnamurti: Let's take the words "good" and "bad." We say "This is bad and that is good." To hate anybody is bad, to love is good. Are they related—the bad and the good?

White: They would seem to be.

Krishnamurti: Therefore it is not good.

White: The good is not good if it is related to the bad?

Krishnamurti: It is not good because it contains the bad. Sir, look: Love and hate: if they are related, then it's not love.

White: One can say it's tainted love or impure love, but it's nevertheless love.

Krishnamurti: It's *not* love.

White: How does one attain to pure, unadulterated love? And how does that relate to enlightenment?

Krishnamurti: It *is* related to enlightenment. You have made the statement that enlightenment is the direct, immediate perception of truth—not "my" truth, "your" truth, "Christian" truth or whatever, but Truth. As long as there is the observer, the perceiver, when he perceives, it is not true. Truth can only be when there is no perceiver, only perception. That's totally different.

White: You mean there's no mental sense of boundary or division between subject and object?

Krishnamurti: And what is the relationship of perception without a perceiver and love? What is love? Is it desire? Is it pleasure? Is something put together by thought? Can there be love where there is ambition? Where there is jealousy, hate, fear—all that? Obviously not. So unless there is freedom from fear, there is no love.

White: And freedom from ambition and lust and so forth?

Krishnamurti: Of course. But what do you mean by "lust?"

White: I mean one of the traditional forms of unvirtuous behavior.

Krishnamurti: A traditional form of behavior is not behavior—it is following a pattern.

White: There can be intelligent conformity.

Krishnamurti: No. If it is conformity, it is no good.

White: Voluntary conformity is nevertheless freedom.

Krishnamurti: Now, wait, sir. Conformity can never bring freedom.

White: I'm saying that freedom can lead to conformity—intelligent conformity.

Krishnamurti: When I go to India, I go in Indian clothes. When I'm in Europe, I wear European clothes. But that's not conformity.

White: But that's the sense in which I'm using the word. I mean abiding by the customs of a place or society.

Krishnamurti: That's a very trivial affair. Look, I get up when a lady comes to the door; that's simply manners.

White: But I mean more than that. It involves the customs codified in law and politics as well.

Krishnamurti: Sir, politics are creating more and more problems. They start to solve one thing and the solution raises a dozen other problems.

White: We're talking about love, freedom, and enlightenment. I make the statement that in freedom, one can voluntarily conform to certain customs and that can be a loving act.

Krishnamurti: Wait just a minute, sir. What do you mean by freedom?

White: I'm using it in the sense I get from your use of it: beyond all biologically-, hereditarily-, and socially-conditioned thought and behavior.

Krishnamurti: Your brain is conditioned by education, by tradition, by television, by newspapers—the whole society you live in—and by environment. And as long as that condition remains, there is no freedom.

White: Agreed.

Krishnamurti: (Laughs) You can agree with anything.

White: For the sake of our discussion, that is perfectly sensible to me.

Krishnamurti: This is not a discussion. A dialogue is what we are having. The meaning of that word "dialogue" is a conversation between two people. Have you gone into the whole question of dialogue? It's very interesting. We are having conversation—a dialogue between us. You put a question to me; I respond to that. You question the response and I respond, back and forth. You respond, I question. In this process you gradually disappear; only the question remains. And the same for me. Because questioning is more important than my answer or your answer.

Sir, look: You ask "What is love?" I reply; you counter-reply to me. You ask; I reply. To my reply, you question; and to a question, I reply. In that process, what's happened? You disappear completely. There is only question and response till we reach a point where there is only question and you can't answer it, nor can I. Let that question flow, so that it is not personal responses. . . .

White: Is it shared inquiry?

Krishnamurti: More than that, sir. It is penetrating, pushing, pushing, pushing till you reach a point where you can't push anymore. When you reach that point you disappear. I disappear. There is only *that.*

White: And how do you name *that?*

Krishnamurti: No, no, no! You see, you are all too eager to name something.

White: (Laughs) But my readers are waiting . . .

Krishnamurti: Is there God? I ask that question and you say, "Yes, there is God." Then I counter that question and say that God is an invention of thought. As long as man is in a state of fear, he'll invent God. So you and I go on, back and forth, till we reach a point: Is there God? You don't know. I don't know, actually.

White: I would respond that I *do* know, that it is the primal fact of my experience, beyond all thought and argument.

99

Krishnamurti: Sir, just a minute. The scientists say human beings began from a small cell and we are the result of that small cell evolving. That's a *fact*. But what you're saying is private, the invention of man. Evolution is not an invention—that all life began in the sea.

White: Well, now, what you're saying is an interpretation . . .

Krishnamurti: Your own thoughts are an interpretation! (Laughs) So what I am trying to point out is this: Question-and-answer is a most extraordinary movement of inquiry till you reach a point where your brain cannot answer. Then that question has its own vitality, its own energy. It's not you answering it. It self-answers.

White: Then in that self-answering experience, does one . . .

Krishnamurti: You're using words! It's not a question; the thing is showing the answer. You're not answering; that question itself brings forth its answer. That's true dialogue. So, you're saying enlightenment is the immediate perception or immediate insight into truth. And I would reply that as long as there is a perceiver in the past, what he perceives is not the truth. It's limited. If I am a Christian or Buddhist or Muslim or Hindu or whatever, I believe in God or Allah or Brahman, whatever. Basically, to me that is an immense reality. Of course, I've grown up with it so I believe in it. You may say, "That's an illusion." To me it's not an illusion. So when I believe in something, that becomes a reality to me. You see, thought is operating there.

So, sir, we're talking about love. Is it not desire, pleasure? Does love contain or relate to jealousy, ambition, greed, fear, and so on? If so, it is not love, obviously. How can I be compassionate if I am attached to some belief, some dogma? Suppose I am a Catholic with a tremendous belief in a certain savior and I think I am compassionate. In reality, I am not compassionate because that belief is holding me, shaping my thought.

White: Can one do the right thing if there is not necessarily the right motive or right reason behind it? Can you nevertheless perform a right action?

Krishnamurti: As long as your motive is not pure, it cannot be the right thing.

White: Let's say the world chooses to disarm itself of nuclear weapons because of fear rather than love. Wouldn't that nevertheless be a right action?

Krishnamurti: But the atom bomb and all the rest of it has been created through fear, through nationalism, and all the rest.

White: Regardless of motives, is it a right action to disarm ourselves of nuclear weapons?

Krishnamurti: Of course. But if we remove those weapons, we'll invent new ones.

White: Granted that may happen, but in and of itself that disarmament would be . . .

Krishnamurti: Beneficial.

White: So one can perform a right action even if one doesn't have the right motive.

Krishnamurti: Now wait a minute. What do you mean by "right act"?

White: You just said nuclear disarmament would be beneficial, even if it were motivated by fear, not love.

Krishnamurti: No, I didn't. That action is based on convenience, safety.

White: But that's not necessarily wrong.

Krishnamurti: I didn't say it's wrong.

White: You just said it's beneficial.

Krishnamurti: Of course, if it helps humanity live another fifty years— before they invent something else! (Laughs)

White: The Mind Bomb.

Krishnamurti: Love can only come when there is freedom.

White: But my point is this: one might perform an act that is loving or compassionate in a partial sense, even though . . .

Krishnamurti: Do you see that as long as there is hate, there is no love? As long as there is fear, there is no love? As long as I am caught in a particular belief, there is no love? As long as I am struggling for my own self, there is no love? As long as I cling to my individuality, there is no love? So can all of that be wiped away, put aside?

White: That is the question.

Krishnamurti: Of course it can!

White: How?

Krishnamurti: When you ask how, you want a map, a system.

White: I only want your response to my question.

Krishnamurti: When you ask "how?", you are asking for a system, a map. Where there is a system, intrinsically there is a deteriorating factor. Any system!

White: But the deterioration may be outside the bounds of that system, not within the system itself.

Krishnamurti: Oh, yes, the system in itself is in decay. Any system.

White: So we're in a dilemma.

Krishnamurti: No! Don't ask for a system.

White: I didn't ask for a system. I only asked, "How?"

Krishnamurti: I'm replying to the word *how*. When you use the word, it means you want to know how to do it. That means you want a method.

White: It may be methodical, it may be chaotic, it may be random. I'm simply asking for your instruction on how to solve the dilemma we have arrived at in our dialogue.

Krishnamurti: Which is what?

White: Which is how to love when we are constantly restricted from loving by all the conditioning influencing us?

Krishnamurti: Leave love alone and uncondition yourself. Uncondition. Can there be freedom from conditioning?

White: Can there be?

Krishnamurti: I say yes. That means you have to find out or become aware for yourself, not according to some psychiatrist or some philosopher. You *are* conditioned—as an American or a Russian or a Briton and so forth. Can you be aware of all that? Is there awareness of how restricted you are, how destructive you are, how poisonous you are? It is creating wars! Can there be freedom from all that? Of course there can be. Such a human being doesn't belong to any country, to any organized religion.

White: Is that part of your response to my question of how?

Krishnamurti: Yes.

White: So, don't belong to any country.

Krishnamurti: Of course! Have a global outlook.

White: You're talking about mental allegiance rather than citizenship.

Krishnamurti: What do you mean by mental allegiance?

White: I mean, I'm a citizen of the United States but . . .

Krishnamurti: Yes, I've got an Indian passport.

White: So you're talking about a global outlook that goes beyond patriotism, nationalism, all that.

Krishnamurti: And you've got economic problems—problems of wealth and poverty, problems of various kinds, because each country wants only for itself and doesn't try to solve the economic problem as a whole.

White: So unless one adopts a global perspective . . .

Krishnamurti: Not adopts! See it! Live it! Otherwise you will destroy yourself.

White: So if one sees it and lives it, then that's love?

Krishnamurti: Now, wait! We said love is freedom from fear. Let's take that one facet of freedom. What is freedom? Freedom from? Or freedom to? If it is only freedom from something, it's not freedom. If I'm a prisoner in a prison—either a self-created one or an actual one—my whole urge is to be free of this limitation of the prison. That's not freedom! It's merely a reaction. So is there a freedom per se?

White: Not in this case. The urge is just a conditioned response.

Krishnamurti: Yes, there is freedom only when there is no conditioned response.

White: Which is the same as no fear, which is the same as love. Now, you've created an equation here which I'm interested in having stated explicitly. You're saying that freedom from all conditioning is the same as freedom from fear, which is the same as love itself.

Krishnamurti: Of course. Sir, the etymological origin of the word "freedom" is also, I believe, the same as for the word "love."

White: My question stands: How does one become love or be love?

Krishnamurti: One cannot be love. Love is outside the brain.

White: Then how does one live as love?

Krishnamurti: How can a petty little mind love? How can a conditioned mind bring love? It can't. When there is freedom from the conditioning, the other thing simply is. It isn't a question of how to live it.

White: Perhaps I should say it lives through me.

Krishnamurti: No! "Me" is limited.

White: The organism is, but the mind . . .

Krishnamurti: The mind is also limited. Brain is also limited.

White: Then that condition you call love must be ultimate reality.

Krishnamurti: No, no! You're using "condition" differently now. The human brain is conditioned by culture, by nationality, by education and so forth. As long as there is that conditioning, love cannot exist. Because that conditioning is fear and all the rest of it. So, when that conditioning is gone, the other is. How can I be ambitious, greedy, envious, and talk about love? I can't. Desire is not love. But we have reduced love to such a sorry little meaning that it is difficult to talk about it. If I say I love my wife, do I really love her? Or is it desire, pleasure, identification?

Now, you've asked about enlightenment. I wonder why we're all interested in enlightenment?

White: It's a term that denotes a condition of being that all people aspire to, however unconsciously at first.

Krishnamurti: Surely, sir, enlightenment means total freedom, complete freedom.

White: I agree.

Krishnamurti: It is total freedom from the self—from fear, from anxiety, attachments, sorrow. So you can publish an article about enlightenment and people will read it and say, "Yes, I agree with it," and carry on with their daily life, unchanged.

White: You're concerned with changing lives.

Krishnamurti: Yes, but it requires a great deal of attention, a great deal of inquiry into oneself, not just reading something and saying "I agree." There are very, very few people who say, "I am going to change." People don't see the danger of nationalism and all the rest.

White: Although there is a growing awareness of it. . . .

Krishnamurti: Which means breaking away, you see—not belonging to any country. The earth is ours to be lived in, not divided, divided, divided. And thought has done this! Americans, British, Russians, Chinese, Indian—it's all the result of the activity of thought. Thought being limited, whatever action follows from thought will also be limited. But global action, global feeling, is something totally different. The content of our consciousness—the biological and physiological reasoning and reactions, fear, all that—is shared by all human beings. You can suffer loneliness, despair, depression. Go to another part of the earth and people experience the same thing, perhaps with different terms for it, but the undercurrent is the same movement.

White: And that undercurrent is conditioned thought?

Krishnamurti: No. Sir, take an example. America suffers—suffers pain. Go to India, Japan, Russia—there is suffering. We share the common thing.

White: You mean common human experience that doesn't depend on national borders.

Krishnamurti: Right. That common current is shared by all of us. Therefore there is no individuality, psychologically. Just look at it. You go to India and you see poverty, enormous poverty, which is degrading and which causes suffering. That suffering is common to all humanity. So you are humanity, not Mr. Smith or Mrs. Jones. Inwardly, psychologically, we are human beings. We are humanity.

White: And you are saying to people: "Look, be aware of your common humanity."

Krishnamurti: Yes, sir. And when you *really* realize humanity, see what happens to you.

White: Is this part of your answer to my question of how—to look at your common humanity, to reject all labels?

Krishnamurti: Look at it first, feel it, see it with your eyes, with your blood, hear the whole thing—that you are not an individual fighting for yourself though all religions say you are an individual soul.

White: But many religions proclaim common humanity as the basis of a peaceful world.

Krishnamurti: But they don't live it.

White: But is that the fault of the religion or the person?

Krishnamurti: It is both the fault of the religion and the fault of human beings. What is important, sir? Not the printed word, not what somebody said . . .

White: But the lived experience.

Krishnamurti: Yes. But to live it without fear.

White: You have said that no guru, no philosophy, no method is sufficient for understanding insight, freedom—understanding yourself.

Krishnamurti: The ancient Greeks said "Know thyself" and before them the ancient Hindus said the same thing. But nobody has said, "Look, I'm going to find out."

White: Many people have said that.

Krishnamurti: They have not done it.

White: Ah, but that's another matter.

Krishnamurti: I'm talking about observing yourself—the fears, the loneliness, the jealousies, the anxieties—and in seeing it, you're free of it. Poof!

White: Many people may set off on a journey seeking a hidden treasure. Most will not find it. But let's say one or a few find it. Can you name individuals in history whom you . . .

Krishnamurti: I can't name personalities.

White: Do you see anyone . . .

Krishnamurti: Perhaps I do. That's of no value.

White: Ah, but their example . . .

Krishnamurti: Their example. That means you follow an example.

White: Not necessarily in a rigid, authoritarian fashion.

Krishnamurti: You are what is more important than anything else— examples, saviors. Understand yourself and be free of fear.

White: But if there is a common humanity and they have realized it in its essence, then one can learn from them.

Krishnamurti: What can you learn? Look, sir. Are you learning from me? Actually learning? Not memorizing?

White: Yes, I understand what you're saying.

Krishnamurti: Good. Very few do. The monk who gets up at three in the morning to pray is as conditioned as the man in the street.

White: Are you hopeful that your message is being heard and acted upon and lived?

Krishnamurti: Sir, I have been talking for the last sixty years or more.

White: How do you assess current world affairs? How do you see the world today? Has there been any awakening to love?

Krishnamurti: Some people do. Some take the journey halfway. There are very few who take the whole journey.

White: Do you think your message would have been responded to more positively by the Egyptians of 4,000 B.C. or the Neanderthals of 50,000 B.C. than by people today? In other words, is the world headed downhill or is

105

there any evolutionary advance in our capacity for insight and love?

Krishnamurti: I think it's becoming more difficult now. The pressures are so great.

White: But that may be the ground for a magnificent breakthrough. Do you think it's possible on a global scale?

Krishamurti: Maybe.

White: People are talking about the coming of a World Teacher and about developing a one-world society based on love and wisdom. Do you see that happening now?

Krishnamurti: I think it's happening on a very slow, small scale. Very, very small scale. Most of the world is preparing for war.

White: But there is a countercurrent that's trying to bring peace.

Krishnamurti: They don't attack war—they attack a particular war. Do you see what that means? They don't say, "Let's stop wars and preparation for war." All the industries are based on wars. So it means: Human beings need to wake up.

White: And I'm asking whether you see that going on around the world in sufficient strength to make a difference.

Krishnamurti: It's sporadic.

White: You hope that the process accelerates.

Krishnamurti: Yes.

White: But do you have a sense that it is, in fact, doing that? That the New Age or the Age of Aquarius is coming?

Krishnamurti: I'm not sure. The ones who talk about it—their own lives do not support that. Their own lives are not peaceful. Sir, I'm not sure that the human brain is not deteriorating. In this country there are specialists expert about everything. Sex specialists, beauty specialists, hair specialists, biological specialists, how-to-dress specialists, specialists about war and how to kill.

White: You mean greater and greater fragmentation in our lives.

Krishnamurti: Americans accept these specialists. If they want to beautify themselves, they say to the specialist, "Tell me how, and I'll copy it." What has happened to human beings who are dominated by specialists, as is happening in this country? They are losing their freedom.

White: Would it be fair to say, then, that you are telling people, "Love, be free, but don't ask me how to do it—find out for yourself"?

Krishnamurti: No, no! I've gone through "how." I've said, "There is no how. Watch. Look at it. Remain with it. See it—all the implications—and don't run away." To me the "how" means system, method. Intrinsically, in any system, there is decay. It doesn't matter what system—ideological, practical, political. Any system must inevitably contain its own decay. This is a law, this is obvious.

White: May I question you on that for a moment?

Krishnamurti: Yes.

White: There are biological systems and physical systems that increase their energy and complexity.

Krishnamurti: Of course. I'm talking mostly about psychological systems. IBM is based on tremendous system. It's one of the greatest systems in the world, apart from the Roman Catholic church. There is decay going on unless the system changes constantly, as IBM does. Sir, there are very, very few people in the world who have brought about a mutation in their condition, but those change the consciousness of humanity. The more, the merrier—you understand?

White: That is precisely what I'm concerned with.

Krishnamurti: There are very, very few, but they can affect the whole of the consciousness of humanity.

White: But if that does not occur, what is the outlook?

Krishnamurti: Grim. You can see what's happening. Look at the newspapers, magazines.

White: Others see hidden currents or undercurrents of change and transformation that they expect to blossom forth on a global scale very soon. They call it an Aquarian Conspiracy or the Age of Aquarius or a transformation of consciousness.

Krishnamurti: Sir, the word "transformation" means to transform from one form to another. We are talking not about transformation but about *radical change,* psychological change—not moving from this to that: the ending of something and the beginning of something totally new.

White: For an individual; but on a global scale . . .

Krishnamurti: No! I said if there are a *few* people, it will affect the whole of consciousness.

White: That sounds like a miraculous savior who's going to do it for us.

Krishnamurti: No, no no! We just agreed we share a common human consciousness, right? If a few people end sorrow, then all of the consciousness is affected.

White: Through people finding out about it and studying it and learning it?

Krishnamurti: Yes.

White: But that's a gradual process.

Krishnamurti: No. That's why time is the enemy of man. We won't go into the question of what is time just now.

White: May I pursue this point for a moment? You have spent sixty years trying to awaken the human race to truth.

Krishnamurti: To danger first, then to truth.

White: There are others who would claim they have been doing the same thing, and still others who would claim that you and those other teachers are having an effect, that there *is* a change going on in the world today, although it's not immediately apparent.

Krishnamurti: Maybe.

White: But you do not subscribe to the notion that there is a transformation of consciousness underway in the world right now?

Krishnamurti: Sir, do you know what is happening in Europe? Their culture is going; their industry is going; everything's declining.

White: Is it the same in America?

Krishnamurti: Not so much. Nevertheless, materialism—the desire for money, position—has become more important.

White: It's been with us for a long time, but I do see evidence that significant numbers of people are beginning to go beyond materialism.

Krishnamurti: What evidence?

White: A Mother Teresa of Calcutta, for example.

Krishnamurti: I don't want to discuss personalities.

White: All right. Without mentioning names, I'll just say there are many humanitarian people and organizations feeding the hungry, treating the sick, clothing the poor and so forth.

Krishnamurti: Humanitarianism is not changing the consciousness of men.

White: Does that mean humanitarian works are no good?

Krishnamurti: No, they partially help to relieve suffering. But they don't alter human consciousness. We're talking about a radical mutation in consciousness.

White: This is precisely what I'm concerned with and what I seek to hear you comment on. Is it possible, and if so, how?

Krishnamurti: I told you, sir: by freeing the conditioning of the human brain—ending that conditioning—which is to be aware, to pay attention to that condition, to be aware that we *are* conditioned, that all human beings are being conditioned by various things, and to be free of that conditioning, totally, not partially here and there, but *completely* free. Otherwise we are going to destroy ourselves. The vast majority of humanity doesn't care about all this. They listen a little, they read a little, but only a very few pay attention. Yet those few can affect all of consciousness in humanity. But those few become rarer and rarer. The world is too much. The world is demanding so much.

White: Granted that the world is demanding so much . . .

Krishnamurti: The world is *me,* demanding. The world is not different from me. I want pleasure, I want position, I want status, I want to have a car, I want this, I want that. Do you follow?

White: Yes, but those are all different aspects of "want," of "desire." And when those desires are fulfilled—as they are being fulfilled here in the United States on a physical, materialistic level . . .

Krishnamurti: Yes, you say they will require something more.

White: Yes, and ultimately one extends desire throughout the whole material level and finds no satisfaction. Nature then forces one to look higher.

Krishnamurti: It hasn't happened for the last 50,000 years.

White: Some would argue, and I am one, that it *is* happening right now. There are opinion polls and surveys that indicate American society is now beginning to place psychological satisfactions above material benefits.

Krishnamurti: I hope so, sir. One wishes that. I'm not depressed about this. I've spoken on it for sixty years. I throw seeds on good soil and bad soil. Some seeds bring flowers, others wither and die. That is life.

ONENESS AND THE TEACHING OF SRI AUROBINDO

SATPREM

One of the spiritual giants of our age—indeed of all ages—is the man whose contribution to the world began in jail at Alipore, India (see his biography in Appendix 4). From then on, Sri Aurobindo rapidly ascended to the summit of self-realization. The depth and comprehensiveness of his achievement is outstanding; it is one of the high points of contemporary spiritual efforts to probe ultimate reality and transform human life into, as he put it in the title of his masterwork, "the life divine." His life and teachings offer a method of self-transformation well-suited to modern times.

Human perfection, Sri Aurobindo felt after his experience at Alipore, would only come through a basic change in the consciousness of the world—a change that allows the oneness of existence to be seen and lived through all the diverse forms the One takes. Toward that end he developed a yoga of transformation that is today spreading around the globe from his ashram in Pondicherry, India and the nearby "City of Dawn" named Auroville, which was founded in 1968 by his coworker, the Mother, to express the legacy of Sri Aurobindo.

His vision is a compelling one, supported by practical instruction and methods for attaining a mighty evolutionary advance in human society. Unlike many earlier yogic endeavors which sought to escape the world through a "leap into nirvana," Sri Aurobindo sought to bring forth the divine potential of humanity into the realm of everyday life and thereby *embody* God in the world. Rather than turn away from Earth and Man, he sought to transform Earth and Man.

SRI AUROBINDO had to pass a year in the jail at Alipore awaiting the verdict. He had had no hand in that unsuccessful attempt; the organization of the rebellion had nothing to do with individual acts of terrorism. *When I was arrested and hurried to the Lal Bazar police station I was shaken in faith for a while, for I could not look into the heart of His intention. Therefore I faltered for a moment and cried out in my heart to Him, "What is this that has happened to me? I believed that I had a mission to work for the people of my country and until that work was done, I should have Thy protection. Why* *then am I here and on such a charge?" A day passed and a second day and a third, when a voice came to me from within, "Wait and see." Then I grew calm and waited. I was taken from Lal Bazar to Alipore and was placed for one month in a solitary cell apart from men. There I waited day and night for the voice of God within me, to know what He had to say to me, to learn what I had to do. . . . I remembered then that a month or more before my arrest, a call had come to me to put aside all activity, to go into seclusion, and to look into myself so that I might enter into closer communion with Him. I was weak and could not accept the call. My work* was very dear to me and in the pride of my heart I thought that unless I was there it would suffer or even fail and cease; therefore I would not leave it. It seemed to me that He spoke to me again and said, "The bonds you had not the strength to break I have broken for you, because it is not my will nor was it ever my intention that that should continue. I have had another thing for you to do and it is for that I have brought you here, to teach you what you could not learn for yourself, and to train you for my work."* [1] This "work" was to be the realization of the cosmic consciousness or Oneness, and the exploration of planes of consciousness above the ordinary mind, or the superconscious, which was to put Sri Aurobindo on the trail of the Great Secret. *What happened to me during that period I am not impelled to say: only that day after day He showed me His wonders. . . . That knowledge He gave to me day after day during my twelve months of imprisonment.* [2]

COSMIC CONSCIOUSNESS

Sri Aurobindo had lived for months in a sort of phantasmagoric and empty dream, standing out against the one static reality of the transcendent; however, strangely enough, it was in the midst of this void and, as if coming out of it, that the world once again burst forth with a new face, as though it were necessary each time to lose all in order to rediscover all in a higher integer: *Overpowered and subjugated, stilled, liberated from itself, the mind accepts the silence itself as the supreme. But afterwards, the seeker discovers that all is there for him contained or new-made . . . then the void begins to fill and there emerges out of it or there rushes into it all the manifold truth of the divine, all the aspects and manifestations and many levels of a dynamic Infinite.* [3] Having seen only a static Infinite, we have seen but one face of God, and we have excluded Him from the world (and perhaps it is better to have a world empty of God, as we say, than a world full of a

---

*For the liberation of India.

solemn and judge-like God). But when the silence has washed away our solemnities, both small and great, leaving us for a time caught in a pure whiteness, the world and God are there once again at every step and at every point as though they had never been separated except by an excess of materialism or spiritualism. It was in the courtyard of Alipore that this new change of consciousness set in, during the hour of walking: *I looked at the jail that secluded me from men and it was no longer by its high walls that I was imprisoned; no, it was* Vasudeva* *who surrounded me. I walked under the branches of the tree in front of my cell, but it was not the tree; I knew it was* Vasudeva, *it was* Sri Krishna* *whom I saw standing there and holding over me his shade. I looked at the bars of my cell, the very grating that did duty for a door and again I saw* Vasudeva. *It was* Narayana* *who was guarding and standing sentry over me. Or I lay on the coarse blankets that were given me for a couch and felt the arms of* Sri Krishna *around me, the arms of my friend and lover. . . . I looked at the prisoners in the jail, the thieves, the murderers, the swindlers, and as I looked at them I saw* Vasudeva; *it was* Narayana *whom I found in these darkened souls and misused bodies.*[4] This experience was never to leave Sri Aurobindo. During the six months the trial lasted, with its two-hundred-odd witnesses and its four thousand filed documents, Sri Aurobindo was shut up every day in an iron cage in the middle of the court, but it was no longer a hostile crowd that he saw nor the judges: *When the case opened . . . I was followed by the same insight. He said to me, "When you were cast into jail, did not your heart fail and did you not cry out to me, Where is Thy protection? Look now at the Magistrate, look now at the Prosecuting Counsel." I looked, and it was not the magistrate whom I saw, it was* Vasudeva, *it was* Narayana *who was sitting there on the bench. I looked at the Prosecuting Counsel, and it was not the Counsel for the Prosecution that I saw; it was* Sri Krishna *who sat there and smiled. "Now do you fear?" he said, "I am in all men and overrule their actions and their words."*[5] For, in truth, God is not outside His world. He has not "created" the world—He has *become* the world. Says the *Upanishad:* "He became knowledge and ignorance, He became the truth and the falschood. . . . He became all this whatsoever that is" (*Taittiriya Upanishad* II. 6). "This whole world is filled with beings who are His members," says the *Swetaswatara Upanishad* (IV. 10). *All to the eye that sees is one; to a divine experience all is one block of the Divine.*[6]

We are inclined to believe that here is an altogether mystical vision of the universe without anything in common with the hard reality of things; at

---

*One of the names of the Divine.

every step we come up against ugliness, against evil. This world is full of suffering; it brims over with obscure cries. Where then is the divine in all this?—the divine, this barbarity ever ready to open its camps of torture? the divine this sordid egoism, this villainy which hides or spreads itself? God is pure of all these crimes, He is perfect, He cannot be all this—*neti neti*—God is so pure that He is not of this world, there is no place for Him in all this squalor where already we are stifling! *We must look existence in the face if our aim is to arrive at a right solution, whatever that solution may be. And to look existence in the face is to look God in the face; for the two cannot be separated. . . . This world of our battle and labour is a fierce, dangerous, destructive, devouring world in which life exists precariously, and the soul and body of man move among enormous perils; a world in which by every step forward, whether we will it or no, something is crushed and broken; in which every breath of life is a breath, too, of death. To put away the responsibility for all that seems to us evil or terrible on the shoulders of a semi-omnipotent devil, or to put it aside as a part of nature, making an unbridgeable opposition between world-nature and God-nature, as if nature were independent of God, or to throw the responsibility on man and his sins, as if he had a preponderant voice in the making of this world or could create anything against the will of God, are clumsily comfortable devices. . . . We erect a God of love and mercy, a God of good, a God just, righteous, and virtuous according to our own moral conceptions of justice, virtue, and righteousness; and all the rest, we say, is not He or is not His, but was made by some diabolical power which He suffered for some reason to work out its wicked will, or by some dark Ahriman counterbalancing our gracious Ormuzd, or was even the fault of selfish and sinful man who has spoiled what was made originally perfect by God. . . . We have to look courageously in the face of the reality and see that it is God and none else who has made this world in His being and that so He has made it. We have to see that Nature devouring her children, Time eating up the lives of creatures, Death universal and ineluctable, and the violence of the* Rudra* forces in man and Nature are also the supreme Godhead in one of His cosmic figures. We have to see that God the bountiful and prodigal creator, God the helpful, strong, and benignant preserver is also God the devourer and destroyer. The torment of the couch of pain and evil on which we are racked is His touch as much as happiness and sweetness and pleasure. It is only when we see with the eye of the complete union and feel this truth in the depths of our being that we can entirely discover behind that mask, too, the calm and beautiful face of the*

*One of the forms of the Divine.

all-blissful Godhead, and in this touch that tests our imperfection the touch of the friend and builder of the spirit in man. The discords of the world are God's discords, and it is only by accepting and proceeding through them that we can arrive at the greater concords of His supreme harmony, the summits and thrilled vastnesses of His transcendent and his cosmic Ananda.† . . . *For truth is the foundation of real spirituality and courage is its soul.*[7]

The wound is then healed which seemed to cut the world forever into two between Satan and the heavens, as though there were nothing else but good and evil; and yet again the evil and the good, and we in between like *an infant coddled and whipped into virtuous ways.*[8] All duality is a seeing in the ignorance; everywhere, there is but *the innumerable One*[9]—and the "discords of God"—to unfold the Godhead within us. Even so, an abyss yet remains between this imperfection, perhaps divine, and the ultimate perfection; this cosmic divine, is he not a rather thinned-out divine? Is it not elsewhere that one must strain towards an untainted divine, transcendent and perfect? *If there is an opposition between the spiritual life and that of the world, it is that gulf which he [the integral seeker] is here to bridge, that opposition which he is here to change into a harmony. If the world is ruled by the flesh and the devil, all the more reason that the children of immortality should be here to conquer it for God and the Spirit. If life is an insanity, then there are so many million souls to whom there must be brought the light of divine reason; if a dream, yet it is real within itself to so many dreamers who must be brought either to dream nobler dreams or to awaken; or if a lie, then the truth has to be given to the deluded.*[10]

But our spirit is not at rest; perhaps we accept to see God in all this evil and suffering, to understand that the obscure enemy who torments us is truly the builder of our force, the secret smith of our consciousness. Perhaps we accept to be the "warriors of the Light" in this darkened world, like the rishis of old, but precisely why this obscurity? Why has He whom we conceive of as eternally pure and perfect, become this world apparently so faintly divine? What need had He of death and falsehood and suffering? if this is a mask, why the mask, and if an illusion, why this cruel game? Perhaps it is a benediction after all that the Lord has not made the world in accordance with our idea of perfection, for we have so many ideas about what is "perfect," about what God ought to be and, above all, about what He ought not to be, that nothing would finally remain behind in our world after clipping all the extra fringes, except an enormous zero which would not even tolerate the impurity of our existence—or a regimented barrack. *Virtue,* observes the

†Divine joy.

114

Mother, *has always passed its time in suppressing many elements in life, and if all the virtues of the different countries of the world were put together, there would remain very few things in existence.* Because, so far, we know only one kind of perfection, that which eliminates, not that which comprehends all; but perfection is a *totality*. Because we see only one second of eternity, and this second does not contain all that we would wish to see and have, we complain and say that this world is ill-made; but if we come out of our second and enter into the totality everything changes and we see perfection in the making. This world is not finished, it is *becoming*, it is a progressive conquest of the divine, by the divine, for the divine, in order to become *the endless more that we must be.*[11] Our world is in evolution and evolution has a spiritual meaning:

Earth's million roads struggled towards deity.[12]

What do we know truly of the great terrestrial journey? It appears to us tortuous, cruel, impure, but we have just been born! We have hardly come out of matter, muddy, small, suffering, like a god in a tomb who knows no longer and who seeks, who knocks against everything—but what other birth, what recollected memory, what rediscovered power does not await us farther down our road? This world is on its way, we do not yet know the whole wonder-tale.

Seek Him upon the earth . . .
For thou art He, O King. Only the night
  Is on thy soul
By thy own will. Remove it and recover
  The serene whole
Thou art indeed . . .[13]

THE CENTRAL BEING.
THE UNIVERSAL PERSON

"Thou are He," this is the eternal truth—*Tat tvam asi*, thou art That. This is the truth which the ancient mysteries taught and the later religions forgot. Having lost the central secret, they fell into all the aberrant dualisms, substituting obscure mysteries for the great all-simple mystery. "I and my Father are one," said Christ, (John 10, 30). "I am He," say the sages of India—*so'ham*—because this is the truth *all* liberated men discover, whether they be of Asia or of the West, of the past or of the present. Because this is the eternal fact which we all have to discover. And this "me," this "I" which declares its identity with God is not that of any privileged individual—as though there were yet room for a small personal and exclusive "I" in this triumphant opening, as though the sages of the Upanishads, the Vedic rishis, or the Christ had annexed for themselves alone the divine parentage—it is the voice of all men fused into one cosmic consciousness and we are all sons of God.

There are two ways of making this discovery, or two stages. The first is to discover the soul, the psychic being, eternally one with the divine, the little light from that great Light: "The Spirit who is here in man and the Spirit who is there in the Sun, lo, it is One Spirit and there is no other," says the *Upanishad;** "whoever thinks 'Other is he and I am other,' he knows not."† It is this discóvery of the Spirit within that the Vedas, some six or seven thousand years ago, called "the birth of the Son": "The red-glowing mass of him is seen: a great god has been delivered out of the darkness" (Rig Veda V. 1.2), and in a language of dazzling power the Vedic rishis affirmed the eternal identity of the Son and the Father, and the divine transmutation of man: "Rescue thy father, in thy knowledge keep him safe, thy father who becomes thy son and bears thee" (Rig Veda V. 3.9).

And the moment we are *born,* we see that this soul in us is the same in all human beings, and not only in beings but in things, latent, unrevealed: "He is the child of the waters, the child of the forests, the child of things stable, and the child of things that move. Even in the stone he is there" (Rig Veda I. 70.2). All is one because all is the One. Did not Christ say, "This is my body, this is my blood," choosing these two most material, most earthy and matter-of-fact symbols of the bread and wine to convey that this matter also is the body of the One, this matter the blood of God?§ And if He had not been already there in the stone, how would He have come to be in man, by what miraculous fall from the skies? We are the result of an evolution, not of a succession of arbitrary miracles: *All the earth-past is there in (our human nature) . . . the very nature of the human being presupposes a material and a vital stage which prepare his emergence into mind and an animal past which molded a first element of his complex humanity. And let us not say that this is because material nature developed by evolution his life and his body and his animal mind, and only afterwards did a soul descend into the form so without soul, no body that is not itself a form of soul; matter itself is*

*Taittiriya Upanishad X.
†Brihadaranyaka Upanishad I.4.10.
§See Sri Aurobindo, *Eight Upanishads,* X, XI.

substance and power of spirit, and could not exist if it were anything else, for nothing can exist which is not substance and power of the Eternal[14]. . . . *The dumb and blind and brute is that and not only the finely, mentally conscious human or the animal existence. All this infinite becoming is a birth of the Spirit into form.*[15]

When we have opened the doors of the psychic, a first stage of cosmic consciousness is unveiled. But the growing psychic, the consciousness-force individualizing itself and becoming more and more compact and dense within, is not for long satisfied with this narrow individual form; feeling itself one with That, it wants to be vast like That, universal like That, and rediscover its inner totality. *To be and to be fully is Nature's aim in us . . . and to be fully is to be all that is.*[16] We need totality because we *are* the totality; the ideal which beckons us, the goal which guides our steps, is not really in front; it does not draw us, it pushes us, it is behind—and before and within. Evolution is the eternal blossoming of a flower which was a flower from all eternity. Without this seed in the depths, nothing would stir, for nothing would have need of nothing—this is the need of the world. This is our *central being*. This is the brother of light who emerges sometimes when all seems lost, the sunlit memory which turns and re-turns us, and will give us no peace until we have rediscovered all our Sun. This is our cosmic center as the psychic was our individual center. But this central being is not located somewhere at a point; it is at all points; it is inconceivably at the heart of each thing and embraces all things at the same time; it is supremely within and supremely above and below and everywhere—it is a *giant point.*[17] And when we have found it, all is found, all is there; the adult soul regains its origin, the son becomes once again the father or more truly, the father, who had become the son, becomes himself once more: *There is a pushing back and rending or a rushing down of the walls that imprisoned our conscious being; there is a loss of all sense of individuality and personality, of all placement in space or time or action or law of nature. There is no longer an ego, a person definite and definable, but only consciousness, only existence, only peace and bliss; one becomes immortality, eternity, infinity. All that is left of the personal soul is a hymn of peace and freedom and bliss vibrating somewhere in the eternal.*[18]

We had believed ourselves small and separated from one another, a man in the midst of separate things, and we needed this separation to grow under our shell else we would have remained an undifferentiated mass in the

§See Sri Aurobindo, *Eight Upanishads*, X, XI.

universal plasma, members of the flock without our own life. Through this separation we have become conscious; through this separation we are incompletely conscious; and we suffer, for our suffering is in being separated—separated from others, separated from ourselves, separated from things, and from all, because outside that single point is where all things unite.

The only way of putting everything right is to become
conscious once more; and this is very simple.
There is but one origin.
This origin is the perfection of the Truth,
for that is the only thing which truly exists.
And by exteriorising, projecting, scattering itself,
that has produced what we see
and a crowd of little heads, very gentle, very brilliant,
in search of that they have not yet found
but which they can find,
because what they seek is within them.

*The remedy is at the centre of the evil.**

When we have suffered enough, lives after lives of this long evolution, grown up enough to recognize that everything comes to us from outside, from a life greater than ours, a mind, a matter vaster than ours, universal, the hour comes to find again consciously what we unconsciously were always— a universal Person: *Why shouldst thou limit thyself? Feel thyself also in the sword that strikes thee and the arms that embrace, in the blazing of the sun and the dance of the earth . . . in all that is past and all that is now and all that is pressing forward to become. For thou are infinite and all this joy is possible to thee.*[19]

KNOWLEDGE BY IDENTITY

We may think perhaps that this cosmic consciousness is a sort of poetic and mystical superimagination, a pure subjectivity without any practical bearing. But first, we could ask ourselves what "objective" and "subjective" signify, for if we take the so-called objective as the sole criterion of the truth, this entire world is in danger of slipping through our fingers as our art, our painting, and even our science for the last fifty years do not cease proclaiming, leaving us only a few crumbs of sure victuals. Certainly roast beef is

*The Mother, in a conversation with the children of the Ashram.

more universally verifiable, and hence more objective, than the joy of Beethoven's Last Quartets; but we have denuded the world, not enriched it. Really this is a false opposition; the subjective is an advanced or preparatory stage of the objective; when everyone will have verified the cosmic consciousness, or even simply the joy of Beethoven, we shall have perhaps the objective phenomenon of a less barbarous universe.

But Sri Aurobindo was not the man to be satisfied with cosmic reveries. The authenticity of the experience and its practical efficacy can immediately be verified by a very simple test, the appearance of a new mode of knowledge, by identity—one knows a thing because one *is* that thing. The consciousness can shift to any point whatsoever of *its* universal reality, can repair to any being, any event whatsoever and know it there and then, intimately, as one knows the beating of one's own heart, because all takes place within, nothing is outside or separate any longer. But the *Upanishad* has already said: "When That is known, all is known."* The first symptoms of this new consciousness are quite tangible: *One begins to feel others too as part of oneself, or varied repetitions of oneself, the same self modified by nature in other bodies. Or, at the least, as living in the larger universal self which is henceforth one's own greater reality. All things in fact begin to change their nature and appearance; one's whole experience of the world is radically different from that of those who are shut up in their personal selves. One begins to know things by a different kind of experience, more direct, not depending on the external mind and the senses. It is not that the possibility of error disappears, for that cannot be so long as mind of any kind is one's instrument for transcribing knowledge; but there is a new, vast, and deep way of experiencing, seeing, knowing, contacting things; and the confines of knowledge can be rolled back to an almost unmeasurable degree.*[20]

This new mode of knowledge is not truly different from ours; indeed, secretly, all experience, all knowledge, of whatever order it be, from the most material level to the metaphysical heights, is a knowledge by identity—we know because we *are* what we know. *True knowledge,* says Sri Aurobindo again, *is not attained by thinking. It is what you are; it is what you become.*[21] Without this secret identity, this underlying absolute oneness, we would be able to know nothing of the world and of beings; Ramakrishna crying out with pain and bleeding from the cut of the whip which lashed the bullock beside him, or the seer who knows that a particular object is hidden in a particular place, the yogi who cures his sick disciple hundreds of miles away, or Sri Aurobindo stopping the cyclone from

*Shandilya Upanishad, II.2.

entering his room, are only striking illustrations of a natural phenomenon—the natural thing is not separation, not differentiation; it is the indivisible oneness of all things. If beings and objects were different from us, separated from us, if we were not in essence this cyclone or this bullock, this hidden treasure, this sick disciple, not only would we be unable to act upon them, to feel them, but they would be quite simply invisible and nonexistent for us. Only the similar can know the similar, only the similar can act upon the similar. We can know only what we are: *Nothing can be taught to the mind which is not already concealed as potential knowledge in the unfolding soul of the creature. So, also, all perfection of which the outer man is capable, is only a realizing of the eternal perfection of the Spirit within him. We know the Divine and become the Divine, because we are That already in our secret nature. All teaching is a revealing, all becoming is an unfolding. Self-attainment is the secret; self-knowledge and an increasing consciousness are the means and the process.*[22]

We have separated from the world and beings across the millenniums of our evolution; we have egotized, hardened some atoms of this great Body, and asserted "we-me-I" against all the others similarly hardened under an egoistic crust. And having separated ourselves, we could no longer see anything of what was *ourself,* formerly, in the great Mother-Unity. Then we invented eyes, hands, senses, a mind to rejoin what we had excluded from our great being, and we believed that without those eyes, those fingers, that head, we could know nothing. But this is our separatist illusion; our indirect knowledge covers up and hides from us the immediate knowledge without which our eyes, our fingers, our head, and even our microscopes would be able to perceive nothing, understand nothing, and do nothing. Our eyes are not organs of vision, they are organs of division; and when the Eye of Truth opens in us there is no longer any need of these glasses or these crutches. Our evolutionary journey, finally, is a slow recovery of what we had exiled, a revival of memory; our progress is not measured by the sum of our inventions, which are so many means of artificially bringing back what we have estranged, but by the reintegrated sum of the world which we recognize as ourselves.

And this is joy—*Ananda*—for to be all that is, is to have the joy of all that is.

The bliss of a myriad myriads who are one.[23]

"Whence shall he have grief, how shall he be deluded, who sees everywhere the Oneness?"*

*Isha Upanishad 7.

References

1. Speeches, p. 54
2. *Ibid.*, p. 61
3. *The Synthesis of Yoga*, p. 133
4. Speeches, p. 57
5. *Ibid.*, p. 58
6. *The Synthesis of Yoga*, p. 341
7. *Essays on the Gita*, pp. 59, 516
8. *The Life Divine*, p. 960
9. *Savitri*, p. 76
10. *The Synthesis of Yoga*, p. 374
11. *Savitri*, p. 296
12. *Ibid.*, p. 702
13. *Collected Poems and Plays*, p. 162
14. *The Life Divine*, p. 677
15. *The Problem of Rebirth*, p. 65
16. *The Life Divine*, p. 1217
17. *Savitri*, p. 29
18. *The Synthesis of Yoga*, p. 415
19. *The Superman*, p. 27
20. *On Yoga II*, Tome One, p. 327
21. *Evening Talks with Sri Aurobindo*, A. B. Purani, (1959), p. 180
22. *The Synthesis of Yoga*, p. 60
23. *Savitri*, p. 369

Man is a transitional being; he is not final. For in man and high beyond him ascend the radiant degrees that climb to a divine supermanhood. There lies our destiny and the liberating key to our aspiring but troubled and limited mundane existence.

SRI AUROBINDO, *The Hour of God*

Beyond mind is a supramental or gnostic power of consciousness that is in eternal possession of Truth. This supermind is at its source the dynamic consciousness, in its nature at once and inseparably infinite wisdom and infinite will of the divine knowledge Knower and Creator. Supermind is superman; a gnostic supermanhood is the next distinct and triumphant evolutionary step to be reached by earthly nature.

The step from man to superman is the next approaching achievement in the earth's evolution. It is inevitable because it is at once the intention of the inner Spirit and the logic of Nature's process.

SRI AUROBINDO, *The Hour of God*

ENLIGHTENMENT AND THE JUDEO-CHRISTIAN TRADITION

J O H N   W H I T E

The global quest for self-transcendence has seen many westerners journey to the East, forsaking their religious roots in this culture for others that explicitly acknowledge the human potential for growth to godhood. Yet, if enlightenment is the core truth of *all* sacred traditions, as Aldous Huxley says, then it should be present in Judeo-Christianity, even if it is not clearly recognized by the keepers of that tradition. And if it is present, then Judeo-Christianity offers an opportunity for enlightenment-seeking westerners to "come home" without turning their backs on their religious heritage.

In this essay, I show that Jesus's teaching was indeed founded on the enlightenment experience. That, and that alone, is the key to the Kingdom of Heaven. Over the centuries, the message has, sadly, become encrusted with dogma, superstition and magical thinking, which veil it from public awareness. Moreover, the body of practices intended to enable followers of Jesus's Way to experience enlightenment have been so distorted, misunderstood or forgotten that the offical forms of Christianity devote their attention to rituals without much insight as to their reason for being.

I hope this clarification of Jesus's teaching—which can be summed up in the Greek word for enlightenment, *metanoia*—will help Christendom to see the transcendent unity of all sacred traditions and the perennial wisdom which rests in the heart of its own particular form of sacramental practice.

The emergence of a higher humanity is a perennial theme in world affairs. The images drawn from this theme vary in form and purity, ranging from the inspired visions of mystics such as Sri Aurobindo to the deranged fantasies of madmen such as Adolf Hitler. Nietzsche's *Übermensch* or Overman was distorted into the racial supremacy doctrines of the Third Reich, and Hitler sought through genocide to create a super-race. Ubermensch also became, in a more benign form, the basis for the comic book hero, Superman. The French Jesuit philosopher Pierre Teilhard de Chardin wrote of this emergence in quasi-scientific terms; the Indian yogi-scientist-philosopher Gopi Krishna addressed it more rigorously in his examination of the next evolutionary development in man via the kundalini experience;

transpersonal psychologist Kenneth Ring finds evidence for it in the widespread phenomenon of the near-death experience. Occult traditions such as Theosophy, Anthroposophy, Rosicrucianism, Freemasonry, alchemy, kaballa and the genuine mystery schools also present the notion of the evolution of humanity to still-higher states. One of the most memorable statements about it was given by the Canadian psychiatrist, Richard M. Bucke, on the last page of his classic *Cosmic Consciousness.*

> . . . just as, long ago, self-consciousness appeared in the best specimens of our ancestral race in the prime of life, and gradually became more and more universal and appeared in the individual at an earlier and earlier age, until, as we see now, it has become almost universal and appears at the average of about three years—so will Cosmic Consciousness become more and more universal earlier in the individual life until the race at large will possess this faculty. The same race and not the same; for a Cosmic Conscious race will not be the race which exists today, any more than the present race of men is the same race which existed prior to the evolution of self-consciousness. The simple truth is, that there has lived on the earth, "appearing at intervals," for thousands of years among ordinary men, the first faint beginnings of another race; walking the earth, and breathing another air of which we know little or nothing, but which is, all the same, our spiritual life, as its absence would be our spiritual death. This new race is in the act of being born from us, and in the near future it will occupy and possess the earth.

For the majority of westerners, however, the most familiar term for this experience was given to it two millennia ago by Jesus of Nazareth.

When Jesus spoke of himself, why did he principally use the term "Son of Man"? Others called him the Son of God, but Jesus most often referred to himself as the Son of Man, the offspring of humanity. Moreover, he told those around him that they would be higher than the angels and that those things which he did, they would do also, and greater (John 14:12), for that is the estate of Man.

The reason for this declaration by Jesus is that he was aware of himself as a finished specimen of the new humanity which is to come—the new humanity which is to inherit the Earth, establish the Kingdom, usher in the New Age. His mission and his teaching have at their heart the development of a new and higher state of consciousness *on a species-wide basis* rather than the sporadic basis seen earlier in history when an occasional adept or avatar such as Buddha or Krishna appeared. Jesus's unique place in history is based upon his unprecedented realization of the higher intelligence, the divinity, the Ground of Being incarnated in him—the ground which is the source of all becoming.

The Aramaic term for the Greek word "Christ" is *M'shekha*, from which we get "messiah." It is a title, not a last name, and although it is conventionally translated as "anointed," it really means "perfected" or "enlightened" or "the ideal form of humanity." Thus, Jesus was an historical person, a human being who lived two thousand years ago; but Christ, the Christos, the Messiah, is an eternal transpersonal condition of being to which we must all someday come. Jesus did not say that this higher state of consciousness realized in him was his alone for all time. Nor did he call us to worship him. Rather, he called us to *follow* him—to follow in his steps, to imitate him, emulate him, learn from him and his example, to live a God-centered life of selfless, compassionate service to the world *as if we were Jesus himself.* This is what is meant by the Latin phrase *imitatio Christi,* "the imitation of Christ." He called us to share in the new condition, to enter a new world, to be one in the supramental consciousness which alone can dispel the darkness of our minds and renew our lives. He did not call us to be Christians; he called us to be Christed. In short, he aimed at *duplicating* himself by fostering the development of *many* Jesuses. He aimed, as the New Testament declares, to make all one in Christ. And who is Christ? St. Paul tells us that Christ is the second Adam, the founder of a new race.

The Kingdom is within us. Divinity is our birthright, our inheritance, nearer to us than hand and foot, but the eye will not see and the ear will not hear. Jesus called people to awaken, to change their ways, to repent. The very first words he spoke to humanity in his public ministry were, "The time is fulfilled, and the kingdom of god is at hand; repent, and believe in the gospel." (Mark 1:14, Matthew 4:17) This is his central teaching and commandment—the kerygma.

But notice the word "repent." Over the centuries it has become misunderstood and mistranslated, so that today people think it merely means feeling sorry for their sins. This is an unfortunate debasement of Jesus' teaching. The Aramaic word Jesus used is *tob,* meaning "to return," "to flow back into God." The sense of this concept comes through best in the Greek word used to translate it. The word is *metanoia* and, like *tob,* it means something far greater than merely feeling sorry for misbehavior. Metanoia has two etymological roots. *Meta* means "to go beyond" or "to go higher than." And *noia* comes from *nous,* meaning "mind." It is the same root from which Teilhard de Chardin developed his term, noosphere, and from which the word noetic, meaning "the study of consciousness," comes. It is also the term Plato used to designate the creative source of the universe prior to the Logos, the Word, which in the gospel of John refers to Jesus. So the original meaning of metanoia is literally "going beyond or higher than the ordinary mental state." In modern terms, it means transcending self-centered ego and becoming God-centered, God-realized.

This is the central experience which Jesus sought for all people. This is the heart of Jesus' life and teaching, although it is now largely absent from the institutional Christian churches. Metanoia indicates a change of mind and behavior based on radical insight into the cause and effect of one's previous actions—insight arising from entry into a condition beyond the realm of time, space and causality. Metanoia is that profound state of consciousness which mystical experience aims at—the state in which we transcend or dissolve all the barriers of ego and selfishness that separate us from God. It is the "summum bonum" of human life. It is a state of *direct knowing, the unmediated perception* of our total unity with God. St. Paul described it as the renewing of your mind in Christ. Jesus said it even more simply: "I am the way" to metanoia.

In its best sense, then, metanoia means a radical conversion experience, a transformation of self based on a new state of awareness, a new state of consciousness—higher consciousness. It means repentence in the most fundamental aspect of our existence—that of "a turning about in the deepest seat of consciousness," as Lama Govinda phrases it. That turning-about is for the purpose of rebinding or re-tieing ourselves to the divine source of our being—the source we have lost awareness of. That is what religion is all about. *Re ligare*: to tie back, to tie again. That is true repentence—when we "get religion" in the sense of becoming aware of our inescapable ties to God, the creator, preserver and redeemer of the cosmos.

When we are rebound to God, the true meaning of sin becomes apparent. Sin means, literally, "missing the mark." Sin is not merely misbehavior. It is transgression of divine law or cosmic principle. It is failure to be centered in God—to be "off target." Religion, then, is in its truest sense *an instrument for awakening us to the evolutionary process of growth to godhood*, which is the aim of all cosmic becoming. When we are guilty of sin, we are fundamentally missing the mark by failing to be God-conscious and all which this means for our behavior and thought.

Thus, the world is indeed in sin, but there is no remedy for it except to change consciousness. For in truth, God does not condemn us for our sins; rather, we condemn ourselves *by* our sins. And thus forgiveness by God is not necessary; it is there always, as unconditional love, the instant we turn in our hearts to God. As *A Course in Miracles* puts it, forgiveness must be offered *from ourselves to the world* for all the offenses, real or imaginary, we have stored in our hearts with rancor, bitterness and longing for revenge. *That* is the turning point; that is when ego transcendence truly begins and the glory of God starts to be revealed to us.

To understand all is to forgive all. God understands all and forgives all and loves all. When we love as God loves—unconditionally—we are beyond the reach of those who are unloving. We are incapable of being hurt or offended in spirit, and therefore are always happy. For this reason, love is the greatest "revenge" we can seek against enemies and those who treat us spitefully and wrongly. Is that not precisely what Jesus taught?

There will never be a better world until there are better people in it, and the means for attaining that condition are democratically available to everyone through the grace and unconditional love of God. If that grace and love were withdrawn for even the slightest instant, the entire cosmos would be annihilated. To become experientially aware of that fact is no easy task, but ther;e is no substitute for growth to higher consciousness: the recognition that all is God and there is only God. The metanoia process, when completed, results in the state of awareness that Jesus himself had when he said, "I and the Father are one."

That is what Jesus taught and demonstrated—cosmic consciousness, the Christic state of mind, the peace that passeth understanding, the direct experience of divinity dwelling in us and all things, now and forever, creating us, living us, preserving us, urging us on to evermore inclusive states of being so that "he that believeth in me, the works that I do shall he do, and greater than these shall he do." That is the human potential—the potential for growth to godhood. That human *potential* is what can change the human *condition* and redeem the world from sinfulness—that alone. It is none other than the omnipresent divine dimension of all existence in which, as St. Paul said, we live and move and have our being.

The institutional Christian churches tell us that Jesus was the only Son of God, that he incarnated as a human in order to die on the cross as a penalty for our sins, and thereby save the world. But that is a sad caricature, a pale reflection of the true story. It turns Jesus into a magical fairy tale hero and Christianity into a degenerate cult of personality. As Emerson pointed out a century ago, institutional christendom has become a religion *about* Jesus, rather than being the religion *of* Jesus. The religion *of* Jesus calls on every human being to grow in awareness to that same state of cosmic unity and wholeness which Jesus himself demonstrated.

Jesus did not "save" people; he *freed* them—from the bondage of ego. The significance of incarnation and resurrection is not that Jesus was a human like us but rather that *we are gods like him*—or at least have the potential to be. The Christian tradition, rightly understood, seeks to have us all become Jesuses, one in Christ—beyond all the darkness of mind that results in the evil and suffering so widespread in the world. Jesus himself pointed out that this is what the Judaic tradition, which he fulfilled, is all about when he said, "Is it not written in your law, 'I said, you are gods'?" (John 10:34)

Jesus showed us the way. He demonstrated in his life and explained in his teaching that we all have the God-given right to enter the Kingdom, to be healed of our sense of separation and alienation, to overcome sin and fear of death—all of which is rooted in the egoic self-sense—and to enter into eternity-timelessness and become whole and holy. We all have this potential, given not by "my" Father but, as the Lord's Prayer says, by *our* Father. Jesus showed in his life, his death and his resurrection that we are eternal celestial beings whose home is the universe. He showed that heaven is a present reality, not a future reward. He showed that the death of the body is not the destruction of our consciousness, that the Christ consciousness which embodied itself in the man Jesus transcends the facts of physics and biology and actually controls physics and biology as conventionally understood. He showed that the Christ consciousness was, is and ever shall be present among us, faithfully calling us to reunion, world without end, for it is the source of all creation.

So rather than saying that Jesus was the Christ, it is more accurate to say: the Christ was Jesus. That allows for *other* Christs: you and me. As Vitvan says in his profound book, *The Christos*,[1] this capacity is a developmental process available to everyone. "If it is not operating in all universally, then it has no value to me."

Jesus, therefore, should not be seen as a vehicle of salvation but as a model of perfection. That is why the proper attitude toward him is one of reverence, not of worship. Jesus showed us the way to a higher state of being and called upon us to realize it, to make it real, actual—individually and as the race. This is the true meaning of being born again: dying to the past and the old sense of self through a change of consciousness. To enter the Kingdom we must die and be born again, we must become as a little child. From the perspective of metanoia, the meaning of Jesus' injunction is clear. To re-enter the state of innocence which infants exhibit, we do not merely regress to an infantile level, forsaking our mature faculties. Instead, we *progress* through transcendence of the illusion of ego and all its false values, attitudes and habits. We attain a guileless state of mind without giving up the positive qualities of adulthood. We grow into what is called "the higher innocence." We optimize, rather than maximize, childhood, becoming childlike, not childish. Superficial values and capriciousness are outgrown, so that we function in the service of a transcendant purpose, offering our life's work to God moment-to-moment rather than seeking self-glorification and some consoling distant reward in this world or the next. We discover that heaven and hell are not remote places; they are states of consciousness. Heaven is union with God, hell is separation from God, and the difference is measured not in miles but in surrender of ego and self-centeredness.

Jesus showed us the way to the Kingdom, but he will not—indeed, cannot—magically take anyone there. That depends on our own effort and willingness to sacrifice ourself—our false self.[1] And even then, the timing is unknown. God's grace is still the final factor in crossing the planes of consciousness. Nevertheless, the effort should be made, *must* be made. Like the climber who went up Mount Everest simply because it was there, sooner or later every human being will feel a call from the cosmos to ascend to godhood. That is our historical love affair with the divine. And as Jesus said, if you ask for bread, you will not be given stones. Knock and it shall be opened unto you.

There is no way to enter the Kingdom except to ascend in consciousness to the Father, to that unconditional love for all creation which Jesus demonstrated. That is what the Christian tradition—and, indeed, every true religion—is all about: a system of teachings, both theory and practice, about growth to higher consciousness. But each of us is required to take personal responsibility for following Jesus on that way. That is the key to the Kingdom. Self-transcendence requires honesty, commitment and spiritual practice to cultivate awareness. The result of such discipline is personal, validating experience of the fact that alteration of consciousness can lead to a radical transformation of consciousness, traditionally called enlightenment. But this, by and large, has been lost to the understanding of contemporary christendom. Instead, Jesus and the Bible are idolized, and heaven is said to be located somewhere in outer space. Awareness of inner space—of consciousness and the need to cultivate it—is sadly lacking. *Exoteric* Judeo-Christianity must reawaken to the truth preserved in its *esoteric* traditions.

For example, the original form of baptism, whole body immersion, was limited to adults. It apparently was an initiatory practice in which the person—a convert who would have been prepared through study of spiritual disciplines—was held under water to the point of nearly drowning. This near-death experience was likely to induce an out-of-body projection such as many near-death experiencers report today. The baptized person would thereby directly experience resurrection—the transcendence of death, the reality of metaphysical worlds and the supremacy of Spirit. He would receive a dramatic and unmistakable demonstration of the reality of the spiritual body or celestial body which St. Paul speaks of in 1 Corinthians 15:40-44 (apparently referring to his own personal experience with out-of-

---

[1] In that regard, I'm sure Jesus the Christ would be in perfect agreement with Gautama the Buddha, who taught his followers to work out their own salvation by steadfastly seeking the truth. For, as Jesus said, "the truth shall set you free."

body projection). The forms of baptism practiced today—even those involving bodily immersion—are from an esoteric perspective debasements of the original purpose and meaning of baptism in the Judeo-Christian tradition. (However, I am not implicitly advocating a return to that esoteric practice; much safer, less risky methods of inducing out-of-body projection are available today. The present symbolic use of baptism is justifiable *if* it is supplemented with the necessary understanding of its true but esoteric significance.)

Matthew 11:29-30 suggests other spiritual practices which Jesus taught to his disciples and an inner circle: "Take my yoke upon you . . my yoke is easy." The word *yoke* is conventionally understood to mean "burden" or "work." However, it is better understood in the sense of the Sanskrit *yug*, meaning "to yoke or join." It is the root from which *yoga* comes, and yoga is a system of spiritual practices designed to accelerate personal growth and development, physically, mentally and spiritually, so that the yogi attains union with the Divine. That yoking with God was precisely the aim of Jesus' teaching. Thus, esoteric Christianity understands the verses to mean "the practices I prescribe for growth to Christ consciousness."

So long as people believe in an unbridgeable gulf between themselves and that which Jesus demonstrated, Christianity will not have accomplished its mission. So long as the focus of attention remains on a naive, romanticized image of the historical person Jesus as the King of Heaven rather than on his transpersonal Christic demonstration of how to bridge the apparent gulf between God and humanity, Christianity will not have carried out its founder's intent. "Building bridges"—should be the main thrust of Christianity. Interestingly, this is explicitly acknowledged in the Roman Catholic tradition whose supreme authority, the Pope, is technically termed the *Pontifex Maximus*, which is Latin for "supreme bridgemaker."

At present, Christianity tends to demand blind faith, rote words and mechanical behavior. This leaves people empty and unfulfilled. But the cosmic calling we humans have will not be denied forever, despite the ignorance of religious institutions which, in effect, prohibit people from direct access to God. The Holy Spirit, the life force, will simply move on to create new forms of religious expression, leaving ruins called churches behind.

But it need not be that way. If the human potential which Jesus demonstrated is understood to be within us, if the capacity to grow to godlike stature is directly experienced by all christendom as the key to the Kingdom, Christianity will fulfill its purpose by encouraging people to evolve, to transform themselves, to rise to a higher state. For we are not simply human beings. We are also human becomings, organisms in an evolutionary process, standing between two worlds, two ages: an old one and a new one. The marvelous thing about us as nature-becoming-aware-of-itself-as-God is that each of us has the latent ability to take conscious control of our own evolution, to build our own bridge, and thereby become a member of the new age, the new humanity. As John recorded the words of Jesus during his visionary experience on Patmos, "Behold, I make all things new." (Revelation 21:5)

There are stages in the course of this transformation which can be presented in a simple formulation: *from orthonoia to metanoia through paranoia.* We grow from orthonia—that is, the common, everyday state of ego-centered mind—to metanoia only by going through paranoia, a state in which the mind is deranged ("taken apart") and rearranged through spiritual discipline so that a clear perception of reality might be experienced. Conventional western psychologies regard paranoia as a pathological breakdown. It often is, of course; but seen from this perspective, it is not necessarily always so. Rather, it can be breakthrough—not the final breakthrough, to be sure, but a necessary stage of development on the way to realizing the Kingdom.[2]

Paranoia is well-understood by mystical and sacred traditions. The disciplines practiced under the guidance of a guru or master or spiritual director are designed to ease the passage through paranoia so that the practitioner doesn't get lost in the labyrinth of inner space and become a casualty. But because metanoia has, by and large, not been experienced by the founders of western psychology and psychotherapy, paranoia has not been fully understood in our culture. It is seen as an aberrated dead end rather than a necessary precondition to higher consciousness. It is not understood that the confusion, discomfort and suffering experienced in paranoia are due largely to the destruction of an illusion, ego. The less we cling to that illusion, the less we suffer.

The world's great spiritual systems, however, understand the psychology of this situation very well and have developed procedures for curing it by disburdening people of their false self-image, their false identity. It is no accident that society's models of the ideal human being include many saints and holy people. These self-transcendent, God-realized individuals have been revered for many reasons: their compassion, devotion and serenity;

---

[2] The stages of spiritual unfoldment have been described well in an excellent article by John T. Chirban entitled "Developmental Stages in Eastern Orthodox Christianity," which appears in *Transformations of Consciousness*, edited by Ken Wilber *et al* (Shambhala Publications: 1986). Chirban delineates the stages as: 1) Image, 2) Metanoia (conversion), 3) Apatheia (purification or transformation), 4) Light (illumination) and 5) Theosis (God-union). This more precise use of the term "metanoia" is a valuable clarification.

their inspirational words of wisdom; their virtuous service to the world. What has been their motivation? Each of them, in his own way arising from his particular tradition or culture, has discovered the secret of the ages, the truth of the saying, "Let go and let God." When the ego-sense is dissolved, when a sense of the infinite and eternal replaces our usual narrow self-centeredness with all its passing, unsatisfying fantasies, there is no longer a mental basis for fear, hatred, anxiety, anger, attachment, desire. Instead, the perfectly harmonious functioning of the cosmos operates through us—and the cosmos is always in balance, always at peace with itself.

The Christian message is essentially a call to be universal—a call to become cosmically conscious. It is not primarily a fundamentalist warning to beware of false gods, but a transcendental urging to *be aware* of true divinity. It is a call to place God at the center of ourselves, not through blind faith but through insightful awareness, not through rigid adherence to ritual and dogma but through graceful expression of cosmic principles. It is a call to recognize god as the transcendent creator of all things, the immanent self of all things, and the omnipresent matrix from which all things arise. This is the true meaning of the Trinity—the three principal aspects of God and the three primary modes of God-Realization: the transcendent Father, the immanent Son and the omnipresent Holy spirit. The christian message is a call to live as that recognition, to "be as gods."

Thus, Jesus could speak of what is called the Second Coming as the end of the age, the end of history, the end of the world. Waking up from the illusion of ego, from the dream of worldly life, into God-conscious reality does indeed end the world. However, it ends the world not as global destruction but as transcendence of space, time and causality, and all false sense of identity based on that. For in reality there is no Second Coming at all. The Bible does not speak of two comings. Aramaic scholar Dr. Rocco Errico points out the true meaning of the phrase is "the coming of Christ." This is confirmed by the passage in Matthew that reports Christ never left humanity: "Lo, I am with you always, even unto the end of the world." (Matthew 28:20)

Thus, the final appearance of Christ will be a worldwide *spiritual* appearance, free from all physical limitations. Errico writes: "At that time the consciousness of mankind will have been raised to a spiritual level so that every eye will see nothing but good. Man will realize the spiritual life and kingdom, and at the coming of the Christ, the whole world will recognize him. His kingdom will be established and the world will be ready to receive him.[3]

---

[3] Rocco Errico, "Light from the Language of Jesus," *Science of Mind*, June 1981, p. 39.

John White

Today the world stands critically close to global holocaust. But a problem cannot be solved at the level that generated it. The answer to this emergency is emergence. That is, the solution the problem of history will not be found within history—i.e., within the state of consciousness that generates time, temptation and trouble: ego. The only way out of history into the Kingdom of God, the only way out of our precarious world situation into a New Age is a change of consciousness, a transcendence of the false sense of self from which all destructive human behavior arises. Only metanoia—the emergence of Christ-in-us—can provide the means whereby reality is seen clearly and an enlightened global culture is possible. And that is precisely what the Son of Man showed us.

TEN SEASONS OF ENLIGHTENMENT
Zen Ox-herding

———

L E X   H I X O N

In the ancient Zen ox-herding pictures described here, the enlightened person is depicted, Lex Hixon tells us, as "a fat, jolly rustic"—seemingly an overgrown, chubby, and playful little boy. In a similar vein, ancient Taoist sages were depicted as having a small babe in their heart; and Jesus said that becoming like a child is necessary to enter the "heaven" of enlightenment.

Now, there is a fundamental difference between being childish and childlike. The difference is ego. Children and sages are appealing because they are so egoless. But since children have not yet developed an ego, their *pre*personal happiness is merely naivete or carefree ignorance. As St. Augustine said, the innocence of infancy is due more to weakness of limb than purity of heart. Sages, however, are *trans*personally happy. They have gone through all the stages of ego/persona formation and transcendence to the discovery of the Supreme identity. The bliss of the enlightened is an expression of their ecstatic release from all the boundaries of consciousness, and is therefore *true* innocence.

None of that would be possible without the prior formation of an ego or separate self which exerts control over the person and urges further development. So two things must be recognized. First, the ego is ultimately a gift from God—a natural part of your development; a means to transcendence. Second, enlightenment doesn't require you to forsake mental experience, regress to infancy, and become childish. You don't cast out knowledge and learning—only the false self-identity which misapplies them. You optimize, rather than maximize, childhood. Mind*ful*ness, not mind*less*ness, is one hallmark of enlightenment. Zen calls it Big Mind. And it is delightfully playful—just like a fat, jolly rustic.

ENLIGHTENMENT is not an isolated attainment of ancient or legendary sages but a process flowering through members of every culture, a process in which our consciousness gradually becomes transparent to its own intrinsic nature. Various traditions have developed subtle languages to describe phases of this process. These dimensions of Enlightenment are not scholastic projections; they reflect the complex tissue of awareness as it gradually becomes purified or clarified by awareness of itself.

The seeker of Enlightenment must become as close an observer of consciousness as the Eskimo is of snow condition. Enlightenment is not simply an expanse of whiteness any more than snow is, but a process developing through various seasonal changes. Ten seasons of Enlightenment are evoked by the Ox-herding pictures, evolved in twelfth-century China, in which the spiritual quest is depicted as the search for an elusive Ox that roams wild in the rain forest. This Ox symbolizes the intrinsic nature of consciousness, the mystery of what we are. In Buddhist teaching, our intrinsic nature is revealed to be that we have no intrinsic nature; that is, the essence of our consciousness is void, free, or open. The dimensions of Enlightenment suggested by these ten pictures become progressively more comprehensive as this essence of consciousness, or what Zen masters call our *True Nature*, becomes clearer and clearer.

The first Ox-herding picture, or phase of Enlightenment, is called Seeking the Ox. This marks the moment when we become explicitly aware of the process of Enlightenment. We now imagine the mystery of our True Nature to be an object of search. Prior to Seeking the Ox, our spiritual growth has occurred in the disguise of ordinary life; for all desires express in more or less clarified ways the longing for ultimate fulfillment, or Enlightenment. Now we have become formal spiritual seekers, a development that is indispensable for focusing our conscious energy toward True Nature. Yet, this development also involves a fundamental illusion which Zen tradition exposes in an uncompromising way. We read from the traditional commentary on the Ox-herding pictures: *The Ox has really never gone astray. So why search for it?* By seeking our True Nature, we are creating an illusory duality between the one who seeks and the object that is sought. Why search for True Nature, which is already present, as the consciousness by which one carries out the search? Our True Nature is never lost and therefore can never be found. We cannot discover a satisfactory answer to the puzzle *Why search?* and this not-finding-an-answer brings about the gradual cessation of search which is the flowering of Enlightenment.

The ancient commentary continues: *Having turned his back on his True Nature, the man cannot see it. Because of his defilements he has lost sight of the Ox. Suddenly he finds himself confronted by a maze of crisscrossing paths.* The seeker is pictured wandering through a mountainous jungle or rain forest. The maze of paths represents the complex possibilities for thought and action in any given culture and within each individual. The seeker assumes that the Ox has taken one of these ways or byways, but no matter how sincerely he follows the various paths, he will never find the Ox of True Nature along any particular path. The Ox is eventually understood to be the entire maze of paths, the infinite rain forest as well as the seeker who wanders through it. Our True Nature is none other than the fundamental principle of Being which Zen masters also speak of as *Original Mind*. The commentary describes this illusory quest for the Original Mind, which can never be lost but from which we have turned away: *Desolate through forests and fearful in jungles he is seeking an Ox which he does not find. Up and down dark, nameless, wide-flowing rivers in deep mountain thickets he treads many bypaths.* There is exhilaration and adventure at this stage of search, yet also a growing sense of desolation and even despair. The seeker has left behind ordinary desires only to become lost in transcendental ambition. This is an impossible quest, for the concept of quest itself obscures the True Nature which we seek and which is not beyond our own present seeing or hearing. The commentary on this first Ox-herding picture ends suggestively: *At evening he hears cicadas chirping in the trees.* The music of the cicadas provides a subtle clue to the seeker's True Nature. This humming sound pervades the jungle as Original Mind pervades all the structures of seeking. The seeker is exploring the trackless wilderness, frustrated and weary, but the soothing song of the cicadas is omnipresent, subtly permeating all dimensions of his mind and senses.

The second Ox-herding picture, or phase, of Enlightenment, is called Finding the Tracks. The commentary reads: *Through the Sutras and teachings he discerns the tracks of the Ox. He has been informed that, just as differently shaped golden vessels are all basically the same gold, so each and every thing is a manifestation of the Self. He has not actually entered the gate, but he sees in a tentative way the tracks of the Ox.* The tracks are the wisdom teachings, expounded by various illumined beings, that the sound of the cicadas, and indeed all phenomena, are the same light of Original Mind, or True Nature. The seeker now becomes the finder, but as there was illusion inherent in the seeking so is there illusion in the finding. The tracks of the Ox are none other than the seeker's own tracks through his own consciousness.

Innumerable footprints he has seen in the forest and along the water's edge. Over yonder does he see the trampled grass? Signs of the Ox's presence are noticed everywhere. The forest no longer seems desolate. Yet, following these tracks will not lead anywhere because, as the commentary continues, *Even the deepest gorges or the topmost mountains cannot hide this Ox's nose, which reaches right to Heaven.* The Ox is the entire realm of consciousness that seekers of the first stage and beginning practitioners of the second stage are exploring, leaving their own tracks everywhere. However, following these tracks is a fruitful and indispensable illusion without which the seeker would not be drawn deeper into the actual practice of meditation on the intrinsic nature of all phenomena as Original Mind.

Children often need to be presented with an incomplete picture to move them in the right direction.

The third Ox-herding picture is called First Glimpse of the Ox. The commentary expands on what was hinted by the song of cicadas: *If he will but listen intently to everyday sounds, he will come to realization, and at that instant see the very Source.* The noise of city traffic is the Ox bellowing. This encounter with the Ox does not come through hearing esoteric teaching or the abstract contemplation of the sutras, but through direct experience. No longer is the Ox imagined to be somewhere out in the jungle. As the commentary suggests: *The six senses are no different from this true Source.* Any of our sense perceptions or thoughts can become a glimpse of the Ox. The commentary continues: *In every activity, the Source is manifestly present. When the inner vision is properly focused, one comes to realize that which is seen as identical with the true Source.* The practitioner who has glimpsed the Ox is consciously Enlightened, for he or she is no longer seeking the Ox or finding its tracks. The Ox is known to be omnipresent, not in abstract contemplation but in direct experience. Reflects the commentary: *The nightingale warbles on a twig, the sun shines on undulating willows. There stands the Ox. Where could he hide?* The Source cannot hide, because it exists through all forms, though they differ in structure and appearance as suns, nightingales, and willows. Yet this third phase of Enlightenment provides only an inebriating glimpse, an ecstatic realization which comes and goes. Further struggle and discipline are required to expand and stabilize such flashes of insight.

The fourth Ox-herding picture is Catching the Ox. *Today he encountered the Ox, which has long been cavorting in the wild fields, and actually grasped it. For so long a time has it reveled in these surroundings that the breaking of its old habits is not easy. It continues to yearn for sweet-scented grasses: it is still stubborn and unbridled. If he would tame it completely the man must use his whip. He must tightly grasp the rope and not let it go, for the Ox still has unhealthy tendencies.* The intransigent character of the Ox experienced in this stage is expressed literally in Japanese as *wild strength.* This is the raw energy of Enlightenment, for which nothing matters, the complete abandon that perceives creation and destruction as one. Such energy must be tempered and refined, a function of advanced spiritual disciplines which cannot begin until one has generated profound insight into the omnipresence of Original Mind. For, prior to such insight, spiritual disciplines are simply an expression of the illusion of seeking. We must now hold and embrace the Ox, sustain our perception of True Nature with such disciplines as total compassion, perfect nonviolence, unwavering truthfulness. These are the *whip* and *rope.* We are dealing with the wild strength of the Ox, which can prove dangerous. Distortions of genuine spirituality are possible at this stage. If discipleship and disciplined practice are prematurely abandoned, the energy of Enlightenment can dissipate into arbitrary and self-willed activity. That the Ox is *still stubborn and unbridled* and *yearns for sweet grasses* reflects the fact that primal awareness has been eternally at play in an infinite field unlimited by human conventions. The conventional surface thinking that operates our daily lives has developed as a byroad, apparently partitioned from the open field of True Nature. When this illusory partition is broken through and the wild Ox enters into conventional human awareness, the advanced practitioner's system of values, and even his physical nervous system, must be reconstituted so as to harmonize the energy of Enlightenment with personal and cultural being.

The fifth Ox-herding picture, Taming the Ox, indicates a more intense intimacy with True Nature. The previous phase, Catching the Ox, is to sustain and control spiritual insight under all conditions. Taming the Ox is more subtle. An effortless intimacy or friendship with the Ox is now being established. All movement of thought is to be integrated into the realization of True Nature. All phenomena are *tamed* by the childlike friendliness of the one who is ceasing to be an advanced practitioner by becoming an illumined sage. Reads the commentary: *With the rising of one thought, another and another are born. Enlightenment brings the realization that such thoughts are not unreal, since even they arise from our True Nature. It is only because delusion still remains that they are imagined as unreal.* We might suppose that Taming the Ox would begin by the elimination of all thoughts, or at least certain thoughts regarded as negative, impure, or unreal. But that is not the way of Enlightenment, which operates fundamentally by inclusion rather than by exclusion. Taming the Ox is the unlearning by the practitioner of convictions concerning discipline, purity, and discrimination that were important in earlier stages. When we follow the tracks of the Ox, which appear as the teachings of various sacred traditions, we learn to discriminate between the unreal and the real, between our inveterate human illusions and the wisdom of the sages. Now we discover all thoughts to be intrinsically the same, since they each arise from Original Mind. Only because traces of illusion remain is any thought imagined to be different from Enlightenment. Yet without this provisional spiritual illusion of discrimination between ultimate truth and relative truth, between insight and ignorance, there would have been no clarification of True Nature but only the chaos of ordinary desire.

Taming the Ox begins to dissipate this illusory discrimination between spiritual life and ordinary life, a distinction that is no longer useful. The one who is becoming a sage makes friends with the limitations of the ordinary ego rather than withdrawing into the transcendental ego of the spiritual seeker or advanced practitioner. This is the first hint of the mysterious ordinariness into which the sage eventually disappears. Describing the Ox at this stage, the commentary reads: *Properly tended, it becomes clean and gentle. Untethered it willingly follows its master.* The point of this taming is to untether the Ox, to release the primal awareness which we have focused as a particular body and mind. The Ox becomes a free companion, not a tool for plowing the field of Enlightenment. This is a graceful process, not a violent unleashing of energy. All movement becomes balanced.

The sixth Ox-herding picture, or phase of Enlightenment, is Riding the Ox Home. The advanced practitioner now becomes the illumined sage: *The struggle is over. Gain and loss no longer affect him. He hums the rustic tune of the woodsman and plays the simple songs of the village children. Astride the Ox's back, he gazes serenely at the clouds above.* In the final film of the Japanese classic, *Samurai Trilogy,* the spiritual warrior prepares for his ultimate duel by becoming a farmer again. Laboring hard in the fields during the day, he carves wooden Buddhas in the evenings by firelight. Eventually he wins his final Samurai encounter, transcending his role as warrior or practitioner, not with a steel but a wooden sword that he carves quickly and surely, drawing on the strength and reverence he developed in the carving of Buddhas. He creates the wooden Buddha and the wooden sword because wood grows directly from the earth. This earthiness of the sage does not mean that he or she is always rural, or rustic. The symbolism here is simplicity, naturalness, spontaneity. The sage, having untethered his own being and the being of all phenomena, begins to blend with the ordinary flow of life. He is pictured sitting comfortably on the Ox: *Riding free as air, he buoyantly comes home through evening mists in wide straw hat and cape. Wherever he may go, he creates a fresh breeze, while in his heart profound tranquility prevails.* The sage begins spontaneously to radiate Enlightenment, which is no longer simply an insight alive privately within him but a breeze of blessing felt by all who come into his presence. Yet while there is no longer any problem of discovering, catching, or taming the Ox of True Nature, this phase still involves subtle illusion. The sage is still relating to the Ox as a separate being, even though this being is now so intimate that one can ride it effortlessly, without having to pay the slightest attention to where it is going. The Ox must disappear utterly as a separate entity. The Ox must be expressed fully through our own person.

The seventh Ox-herding picture is called Ox Forgotten, Self Alone. The sage finally regards himself as the full expression of True Nature: *There is no twoness. The Ox is his Primal Nature: this he has now recognized. . . . Only on the Ox was he able to come Home. But lo! the Ox has now vanished, and alone and serene sits the man. . . . Yonder, beneath the thatched roof, his idle whip and idle rope are lying.* All spiritual practices and concepts are now idle. There is no longer any question of having to attain or to discipline. The contemplative way has become indistinguishable from daily life. Meditation, nothing more special than walking or breathing, has become the natural activity of the sage and no longer implies any sense of separation or motivation. *Only on the Ox was he able to come Home.* That lingering twoness between the practitioner and his or her True Nature was necessary all along the way until this stage of Coming Home. A new image emerges here. The Ox symbolized True Nature during the period of illusory quest, discipline, and attainment, but the image of Home no longer contains these illusions. Yet, although the separate Ox has disappeared, the Enlightened sage himself still exists as a particular embodiment of True Nature. He enjoys serenity and solitude. This subtle twoness created by the separate existence of the sage himself is yet to be dissolved into the perfect singleness of Original Mind. As the roles of seeker and practitioner gradually disappeared, so also the role of sage must cease to limit illumination.

The eighth Ox-herding picture is called Both Ox and Self Forgotten. The final illusory barrier has evaporated: *All delusive feelings have perished, and ideas of holiness, too, have vanished.* The sage of the previous level has no personal sense of his own holiness but does entertain a sense of reverence for True Nature as expressed through his own conscious being. Instead of blending completely with True Nature, he remains in a contemplative mood and experiences a bliss that still retains a trace of twoness. But on the eighth level, represented by empty space, there is only awakened Enlightenment: no contemplator and no contemplation, no serenity and no disturbance. *He lingers not in Buddha and passes quickly on through not-Buddha.* Awakened Enlightenment itself cannot assert, *I am Buddha,* any more than it can assert, *I am not Buddha.* Any such assertion implies the existence of someone who frames the assertion. Here there is no one, not even the sage. Both Ox and Self Forgotten is represented by the traditional Zen circle, the single brushstroke leaving the paper shortly before the point of closure. If there were not that opening, further growth could not occur and the process of Enlightenment would be frozen into empty space. This profound state of emptiness needs to open into fullness. Otherwise it would be excluding the flow of life outside itself, and another illusory sense of subtle duality would arise. The empty circle should contain a landscape. The stream of life-forms continues to flow as trees, fish, insects. Life is not to be locked out by Enlightenment.

The ninth Ox-herding picture is called Return to the Source. Mountains and pine groves, clouds and waves are appearing from nowhere. The open space of emptiness is melting into a kind of springtime: formless awareness is growing back into forms again without losing its formless, or perfectly unitary, nature. The Enlightened being is no longer faced with the illusion of Enlightenment: *From the very beginning there has not been so much as a speck of dust to mar the intrinsic purity.* After the First Glimpse of the Ox, the practitioner senses every activity as emerging directly from the Source, yet must traverse all the subtle intervening levels of development in order actually to return to that Source. The sage's homecoming had to dissolve into the circle of emptiness before he could completely disappear and simply *be* the Source. But there is no annihilation. All manifestation is now observed by awakened Enlightenment as its own emanation: *This waxing and waning of life is no phantom or illusion, but a manifestation of the Source. Why, then, is there a need to strive for anything? The waters are blue, the mountains are green.* Enlightenment simply *is* the blue lake and the green mountain. In earlier stages there has been a dramatic quality of realization; but in the ninth stage this drama fades, leaving only freshness or plainness: *The waters are blue, the mountains are green.* But where are the human beings? There remains a subtly transhuman flavor in this Return to the Source. The process of Enlightenment has come so far, through so many simplifications, that there is difficulty in recognizing and accepting the constructions of human personality and society: *It is as though he were now blind and deaf. Seated in his hut, he hankers not for things outside.* There is a subtle twoness here between the Source flowering as pine or cherry trees and its manifestation as the chronic delusion and suffering of human civilization. This very Return to the Source must deepen to include the return to mundane life.

The tenth Ox-herding picture, which obliterates oneness as well as twoness, is called Entering the Marketplace with Helping Hands. Awakened Enlightenment takes the form of a fat, jolly rustic who wanders from village to village, from mundane situation to mundane situation. His body is overflowing with life-energy. His being is full of compassionate love. His open hands express perfect emptiness. *The gate of his cottage is closed, and even the wisest cannot find him.* He has gone beyond, gone completely beyond, not to move farther away from humanity but to return completely into the human world. He has even abandoned the Source as a citadel where Enlightenment may subtly isolate itself. *The wisest cannot find him,* because it is not he that wanders about but simply the activity of awakened Enlightenment. He does not experience any intrinsic difference between himself and the villagers, or even the village landscape: *His mental panorama has finally disappeared. He goes his own way, making no attempt to follow the steps of earlier sages.* Advanced practitioners and even sages feel intense reverence for previous sages, and thereby may regard themselves as subtly separate from those Great Ones. But the awakened Enlightenment expressed in this tenth stage is fully identical with the Enlightenment of all Buddhas, past, present, and future. Who is there to follow? The cheerful one who fully manifests Enlightenment follows no path. He carries a wine gourd, symbol of the Tantric ecstasy which transforms the wine of the delusive human world from poison into nectar. *Carrying a gourd, he strolls into the market. He leads innkeepers and fishmongers in the Way of the Buddha. Bare-chested, barefooted, he comes into the marketplace. Muddied and dust-covered, how broadly he grins! Without recourse to mystic powers, withered trees he swiftly brings to bloom.* By being perceived as intrinsically Buddhas, not only fishmongers and innkeepers but all human beings in the marketplace of desire are swiftly brought to bloom.

> Who is the teacher and who is the taught?
> You think you're the seeker and find you're the sought.

> Plant a thought, harvest an act.
> Plant an act, harvest a habit.
> Plant a habit, harvest a character.
> Plant a character, harvest a destiny.

MINNETAREE INDIAN CHANT

> I sought my soul—my soul I could not see;
> I sought my God—my God eluded me;
> I sought my brother—and found all three.

EXCEPTIONAL MENTAL HEALTH
Ancient Images and Recent Research

R O G E R   N.   W A L S H

Enlightenment sees the underlying unity of all things. Wherever there is boundary and rift, it tries to dissolve them insofar as they are based on ego and ignorance. It does not try to eliminate diversity and difference—only division.

In that spirit, Roger N. Walsh, a transpersonally-oriented psychiatrist, demonstrates here the compatibility of an eastern psychological system (drawn from Theravadin Buddhism) with western psychological and social concerns. Although there is presently a large division between eastern and western views of the nature of the human being, bridges are being built by far-seeing individuals such as Walsh whose efforts correct and enlarge the views of conventional western psychologies. Since transcendence is the essential process in growth to enlightenment, and since transcendence does not merely negate but also includes lower levels while purifying or correcting them, studies such as this one are a powerful antidote to the impurities of conventional psychological models. At the same time, however, they preserve what is right and true in those models, giving due credit while showing new directions for research and application. For example, Walsh cites meditation studies that grew out of western investigative science and a current interest in Eastern phenomena. These studies, he says, point in a preliminary fashion beyond some of the most fundamental assumptions of western psychology. Those assumptions concern higher human development—assumptions which essentially deny the possibility of it. If there are historical examples of people who have actualized the human potential for "the ten perfections" named here, if these assumptions are incorrect, and if techniques exist for assisting humanity at large to attain such a condition, then the means are at hand for psychotherapy and the care-giving professions to make a mighty evolutionary leap forward in their contribution to human well-being.

"WE HAVE," lamented the great psychologist Gordon Allport, "on the psychology of liberation—nothing."[1] His lament was that western clinical psychology and psychiatry are primarily oriented toward pathology and have little knowledge of psychological health, let alone of the topic of this book—enlightenment. Indeed, these topics are widely misunderstood. Many mental health professionals still regard phenomena such as psychological maturation beyond cultural norms, mystical experiences, and enlightenment as mythical at best and pathological at worst; "psychological regression at its most extreme,"[2] as one well-known psychiatric textbook describes them.

This attitude is understandable. Until very recently there has been remarkably little reliable information available on the eastern traditions and psychologies which originated the idea of enlightenment.

In addition, the available information has frequently been distorted by linguistic, cultural, and paradigmatic barriers.[3,4] However, within the last decade a considerable body of theoretical and research evidence has accumulated which suggests that we may have seriously underestimated the possible validity and value of some eastern psychologies. Integrations among eastern and western systems have begun to appear, and the works of Ken Wilber, who is perhaps today's foremost theoretical psychologist, have been particularly successful in this regard.[5,6,7,8,9]

Likewise, there has also been a significant increase in interest and research on psychological health and well-being.[10,11] Though pathology remains the major focus of western behavioral sciences, there is a growing recognition that health is more than just "not sick." Respected thinkers such as Abraham Maslow,[12] Eric Fromm,[13] Lawrence Kohlberg,[14] and Ken Wilber,[5,7] among others, have acknowledged, respectively, levels of motivation, attitude, moral thinking, and cognitive development beyond what have traditionally been taken to be "normal," or the upper limits, of psychological maturity.

Eastern psychologies, on the other hand, represent almost mirror images to their western counterpart. Hindu, Buddhist, and Sufi systems, for example, are derived from pragmatic concerns having to do with cultivating well-being. Consequently, they contain relatively little in the way of systematic analyses of psychopathology but do provide sophisticated cartographies of stages of psychological development which they claim lie beyond the boundaries of traditional western psychological models.

It is generally agreed that, as Huston Smith puts it in his essay reprinted here, "of the great traditions it is Buddhism which puts its message most psychologically."[15] In Buddhism we find rich descriptions of psychological health and development, and of states of consciousness.

Like all the great religious traditions, Buddhism has split into numerous and diverse schools. The oldest surviving school is the Theravadin, found today predominantly in Southeast Asia. The Theravadins represent the Buddhist conservatives whose major authority is the earliest Buddhist writings which date back almost 2,000 years. Other schools also value these writings, but in addition have incorporated many new ideas and texts. The net effect is that the Theravadin tradition and ideas are shared by virtually all contemporary schools of Buddhism but are accorded different values.

The following model of the qualities of exceptional psychological well-being is derived from this Theravadin tradition. This model describes ten traits, qualities, or attributes said to characterize healthy people. In the fully enlightened person these traits are said to have been brought to their highest possible fruition or perfection, and hence are called "the ten perfections." All of us possess these qualities to varying degrees, and all of us are said to be capable of cultivating them by practicing an ethical life-style and meditation, and by developing wisdom.

Students of comparative religion and practice will recognize in the ten perfections goals common to all the great religious/philosophical/consciousness disciplines. They are not an exhaustive list of the qualities which these disciplines attempt to cultivate, but they do provide one vision of the heights of human development. Let us now examine these ten qualities: determination, energy, ethicality, truthfulness, renunciation, patience, equanimity, generosity, loving kindness, and wisdom.

1. Determination

Buddhism states repeatedly and explicitly that one's degree of attainment and depths of realization are self-determined. There is, it says, no outside agency, god, or guru who can do our work for us, and the attainment of true mental health demands intense determination and effort. The Buddha claimed that his path was rewarding but by no means easy, and regarded unyielding determination as essential for success.[16,17,18] Fortunately, the ten perfections are both means and end, and are said to be strengthened as one progresses so that determination is developed with practice.

2. Energy

Closely related to determination is the quality of energy, which also has connotations of effort and striving. Indeed, the Buddha spoke of the necessity of effort more frequently than any other quality.[18] The quality of energy-effort is regarded as essential for overcoming one of the five major hindrances to progress, namely, the tendency toward laziness, inertia, and hypoarousal which the Buddhists have so picturesquely labeled "sloth and torpor." This is said to be a common trap for beginners on the path, and recent electroencephalographic studies have sometimes revealed low levels of brain arousal and the initial stages of sleep in beginning meditators.[19,20]

3. Ethicality

"See yourself in others
Then whom can you hurt?
What harm can you do?"

THE BUDDHA[17]

Ethicality, as it is implied in Buddhism and other consciousness disciplines, has been much misunderstood in popular thinking and institutionalized religion. In the consciousness disciplines ethicality is recognized as a functional and skillful device which is essential for mental training and is not to be confused with externally imposed moralism or sanctions. No one deeply involved in an intensive mental training program can long remain ignorant of the harmful effects of unethical behavior on mental activity and control. The practitioner soon recognizes that unethical behavior is motivated by powerful emotions such as greed, anger, or aversion which grip the mind and render it hard to control.[18,21,22] While unethical behavior stems from such motives, it also conditions and reinforces them, thus leaving the mind more deeply entrapped in counterproductive conditioning. This, in turn, produces still more disruptive states such as agitation and guilt.

The practice of ethicality, on the other hand, is designed to reverse this process and to extinguish those addictions and emotions which produce it. The final result is the mind of the arahat (the fully enlightened individual), which is said to be totally freed of such states, and hence to be quite incapable of unethical behavior.[22,23]

Ethicality is a particularly clear example of the synergistic nature of the perfections. That is, they necessarily serve both the practitioner and others so that selfish or sacrificial, you-or-me, zero-sum, win-lose dichotomies become meaningless.

4. Truthfulness

The Buddha is said to have admonished his son to "Never lie, even in jest." This stringent advice seems to reflect the Buddha's deep insight into the powerful influence of speech on our mental functioning and behavior.

Like unethicality, of which it is a part, lying is said to reinforce the addictions, fears, and other unskillful behaviors which motivate it, and to

145

result in further disruptive emotions such as guilt, agitation, and anger. Further lying and unethicality to protect the original lie frequently follow.

The impeccable practice of truthfulness, on the other hand, is said to serve several functions. It encourages ethicality, requires precise awareness of speech and motivation, enhances clear perception and memory of events which might otherwise be distorted by lying, frees the mind of guilt and fear of discovery, and consequently reduces agitation and worry.

The fully enlightened individual, freed from greed, anger, and other unskillful mind states, has neither desire nor need to distort the truth or act unethically. Those who are fully ethical have nothing to hide, and truthfulness, like all the other perfections, is said to ultimately become a spontaneous and continuous expression of the arahat's essential nature.

"Like a lovely flower,
Bright and fragrant
Are the fine and truthful words
Of the man who says what he means."

THE BUDDHA[17]

5. Renunciation

Renunciation is an attribute somewhat foreign to our western thinking; it calls up images of asceticism, sacrifice, and the relinquishment of pleasure. However, a deeper understanding of the term as it is used in Buddhist psychology suggests that it really means the voluntary relinquishment of one source of pleasure in order to gain access to pleasures of a deeper and more permanent nature.

Contrary to our traditional western models, Buddhist psychology recognizes four types of pleasure: sensory pleasures; pleasures arising from states of extreme mental concentration; the pleasures of insight, i.e. those which arise as a result of mental clarity; and the pleasure of nirvana.[18] These pleasures are supposedly of increasing refinement, sensitivity, and degree. Those recognized by our western models are confined to the first type, the sensory realm, which in Buddhist psychology include mental pleasures such as memory and fantasy, since in Buddhist psychology these are regarded as sensory inputs.

Renunciation can be viewed as a relinquishment of addiction to sense pleasures in order to cultivate the remaining three. This choice can also be seen in terms of Maslow's hierarchy of needs. Lower order needs are primarily concerned with material objects and sensory stimulation, whereas higher order needs are more concerned with internal self-produced stimulation and are held to be inherently more satisfying to the individual who has experienced them.[12,24,25] Thus, renunciation can be viewed as a voluntary relinquishment of lower order needs in order to cultivate the higher ones.

Renunciation also facilitates a life-style of voluntary simplicity.[26] With deepening perceptual sensitivity, practitioners of the consciousness disciplines are said to recognize more clearly the disrupting effects of greed and attachment. At the same time, they find themselves better able to generate a sense of well-being and positive emotions which formerly depended upon external possessions and stimuli. Greater pleasure is now found in a deepening sensitivity to the moment-to-moment flow of experience; and each moment, no matter what one is doing, becomes a source of rich and multifaceted stimulation. Thus, from this perspective, renunciation is seen not as an ascetic practice demanding sacrifice and suffering, but rather as a skillful means for removing distractions to the attainment of higher pleasure.

In the individual who has perfected this quality, the mind is said to be free of attachment and aversion, and therefore, to no longer covet or avoid any experience. Rather, all situations and stimuli are viewed with equanimity, itself also one of the perfections, and the individual's sense of well-being is no longer so dependent on the environment.

> "If you are filled with desire
> Your sorrows swell
> Like the grass after the rain.
> But if you subdue desires
> Your sorrows fall from you
> Like drops of water from a lotus flower."
>
> THE BUDDHA[17]

6. Patience

> "At the end of the way is freedom.
> Till then, patience."
>
> THE BUDDHA[17]

Impatience reflects dissatisfaction with present experience and addiction to anticipated experience. The result is, as almost all of us are aware, an agitated mental state characterized by discomfort and fantasy. Yet, the work of mental training is to be open to, accept, and be deeply aware of experience moment by moment, neither resisting what is present, fantasizing about what could be, or comparing the two.[13]

Yet "patience" is not really a sufficient translation, for the Buddhists also imply ideas such as tolerance, forbearance, and forgiveness of others.

The patient mind is slow to anger and quick to forgive, committed to ethical, compassionate behavior itself, yet forgiving of those who are not; patient, in other words, not only with situations and things but also with people and their shortcomings.

7. Equanimity

The mind which responds with conditioned, automatic likes and dislikes is dominated by reactive pleasure and pain. Such a mind is at the mercy of its environment and is said to be turbulent, hard to control and concentrate, inconstant in purpose and direction, and insensitive in perception and insight.[16] With training, the conditioned reactivity of strong affective responses is reduced and the mind gradually becomes less reactive and more calm. As such, it becomes more easy to control and remains unperturbed in the face of an increasingly broad range of experience. Finally, it is said to be able to encompass all experiences and to allow "the one thousand beatific and one thousand horrible visions" to pass before it without disturbance. Of such a mind, it is said that "the eight vicissitudes,"

> "Pleasure-pain
> praise and blame
> fame and shame
> loss and gain,
> are all the same."

8. Generosity

The Buddha said that if we understood the power of generosity as deeply as he did that we would not sit down to a meal without sharing it.[18] Generosity has long been recognized as both means and end in all the major consciousness disciplines and great religions. It appears to be a powerful inhibitor of such unskillful mental habits as greed, addiction, and hatred. It is interesting that contemporary research has found evidence that psychologically mature people contribute more to charity than do the immature,[10] and that their lives tend to be more oriented toward service.[27]

Buddhism describes three levels of generosity: beggarly, brotherly, and kingly. In beggarly giving, we give with great hesitation and consideration the worst and least valued of what we have. In brotherly giving, we share equally, while in kingly giving, we unhesitatingly offer that which we most value for the pleasure and enjoyment of others.[18]

The fully enlightened individual, it is said, is no longer driven by egocentric motives of any kind. Rather, behavior is said to emerge spontaneously and appropriately in any situation in such a way as to most effectively serve and contribute to others. Freed of unhealthy mental factors,[28] generosity is now the only possible response for such an individual. As such, giving is no longer experienced as a sacrifice, but rather as a natural and joyful expression of the perfections of loving kindness, renunciation, and ethicality which usually accompany it.

9. Loving Kindness

Buddhist psychology describes several practices for the cultivation of loving kindness. Some appear to be analogs of certain behavior modification techniques such as systematic desensitization. However, instead of replacing anxiety with calm as desensitization usually does, the Buddhist practices of loving kindness replace unskillful states such as anger and hatred with loving kindness.[16,29] This suggests that some of the principles of behavior modification were identified 2,500 years earlier than has usually been recognized.[29]

One family of practices for the cultivation of this quality is described for use by advanced practitioners with extreme powers of concentration. Such people are said to be able to fill their awareness with the experience of loving kindness, or other desired qualities. Four such qualities are particularly recommended, namely universal loving kindness, universal compassion, sympathetic joy (joy which derives from the well-being of others), and another of the ten perfections, equanimity.[18] When these qualities are held alone and without fluctuation in the fully concentrated mind, they are said to result in extremely positive and beneficial states. When the extreme concentration is released, the qualities tend to dissipate in part, though they do result in certain trait changes, including readier access to them in the future and inhibition of unhealthy factors such as anger. When perfected, the quality of loving kindness is no longer dependent upon entering specific states of consciousness, but arises spontaneously.

10. Wisdom

Like the other perfections, wisdom has many levels; a certain amount of it is considered necessary even to begin some type of mental training. Through this training, the mind is gradually brought under greater control, and perceptual distortions, unskillful habits, disruptive affects, and unskillful behavior of any type are gradually pared away. This leads to clearer perception and greater concentration, which in turn allow the recognition of still more subtle levels of unskillful habits which are pared away in their turn. The result is said to be a positive feedback cycle in which wisdom leads to the recognition of the need for removing unskillful habits and cultivating skillful ones which in turn lead to greater wisdom.

One of the results is a deep insight and understanding, born of direct experience, of what are called "the three marks of existence": *ducca, annica,* and *annata.*[18] *Ducca* is the recognition of the extent to which dissatisfaction and suffering pervade the untrained mind, and that no possession or stimulation can completely or permanently remove it. This recognition is analogous to the *angst* of the existentialists. *Annica* is the recognition of impermanence, that everything is in constant flux, that nothing remains the same, and hence, that there is no ultimate source of security in the world on which we can rely. *Annata* refers to an insight that there is no permanent, unchanging self or ego. Rather, what the advanced practitioner is said to recognize is that in the psyche there exists only an impersonal, continuously changing flux of thoughts, emotions, and images.[17] The untrained mind identifies with these mental components and illusorily perceives them : evidence of the existence of a solid self, much as a moviegoer perceives an illusory sense of continuity and motion even though there actually exists only a succession of still frames.

The deep recognition of these three marks of existence is said to result in a radical wrenching of one's cognitive system. Seeing the transitory and ultimately less than fully satisfying nature of sensory pleasures, and the illusory nature of our usual egoic identification, undermines egocentric motivation, thus enhancing renunciation and equanimity. Out of this wisdom springs a compassionate understanding of the counterproductive nature of the means by which people usually seek happiness, but all too often only sow the seeds of further discontent. This, in turn, is said to lead to the desire to serve others and alleviate suffering whenever possible, and the recognition that the cultivation of the ten perfections may be a strategic way of best fitting oneself for the task. With this realization, the individual has become a *Boddhisattva,* one committed to both full enlightenment and selfless service to others.

DISCUSSION

Taken together, the ten perfections point to a level of mental health far exceeding that usually considered possible by traditional western psychological models. Moreover, these perfections are described as the goal of specified practices. The Buddhist claim is, therefore, not only that we in the west have underestimated the human potential, but that the means for realizing this potential are available to anyone willing to test these practices.

These claims present a major challenge to some of the most fundamental assumptions of western psychology. Moreover, a small number of empirical studies, such as of meditation, lend some support, though only preliminary, to certain of the claims of Buddhism and the other perennial traditions.

However, no matter how theoretically interesting such studies may be, the most important implications of these perennial claims are practical and experiential. No theoretical paper on well-being can be as meaningful as its experience, and the most important place to test the claim of eastern psychologies that they can enhance mental health is in our own lives. We are the ultimate testing ground for these practices, and no amount of reading or writing can take the place of doing them. In the words of an ancient Buddhist sage: "To see if this be true look within your own mind."

Eastern psychologies and the ten perfections may also hold important social and global implications. It is no secret that humankind has reached a critical period in its history, a period which may well determine the fate of both our planet and our species. Our well-being and very survival are threatened by rapidly growing ecological, resource, and nuclear threats. Some fifteen million of us die each year of malnutrition-related causes; wastes pollute the atmosphere and water; agricultural and natural resources are strained; and nuclear warheads amounting to twenty billion tons of TNT sit awaiting launch at a moment's notice.[30]

These global problems are unique, not only in their urgency, scope, and complexity, but also in that for the first time in human history all the major threats to our well-being and survival are human-caused. What this means is that they all stem from our individual and collective behavior, and hence, are largely psychological in origin.[30] Greed, hatred, fear, defensiveness, ignorance, psychological immaturity: these, and more, are among the basic causes of our current crises.

What this means is that if we are to successfully resolve these crises we must correct not only the overt problems, such as malnutrition, but also the psychological forces which create them.[30] Yet, it is very, very rarely that these psychological factors are taken into consideration, in part because their role is not appreciated, and in part because there is little understanding of how to counteract them. It is therefore significant that eastern psychologies claim to possess techniques for cultivating mental qualities, such as the ten perfections, which would seem to be effective antidotes for these problematic psychological factors. If there is even a slight possibility that these eastern claims are correct, then, given the urgency of our situation, presumably we ought to place a high priority on testing them, both personally and experimentally. Human survival is going to require tremendous psychological resources and maturity, and the techniques which cultivate them may be crucial.

References

1. Allport, G. In H. Smith *Forgotten Truth: The Primordial Tradition.* New York: Harper and Row, 1976.
2. Kaplan, H. I. and B. J. Sadock (eds). *Modern Synopsis of the Comprehensive Textbook of Psychiatry* (3rd ed). Baltimore, MD: Williams and Wilkins, 1981.
3. Walsh, R. The consciousness disciplines and the behavioral sciences: Questions of comparison and assessment. *American Journal of Psychiatry 137*:6, 1980.
4. Walsh R. and F. Vaughan (eds). *Beyond Ego: Transpersonal Dimensions in Psychology.* Los Angeles, CA: J. P. Tarcher, 1980.
5. Wilber, K. *The Spectrum of Consciousness.* Wheaton, IL: Theosophical Publishing House, 1977.
6. Wilber, K. *No Boundary.* Los Angeles, CA: Center Press, 1979.
7. Wilber, K. *The Atman Project.* Wheaton, IL: Quest, 1980.
8. Wilber, K. *A Sociable God: A Brief Introduction to a Transcendental Sociology.* New York: McGraw-Hill, 1983a.
9. Wilber, K. *Eye to Eye: The Quest for the New Paradigm.* Garden City, NY: Anchor/Doubleday, 1983b.
10. Heath, D. The maturing person. In R. Walsh and D. H. Shapiro (eds) *Beyond Health and Normality: Explorations of Exceptional Psychological Well-being.* New York: Van Nostrand Reinhold, 1983, pp. 152–205.
11. Walsh, R. and D. H. Shapiro (eds). *Beyond Health and Normality: Explorations of Exceptional Psychological Well being.* New York: Van Nostrand Reinhold, 1983.
12. Maslow, A. H. *The Farther Reaches of Human Nature.* New York: Viking Press, 1971.
13. Fromm, E. *Wellbeing of Man and Society.* New York: Seaburg, 1978.
14. Kohlberg, L. *The Philosophy of Moral Development.* San Francisco, CA: Harper and Row, 1981.
15. Smith, H. The sacred unconscious. In R. Walsh and D. H. Shapiro (eds) *Beyond Health and Normality: Explorations of Exceptional Psychological Well-being.* New York: Van Nostrand Reinhold, 1983, pp. 265–271.

16. Buddhagosa (P. M. Tin, trans). *The Path of Purity*. Sri Lanka: Pali Text Society, 1923.
17. Byrom, T. *The Dhammapada: The Sayings of the Buddha*. New York: Vintage, 1976.
18. Goldstein, J. *The Experience of Insight*. Boulder, CO: Shambhala, 1983.
19. Shapiro, D. *Meditation: Self Regulation Strategy and Altered State of Consciousness*. New York: Aldine, 1980.
20. Shapiro, D. H. and R. Walsh, (eds.). *Meditation: Classic and Contemporary Perspectives*. New York: Aldine, 1984.
21. Walsh, R. Initial meditative experiences: Part I. *Journal of Transpersonal Psychology 9*:151–192, 1977.
22. Goleman, D. *The Varieties of the Meditative Experience*. New York: E. P. Dutton, 1977.
23. Goleman, D. and M. Epstein. Meditation and well-being: An eastern model of psychological health. In R. Walsh and D. H. Shapiro (eds) *Beyond Health and Normality: Explorations of Exceptional Psychological Well-being*. New York: Van Nostrand Reinhold, 1983, pp. 229–252.
24. Roberts, T. Beyond self actualization. *ReVision 1*:42–46, 1978.
25. Walsh, R. and F. Vaughan. Towards an integrative psychology of well-being. In R. Walsh and D. H. Shapiro (eds) *Beyond Health and Normality: Explorations of Exceptional Psychological Well-being*. New York: Van Nostrand Reinhold, 1983, pp. 388–431.
26. Elgin, D. *Voluntary Simplicity*. New York: William Morrow, 1981.
27. Waterman, A. Individualism and interdependence. *American Psychologist 36*:762–773, 1981.
28. Goleman, D. Mental health in classical Buddhist psychology. In R. Walsh and F. Vaughan (eds) *Beyond Ego: Transpersonal Dimensions in Psychology*. Los Angeles, CA: J. P. Tarcher, 1980, pp. 131–134.
29. Shapiro, D. *Precision Nirvana*. Englewood Cliffs, NJ: Prentice-Hall, 1978.
30. Walsh, R. *Staying Alive: The Psychology of Human Survival*. Boulder, CO: New Science Library/Shambhala, 1984.

THE TRUE AIM OF YOGA

G O P I   K R I S H N A

Yoga is not a religion but a sacred tradition. Its Sanskrit root, Gopi Krishna points out, is *yuj* (or *yug*), meaning "to yoke or join." The individual practitioner of yoga aims to be yoked or joined with the cosmos in a transcendent state—samadhi or moksha.

Thus, yoga is both a means and a goal. It has many lines or forms with regard to methodology and emphasis, but all theoretically lead to the same condition of liberation. Yoga can be adapted to any culture or religious setting or work situation or lifestyle. There are Hindu yogis, Christian yogis, Buddhist yogis, Taoist yogis; there are yoga programs in YMCAs, in psychiatric hospitals, in prisons, in reducing salons.

As Sri Aurobindo said, "All life is yoga." He meant that insofar as you try to become enlightened human beings, anything you do in your life is an opportunity for the practice of consciousness expansion and self-transformation—an opportunity to attain yoga. And thus Jesus's statement, "My yoke is easy," in Matthew 11:30, has deeper meaning than is ordinarily understood. Conventional/exoteric Christianity interprets "yoke" to mean "burden" or "work," but esoteric Christianity interprets it as "the practices I prescribe for growth to Christ consciousness."

In his thirties Gopi Krishna experienced a remarkable transformation in consciousness. Thereafter he studied the phenomenon—referred to in yogic texts as kundalini—and sought to bring it to the attention of science, claiming it is the key to understanding evolution and enlightenment. His research showed that ancient records from sacred traditions and cultures around the world refer to the kundalini phenomenon. Moreover, his personal experience convinced him that the phenomenon had a biological basis, and therefore was accessible to scientific investigation. In the fields of religion and science, Gopi Krishna brought *new* knowledge of human transformation—knowledge that might be termed transpersonal physiology, parallel to transpersonal psychology.

Gopi Krishna himself beautifully exemplified many of the qualities and experiences he notes here as characteristic of enlightenment. I met him on several occasions over a seven-year period and always observed him to be a sweet and saintly man. Moreover, he had a remarkable erudition for someone without formal higher education. His patient, dedicated research and literary efforts show the mark of a mind of genius, and are most worthy of examination.

154

The True Aim of Yoga

IN ALL THE ANCIENT LITERATURE of India, yoga adepts hold a place unequaled by any other class of men. The amount of literature on yoga is enormous. Only a fraction of it has been translated into the languages of the west, and one of the results of this lack of sufficient information on the subject has been that the real significance of yoga is not yet clearly understood.

Broadly speaking, all systems of yoga in India fall into two categories: raja yoga and hatha yoga. Raja in Sanskrit denotes king, and hatha means violence. Raja yoga implies the kingly or easy way to self-realization, and hatha the more strenuous one. Both systems base their stand on the *Vedas* and the *Upanishads*; the main practices and disciplines are common to both.

In hatha yoga the breathing exercises are more strenuous, attended by some abnormal positions of the chin, the diaphragm, the tongue, and other parts of the body, to prevent expulsion or inhalation of air into the lungs in order to induce a state of suspended breathing. This can have drastic effects on the nervous system and the brain, and it is obvious that such a discipline can be very dangerous. Even in India, only those prepared to face death dare to undergo the extreme disciplines of hatha yoga.

It should not be thought, even for a moment, that yoga in these forms has provided the only channel for self-realization. On the contrary, there is hardly any mention of yoga in the *Vedas*, the oldest written religious scripture in the world. Even in the principal *Upanishads*, the fountainhead of all philosophical systems and spiritual thought in India, there is only a passing reference in two or three of the older ones. The most popular scripture of India—the *Bhagavad Gita*—and some of the greatest spiritual teachers recommend other disciplines for the attainment of the goal. These are: nishkama karma (selfless action as service to God); bhakti (an attitude of intense devotion to the divine power); jnana (exercise of the intellect in distinguishing the real from the false); and upasana (worship and other forms of religious discipline prescribed in almost all great religions of the world).

However, yoga has its own value and importance. It combines a number of disciplines in an intense course of training with the aim of making spiritual enlightenment possible in the span of one lifetime. In India, it is told that the human soul undergoes a long series of births and deaths, coming again and again into this world of happening and sorrow to reap the fruit of action done in previous lives. The cycle continues, with the practice of religious discipline, until one succeeds in cutting asunder the chain of cause and effect to reach the final state of union with the all-pervading, all-knowing First Cause of the Universe.

The most authoritative book on raja yoga is Patanjali's *Yoga Sutras*, a highly respected work more than two thousand years old. The authoritative books on hatha yoga are *Hatha Yoga Pradipika, Siva Samhita,* and others that take their stand on the Tantras. There are hundreds of books on tantric philosophy and tantric modes of worship.

The yoga expounded by Pantanjali consists of eight steps, or parts, and is, therefore, known as ashtanga yoga—that is, yoga with eight limbs. Hatha yoga has also the same eight sections, with minor differences in detail.

The eight limbs of yoga are: yama, which means abstention from all kinds of evil thought and deed; niyama, which means daily religious observances such as purity, austerity, contentment, study of scriptures, devotion to God, etc. The third is asana, which means posture or, in other words, the most healthy and convenient way to sit for the practice of yoga. The fourth limb is pranayama, which means the regulation and control of breathing. The fifth is pratyahara, which means the subjugation of the senses to bring them within the control of the mind, a very necessary preparation for concentration. The sixth is concentration of the mind, known as dharana. The seventh is dhyana, which means a steady, unbroken concentration for a certain length of time or deep contemplation. The eighth is samadhi, which means the state of ecstatic, or rapt contemplation of the inner reality.

It will thus be seen that yoga is more comprehensive and complex than is sometimes supposed. It is not only asana, or posture, which is but a method to keep the body steady and straight when practicing meditation. The practice of various asanas is an exercise for health, and it is incorrect to say that one who is practicing several asanas efficiently is practicing yoga. The correct thing would be to say that he is practicing these exercises to keep his body in a healthy and flexible condition.

The reason why such a large variety of asanas is prescribed in the books on hatha yoga lies in the fact that neophytes had to sit for hours at a time in intense concentration. Some sort of exercise was necessary for them to keep their bodies in a fit condition. The books on raja yoga generally leave it to the student to choose an asana for which he has a preference. The most common are the padamasana and siddhasana.

Similarly, mere concentration, or even concentration with asana and pranayama, is not yoga. There are ascetics in India who can perform all the eighty-four asanas to perfection and continue performing them all their lives, but they never attain to enlightenment. There are also ascetics who can suspend their breathing for days so that they can be buried underground, or placed in hermetically sealed chambers for days and weeks without being suffocated. But despite such drastic measures, they often awake as one awakes from a deep sleep or a swoon without experiencing the least enlargement of consciousness or gaining any insight of a transcendental nature. This is called jada-samadhi, which means unconscious samadhi. It is a kind of suspended animation similar to that of bears and frogs when they hibernate during winter.

There are also ascetics in India who sit in meditative postures twenty-four hours a day. They sleep while sitting upright, and on awakening after a few hours continue their meditational practices. They live austere lives, occupying all their time with meditation or the recitation of mantras prescribed by their gurus, and continue the practice for scores of years without ever rising above the human level of consciousness or experiencing the divine.

There are ascetics in India who resort to extreme self-torture and even mutilation to assuage their burning thirst for spiritual experience. They lie with naked flesh on beds of nails or keep one of their arms constantly upraised until the limb becomes atrophied and withers to a stump. Some hang from trees with their heads downward, inhaling acrid fumes from a burning fire. Others stand on one leg for days and weeks, and there are even those who gaze fixedly at the blazing sun until their eyesight is lost.

There are also ascetics in India who smoke or eat preparations from the hemp plant (hashish and marijuana) in enormous doses, often remaining under the influence of the drug day and night. These practices have been in vogue in India for many centuries without producing a single enlightened spirit. Drug-taking hermits number in the hundreds of thousands and are a source of unhappiness to themselves and to others. Narcotics, hallucinogens, and intoxicants are not a help but an insuperable barrier in the path of God-realization.

Interestingly, the word "yoga" is derived from the Sandskrit root *yuj*, which means to yoke or join. Yoga, therefore, implies the union of the individual soul with the universal spirit or consciousness. According to all authorities, the final state of union with the divine is extremely hard to achieve. "After many births," says the *Bhagavad Gita*, "the discriminating seeker attains to me, saying all this (creation) is the Lord. Such a great soul is hard to find." According to the tantras, out of thousands who take to hatha yoga, hardly one succeeds.

Let us examine this difficult "union" more closely. Out of the millions who have been practicing meditative techniques of yoga, how many have attained to enlarged consciousness in the West? How many have gained that state of beatitude and spontaneous flow of higher wisdom which from immemorial times has been associated with the success of this holy enterprise? How many have published their spiritual experiences to afford a glimpse of the transcendental to other seekers in order to inspire them and to provide guidance on the path?

In India, the number of enlightened during the last one hundred years can be counted on the fingers of one hand. In ancient days, self-revelation was the first test of the spiritually illuminated. The famous seers of the *Upanishads*—and even Buddha—had to produce proofs for the authenticity of their own experiences.

The aim of yoga, then, is to achieve the state of unity or oneness with God, Brahman, spiritual beings such as Christ and Krishna, Universal Consciousness, Atman, or Divinity . . . according to the faith and belief of the devotee.

From the recorded experiences of Christian mystics such as St. Paul, St. Francis of Assisi, St. Teresa, Dionysius the Areopagite, St. Catherine of Siena, Suso, and others, and from Sufi masters including Shamsi-Tabrez, Rumi, Abu Yazid, al-Nuri, and al-Junaid, and from the experiences of Yoga-adepts such as Kabir, Guru Nank, Shankaracharya, Ramakrishna, Ramana Maharshi to name a few, it is obvious that in the basic essentials the experience is the same.

During the ecstasy or trance, consciousness is transformed and the yogi, sufi, or mystic finds himself in direct rapport with an overwhelming Presence. This warm, living, conscious Presence spreads everywhere and occupies the whole mind and thought of the devotee; he becomes lost in contemplation and entirely oblivious to the world.

The mystical experience may center around a deified personality such as that of a saviour, prophet, or incarnation, or around a shunya, void, or the image of God present in the mind of the devotee, or it may be centered on an oceanic feeling of infinite extension in a world of being that has no end. It is not merely the appearance of the vision that is of importance in mystical experience. Visions also float before the eye in half-awake conditions and in hysteria, hypnosis, insanity, and under the influence of drugs and intoxicants.

It is the *nature* of the vision—the feelings of awe and wonder excited by the spectacle that transcends everything known on earth. The enlargement of one's being, the sense of infinitude associated with the figure or the Presence, and the emotions of overwhelming love, dependence, and utter surrender mark the experience and make it of paramount importance as a living contact with a state of being which does not belong to this earth.

Even a momentary contact with the divine is a stupendous experience. Some of the most famous men on earth—the greatest thinkers and the ablest writers—such as Plato, Plotinus, Parmenides, Dante, Wordsworth, and Tennyson had the experience. Emerson and many, many other renowned men and women had this singular experience thrust upon them, often to their grateful amazement. Most of them had undergone no spiritual discipline, and there were even some who had no firm belief in God. For even when unexpected, the experience leaves a permanent mark on life which uplifts the individual and grants him insights into the nature of things that are not possible for those who never see beyond the veil.

The experience always has the same basic characteristics. It is incredible that so many learned men and women, both scientists and scholars, should ignore a phenomenon as widespread as mystical experience has been. The phenomenon becomes even more surprising when we observe that all great founders of religion and some of the greatest philosophers, writers, and artists were endowed with beatific vision. All of them recognized it for what it was—a fleeting glimpse of another life and another world.

Yoga signifies a momentary glimpse of ourselves, unfettered by flesh and the allure of the earth. For a short time we are invincible, eternal—immune to decay, disease, failure, and sorrow. We are but drops in an ocean of consciousness in which the stormy universe of colossal suns and planets looks like a reflection that has absolutely no effect on the unutterable calm, peace, and bliss that fill this unbounded expanse of being. We are a wonder, an enigma, a riddle; even those who have access to it some time in their lives cannot describe mystical experience in a way others can understand. For the soul belongs to another realm, another state of existence, another plane of being where our senses, mind, and intellect flounder in the dark.

Yoga also signifies the fact that this metamorphosis of consciousness is not only bone and flesh, but a thinking, feeling, knowing entity whose true nature is still hidden from the scholars of our age as it was hidden from the wise men of the past. Consciousness is something intangible to our senses and mind. "Neti, neti" (not this, not this) say the *Upanishads,* for it cannot be described in terms of anything perceived by our senses, or apprehended by our minds.

Can you explain to yourself what or who you are? What is the nature of this thinking, knowing, feeling entity in you which is conscious of the world around it and which is never able to answer the question whence it came and where it has to go.

Material progress is a preliminary step to spiritual awakening. In every civilization of the past, when the smoke and dust of the battles and struggles for supremacy died down, the eternal questions—Who am I and what is the mystery behind this creation?—began to agitate the more intelligent and evolved individuals of the populace.

The answers furnished by wise men among the Egyptians, Babylonians, Indo-Aryans, Chinese, Persians, Greeks, and Romans are still on

159

record, and it is obvious that it is only this restless hunger of the soul to discover itself that has prompted most of man's mental, artistic, and scientific growth. In fact, at the beginning all knowledge originated from the pressures exerted by the religious thirst in man. There is nothing so erroneous as the opinions expressed by some scholars and men of science that religious experience is a pathological condition of the brain or an invasion from the unconscious. This irresponsible attitude destroys the very foundation of the precious urge responsible for the progress of mankind.

Yoga aims to give these momentous questions answers which cannot be furnished by skeptical denials, drug use, asanas or mantras, breathing exercises, or meditation without other moral virtues. In order to be effective, Yoga must be practiced in the fullness of all its eight limbs or branches. Everyone who aspires to the supreme experience must strive for perfection; he must begin first with the development of his personality.

"I call him alone a Brahman, that is, a spiritually awakened person," says Buddha, "from whom lust, anger, pride, and envy have dropped off like a mustard seed from the point of a needle." Mere recitation of the well-known mantra, "Om mani padme om," popular among the Buddhists in Tibet, or its rotation millions of times on prayer wheels, could not bear any fruit in one who did not follow the other teaching of Gautama the Buddha. The tragedy is that people do not often understand what "enlightenment" or "self-realization" means. It is a colossal achievement.

According to the records available, all the men who had the genuine experience through the whole course of history do not number more than a few hundred. They are far fewer in number than the men of talent and genius in all other branches of knowledge and art; but they created the revolutions in thought which continue to affect the world to this day. The spiritual adept or religious genius is extremely rare for this reason. "Illumination" represents a transformation of consciousness, the opening of a new channel of perception within, by which the deathless and boundless universe is opened to the vision of the soul.

Just as every atom of matter represents a unit of basic energy forming the universe, every human soul represents a drop in an infinite ocean of consciousness which has no beginning and no end. The average man, oblivious to his own divine nature and unconscious of his own majesty, lives in permanent doubt because of the limitations of the human brain. He is overwhelmed by uncertainty and sorrow at the thought of death and identifies himself with the body from the first to the last. He does not realize that he has a glorious, unbounded, eternal existence of his own.

All the systems of yoga and all religious disciplines are designed to bring about those psychosomatic changes in the body which are essential for

160

the metamorphosis of consciousness. A new center—presently dormant in the average man and woman—has to be activated, and a more powerful stream of psychic energy must rise into the head from the base of the spine to enable human consciousness to transcend the normal limits. This is the final phase of the present evolutionary impulse in man. The cerebrospinal system of man has to undergo a radical change, enabling consciousness to attain a dimension which transcends the limits of the highest intellect. Here, reason yields to intuition and revelation appears to guide the steps of humankind.

The syllable "aum" represents the music of the soul. This melody is heard only when the Divine Power Center in man is roused to activity. Then, a sublime radiation floods the brain like a stream of golden nectar, lighting what was dark before. As the luster spreads, the soul is filled with an inexpressible happiness and finds itself growing in dimension, extending outward like rays from the sun. It reaches all nearby objects, then spreads to the distant boundaries, including the horizon and the visible universe. There is no confusion or distortion, as happens with drugs, and no loss of memory as happens in hypnosis. The intellect remains unaffected, and there is no overlapping or aberration. The inner and outer worlds stand side by side, but with one momentous difference: from a point of consciousness the soul now seems to stretch from end to end, an ineffable and intangible intelligence present everywhere.

The goal of yoga is this union with the universe of consciousness, enabling man to understand his origin and destiny in order to shape his life and the world accordingly. It is a herculean achievement, more full of adventure, risk, and thrill than the longest voyage in outer space. This is the greatest enterprise designed by nature for the most virile and most intelligent members of the race when they attain to the zenith of material knowledge and prosperity.

It is because of the extremely arduous nature of the undertaking that Buddha prescribed celibacy and a monastic life for the aspirants. This is the Kingdom of Heaven spoken of by Christ, into which only the pure of heart can enter. "I call him alone a Brahman," says Buddha, "who has gone past this difficult road, the impassable and deceptive circle of existence, who has passed through it to the other shore; who is meditative, free from desire and doubt, and released from attachment, gaining a transhuman state of consciousness." In his knowledge of the spiritual and evolutionary needs of mankind, he must tower head and shoulders above the greatest intellects of the age.

"One who has attained to union with the divine," says an Indian sage, "will not change his position even with a king." "That state is called yoga," says the *Gita,* "which having obtained, one does not reckon any other gain to be greater, and established in which, one is not disturbed even by great sorrow." Once again, Jesus addressed the people: "I am the Light of the world. No follower of mine shall wander in the dark, he shall have the light of life."

"I am a king, O Sela," Buddha said to the Brahman of that name. "I am supreme king of the Law. I exercise rule by means of doctrine—a rule which is irresistible."

"In this state, that is the last state of love," says St. John of the Cross. "The soul is like the crystal that is clear and pure; the more degrees of light it receives, the greater concentration of light there is in it. This enlightenment continues to such a degree that at last it attains a point at which the light is centered in it with such copiousness that it comes to appear to be wholly light and cannot be distinguished from the light . . . for it is enlightened to the greatest possible extent, and thus appears to be light itself."

Christ and Buddha spoke but the truth. They were the Light.

True enlightenment consists of reaching beyond the highest intellects of the time to grasp and proclaim the law. There is no uncertainty and vacillation, because the truly enlightened one is as sure of his perception of the higher truths revealed to him as he is of the existence of the physical world seen with mortal eyes. This is why Buddha said that his doctrine was irresistible.

The laws revealed to the illuminati provide solutions to the evolutionary problems of humanity, because it is possible to look into the future and discern the turns and twists of the *predestined* path. For this reason, the "enlightened" and the "awakened" have been and always will be the spiritual guides of mankind.

It is a historic fact that the law proclaimed by Buddha, Christ, and the *Gita* persisted for two thousand years and more, and is still honored today by millions. After only a century of domination, however, cracks have begun to show in the façade of agnostic science.

It should also be remembered that idea, intuition, and inspiration are as much a gift from universal consciousness as are the revelations of the "enlightened." The life-energy stimulating the brain in both instances is Kundalini. The same biological center of energy in the body is responsible for both mystical experience and genius. The spiritually enlightened person is simply more evolved than the talented man of science or the gifted master of art. Nature is as consistent in the realm of mind as she is in the physical world. Stern psychosomatic laws govern the evolution of man and will remain outside human understanding until they are thoroughly demonstrated in a scientific laboratory.

The enlightened prophets and seers of all nations appeared from time to time not as the result of an accident, but under the same laws as did the men of extraordinary talent and genius. They are the creations of the collective consciousness of the race which governs the survival and the evolutionary drive of the entire mass of human beings. Unknown biological laws regulate the behavior and group instinct in ants, mice, bees, baboons, migratory birds, elephants, and other forms of life. These laws are still unknown because life remains a riddle, and scientists are divided among themselves about its nature and status in the universe.

At opportune times or a critical junctures, the enlightened are vouch-safed insights into supernal laws in the same way that men of genius and talent gain knowledge of laws ruling the material world. "By making Samyama on the Inner Light, one obtains knowledge of what is subtle, hidden, or far distant," says the sage Patanjali in *Yoga Sutras*. Samyama means the state of mind in the last three phases of ashtanga yoga: concentration and ecstatic contemplation combined.

It has been known for thousands of years that in the higher state of consciousness hidden knowledge can pour into the mind independent of experience, education, or understanding. Oracles in ancient Rome, Greece, and Egypt were expected to prove the validity of this belief. The ability to come into occasional contact with this blissful ocean of perfect knowledge and infinite wisdom is the final achievement of Yoga. There are many stages, but so long as the final stage is not reached, one cannot be said to have been stabilized in yoga; he still belongs to the normal class of human beings. It is only when he has gained access to superhuman levels of consciousness and is receptive to revelation that he is considered to be "illuminated." The soul of every man and woman is capable of this prodigious leap from the human to the superhuman level of knowledge when the brain is properly attuned. In dreams, in reverie, in meditation, or while listening to music, praying, walking, or even working, the window of the soul may be thrown open. Often there is a brief glimpse of the transcendental world, but many people stand face to face with the ineffable and never understand the nature of the experience.

Yoga exercises can also be directed toward worldly objectives. There are exercises that are conducive to the health and efficiency of the mind, others that lead to psychic gifts, and still others that strengthen the will and improve the ability to deal with problems. However, no single achievement of this kind—or even several of them taken together—is yoga.

Therefore, yoga is a transhuman state of mind attained by means of the cumulative effect of all practices combined, carried on for years, and supplemented by grace. The window of the soul cannot be forced open. The aspirant, trying his best year after year, has to wait patiently for grace. The window must be opened from the inside. The custodians of the window, in the shape of hidden devices in the brain, know exactly when the shutters are to be opened. Thus, the ascent to the next state of consciousness is difficult to achieve.

Those who have not attained to the supreme state of yoga, and validated their experience, cannot be considered to be yogis, yoga-adepts, or enlightenment. They are hoga-practitioners or sadhakas. The true yoga is one who has attained to the state of union with the ocean of divine consciousness—call it Brahman, Atman, God, Nirvana, Allah, Ishwara, or what you will. He must have pierced the veil and gathered knowledge not available to the intellect alone. The others can be oracles, physical trainers, acrobats, dispensers of spells and charms, mantra specialists, necromancers, miracle workers, magicians, mental healers, clairvoyants, psychics, mediums, astral travelers, occultists, and the like, but they cannot be held to be yogis or the "awakened" as long as they do not transcend the human level of consciousness and present their credentials to the world. Such people are useful in their way by meeting the needs of those who are fascinated by Yoga, the occult, or the spirit world; seekers who wish to develop psychic gifts, or satisfy their curiosity about the supernatural. But they should not confuse these desires for gifts and experiences with self-knowledge, mystical experience, or union with God. Above all, they should not confuse it with the supreme experience which reveals the majesty, infinite awareness, and immortal nature of the soul.

There are hundreds of thousands of men and women in this world who are intensely attracted by the occult and the supernatural. There are also hundreds of thousands for whom the riddle of existence holds an irresistible fascination, and many others who have an uncontrollable desire for occult powers and psychic gifts. The seekers of all the three categories take to Yoga, spiritualism, psychical research, occult practices, and spiritual disciplines to satisfy their respective urges. This is natural and, from their point of view, correct. But there is often confusion in the interpretation of this urge, and the confusion is made worse by the professionals who specialize in these three departments.

The aim of yoga and of every religious discipline is a fruitful, righteous life and union with God.

When successful, this is designed to lead to super-rational knowledge and a higher state of consciousness. The visionary experience, as has been confirmed by almost every mystic, sufi, and yogi of the past, proves to be a source of unspeakable happiness. It provides the seeker with unwavering strength and faith, unshakable conviction of immortality, transcendental knowledge, and a blissful union with an ocean of life, beauty, grandeur, compassion, love, peace, and calm. There is no parallel on earth.

"Men of sattvic (pure) disposition worship the gods," says *Bhagavad Gita*, "those of rajasic (worldly minded) disposition worship nature-spirits and demons, while others of tamasic (dark or undiscerning) disposition worship disembodied souls and ghosts."

The difference between the genuine quest of the soul, or God, and the hunger for psychic phenomena and miracles, has been clearly recognized by the illuminated from immemorial times. The practices of fortune-telling, astral projection, mental healing, witchcraft, etc., were in existence from the very beginning of culture in Sumer and Egypt, more than five thousand years ago. Since then, countless men and women in all parts of the earth have tried to benefit from them in some way. Millions have tried to become proficient in these activities in order to win power, gain fortunes, communicate with spirits, destroy enemies, work miracles, or to prolong life and conquer death. But are there any instances to prove that they succeeded or set examples for others to follow?

The miracles attributed to Christ might have benefited a few thousand persons in his time, but what has been of lasting value to mankind is the impact of both his priceless teachings and the life he lived. The miracles he is said to have performed, and those ascribed to his birth, now constitute one of the main factors responsible for creating doubts about the reality of his very existence. Nothing that is not in accordance with divine law survives for long. His teachings were in accord with these laws and they survive intact. His miracles were not and their importance has ended; they are not even accepted now by the rational intellects of our time.

This situation is not peculiar to Christ alone. All the phenomena attributed to Buddha, the yoga-adepts, the Christian mystics, or other spiritual teachers of the earth, by the churches are not only rejected outright by most informed people, but are also used by the skeptics as a weapon to attack the very foundation of the faiths they were intended to fortify.

Many of the miracles attributed to holy men, such as levitation and flying through the air, have not only been duplicated but surpassed by science. There is nothing in the annals of antiquity relating to the miraculous or magical performances of spiritual men that can even approach the miracles wrought by the intellect. The only miracle that has survived through the onslaught of time to stand unparalleled today is the miracle of reformation—the great revolutions in thought and conduct of generations and generations of human beings. It gives testimony to the solace and strength given to the soul, to sorrow and suffering mitigated through faith, and of hope sustaining them through darkest despair toward a glorious future. Most of these are necessary medicaments and props for the human mind to maintain its confidence and courage through the laborious evolutionary ascent. This is the one miracle which science cannot ever duplicate.

The desire to solve the riddle of existence, to reach into the dark and mysterious, and look into the beyond, owes its origin to the deep-seated evolutionary impulse in the human mind. By means of this urge, nature plans to draw the intellect toward the investigation of the supernatural and the numinous, ultimately leading to the discovery of the superphysical forces pervading the universe.

The main purpose is to draw the soul toward an investigation of its own mystery, to answer the questions that arise perennially in the minds of almost every man and woman about the problem of their own existence. The final end in view is emancipation or awareness of the soul about itself.

It is infinite, eternal, an ocean of bliss, one with the sun, stars, and planets, and yet untouched by their ceaseless motion. It is the light of the universe, free from every chain that binds the human body to earth. The aim of this evolutionary impulse is to make man aware of himself. With this sublime awareness, he will regulate his life as a rational human being, free from egotism, violence, greed, ambition, and immoderate desire. The aim, therefore, of nature is that every child born on earth should have the capacity to win higher consciousness and live a glorious life aware of his immortal, divine nature within while maintaining peace and harmony with every human being without.

From the zenith of material prosperity—at which mankind now stands due to the achievements of science—the ascent toward spirituality will begin. Modern knowledge, now almost at the frontier of its survey of the physical world, has but a short distance to cover to gain knowledge of the entrance to the spiritual realm. This is the biological mechanism of evolution in every human body. It has been known and worshiped for thousands of years. The activation of this mechanism through Yoga or other religious discipline leads to biochemical changes in the composition of the psychic energy feeding the nervous system and the brain, resulting in the transformation of consciousness. This transformation is of such an extraordinary nature that the individual who has the experience in its fullness is actually lifted from the level of mortals to the sphere of gods, while retaining all the noble years. The activation of this mechanism through yoga or other religious true mystics, sages, and seers had this divine organ active from birth, or activated it with appropriate disciplines and a righteous life.

This life—this thinking, feeling, knowing, being whom we think is born, grows old, and dies—is, in fact, the cream of the universe. It is a spark from a boundless ocean of fire, a ray from a living sun of unlimited dimensions, unbounded knowledge, and inexpressible bliss. It is a deathless atom from an infinite universe of consciousness. It must experience itself to know its stature in order to live in unutterable peace and bliss for the appointed span of life on earth.

This, I think, is the goal of every one of us, a goal designed by nature from which there can be no deviation except at the painful price of terrible suffering and disaster. Our evolutionary course is predetermined. Our transgressions can only delay the beatific consummation, but can never change or shape it according to our choice.

This, I believe, is the purpose for which you and I are here—to realize ourselves. We must know the truth: this colossal universe of matter is but a ripple in the ocean of life to which we belong. This is the reason why every great spiritual luminary laid the greatest stress on a righteous life. This condition is not imposed by man. It is the revealed injunction from the collective consciousness of the race; it is the law imposed by nature, enabling us to cross the boundary to higher consciousness.

When the vision of the lower Samadhi is suppressed by an act of conscious control, so that there are no longer any thoughts or visions in the mind," says Patanjali in the *Yoga Sutras,* "that is the achievement of control of the thought waves of the mind. . . . when this suppression of thought waves becomes continuous, the mind's flow is calm." Almost all great spiritual teachers have pointed out the dangers of succumbing to the lure of psychic powers or visionary experiences on the astral or mental plane, for these constitute entanglements for the soul as confusing and as hard to shake off as the entanglements of the earth.

"As time passes," says the Taoist master Chao Pi Ch'en, "demonic states will occur to the practiser in the forms of visions of paradise in all its majesty, with beautiful gardens and pools, or of hells with frightful demons with strange and awesome heads and faces, constantly changing their hideous forms. If he is unable to banish these apparitions caused by the five aggregates, as well as the visions of women and girls which disturb him, he must compose his mind which must be clear within and without." Keeping the mind clear within and without is indispensable in order to behold the majesty of the soul. Buddha is even more explicit in advising the suppression of the desire for psychic gifts of a miraculous kind. The desire for visionary flights, psychic gifts, and miraculous powers implies a wish to continue under the domination of the ego, mind, and senses in order to experience on subtler planes what one experiences on earth. To perform surprising feats with invisible psychic or other cosmic forces is descending again to the plane of earth.

The aim of the evolutionary impulse, on the other hand, is to bring about a state which is the very antithesis of this; it is to bring the soul to a clear realization of its own divine nature, beyond anything associated with this world. We come to earth to know ourselves. The unique mirror of life in us which reflects the universe never reveals its own amazing substance, and never reflects its own world. The whole of human evolution is designed to make us aware that we are gems clothed in flesh; this awareness is not only possible but obligatory for every human being born on the earth. It may take centuries, but every human activity and every social, political, or religious order is taking part in this mighty spiritual plan.

If properly carried out, the system [of yoga] will explain the nature of man's spiritual destiny to the world of science. Man must know himself to rise above the sorrow and misery, defeat and despair, distress and distraction of this world. There is nothing that can sustain him more firmly in his earthly battles than an occasional glimpse of his own majesty and immortality hidden within him by nature.

> Actually it is not necessary to renounce the objects of the world because a human being does not actually own or possess anything. Therefore, it is not necessary to renounce anything, but the sense of possessiveness should be renounced. Whether you live in the world or outside it does not make much difference. Attachment to the objects of the world is the cause of misery. One who practices non-attachment faithfully and sincerely obtains freedom from the bondage of karma.
>
> SWARMI RAMA *Living with the Himalayan Masters*

"HUMAN, ALL TOO HUMAN" AND BEYOND

D A N E   R U D H Y A R

Enlightenment is not strictly psychological; there is an associated physical transformation of the organism. It certainly includes changes in the operation of the nervous system, endocrine system and blood chemistry, as Gopi Krishna points out. But certain occult and spiritual traditions indicate that enlightenment in the most advanced stages involves a transformation of the actual substance of the body, so that the consciousness of an individual operates through a form composed of subtler material than gross flesh. Sri Aurobindo points to the final stage of yoga as one in which, after attaining union with the Supermind, the yogi begins a structural reorganization of his body on the molecular level.

To put it another way, would evolution cease if all members of the human race reached the state of Jesus or Buddha? The answer is no. There are states of being beyond even that. Enlightenment means at some point literally becoming light.

Dane Rudhyar, one of the great souls of our time, investigated the dynamics of spiritual unfoldment for more than seven decades. He writes here primarily as an occult psychologist, and what he has to say concerns stages of enlightenment beyond "ordinary" mysticism. What he terms the *Pleroma* state is, in the title of one of his many writings, "beyond personhood." It is a state beyond Nietzsche's designation of our present evolutionary condition as "human, all too human" in which the biophysical functions and drives—for breath, food, sex, and so on—are no longer operative and even the feeling of "individual" existence has only a secondary meaning. The body, transphysicalized, is composed of etheric matter. "Food" is obtained directly from space through different modes of energy. The details are not wholly clear to us, but traditions such as Theosophy speak somewhat about the subject. It will become clearer in time. What is important at the moment is to recognize that the Pleroma is an evolutionary potential of us all in our growth to godhood.

WHEN ONE ATTEMPTS to interpret the meaning of states of consciousness to some extent transcending the high normal level in any particular society, at any particular time, the greatest source of confusion and misunderstanding is the failure to properly define the relation of such states to the fundamental character and basic assumptions (or paradigms) of the culture. Moreover, such relatively transcendent states of consciousness (as well as feeling-responses and modes of interpersonal behavior) can belong to one of two basically different categories, even if, superficially and intellectually, these states may appear similar. Succinctly and symbolically stated, such states may be interpreted as the "flowering" of the culture in and through extraordinary persons—or as the earliest manifestations of "seeds" whose development was synchronous with the slow dying of the annual plant (the culture), and whose destiny it is to leave the plant which bore them.

A seed is formed in a particular plant, but it is not essentially connected with the character of that particular plant; its allegiance is only to the species as a whole. If we symbolically equate a particular human culture with a particular plant, the "seed person" formed within and by the culture fulfills his or her destiny (or function) most characteristically only when he or she "leaves," or becomes spiritually separate from the culture. The latter, having then evolved *past* its flowering period of collective fulfillment, is therefore already disintegrating or becoming increasingly sclerotic. The seed person's allegiance is not to his or her culture but to the human species as a whole. Because humanity's essential archetypal character and destiny is to be an agent for transformation on the planet earth, the seed person can be considered a "mutant." He or she becomes (or at least may become) the visionary formulator, and spiritually or mentally the "ancestor," of a *new* type of culture.

This symbolism certainly should not be taken literally as it omits several factors. Nevertheless, it may convey several points of essential significance. It illustrates a basic distinction which Western, Euro-American culture (some would say "civilization") fails to recognize or accept, and which Asian religious philosophies, for valid reasons, approach rather ambiguously, especially when dealing with westerners or their own westernized students. The distinction is between *mystics,* who are truly the flowering of the basic religious spirit of a culture, and those seed persons who are *true occultists,* or at least visionary and Promethean minds. As philosophers, creative artists, and statesmen, the essential destiny of these seed persons is to radically transform *both* the sociocultural assumptions of at least a section of mankind and certain aspects of generic human nature.

The western mind has difficulty considering and, even more, under-standing this distinction because the term "occultism" has been dreadfully debased. True occultism has essentially nothing to do with what have come to be known as "occult powers" and strictly "psychic" experiences, even though such powers and experiences may have a very effective reality in some cases. A true occultist is an individual seeking to effectuate the very difficult and extremely dangerous *transition* between two levels of reality: the human level—as we know it today in its dependence upon what we perceive as "physical" matter and biological systems of organization of material entities—and a superhuman, superindividual, and "planetary" level not only of consciousness but also of activity (and of will and feeling) at which matter, too, takes on a transcendent yet still "physical" character.*

MYSTICISM AND EMPIRICISM

Since 1400 A.D., and especially since the days of Francis Bacon, and soon after him Newton and Descartes, western civilization—which I prefer to characterize as Euro-American culture—has been based on the belief that reality can be approached only through the empirical and quantitative (and later on, statistical) methods of science. During the preceding five centuries, the religious approach to reality, pursued and dominated by the Catholic church, had relatively indisputably dominated the collective mentality of Europe. This approach was inspired or dynamized by what I might call, in an objective sense, the Christ mythos. It was given a definite form by a number of basic symbols and more or less dogmatic assumptions. Most Europeans (whether priests, monks, or laymen) were bound mentally and emotionally by these dogmas and forms, and the church and its inquisitors saw to it that they remained so. However, mainly after this first phase of the European culture reached its full development under a process of cultural cross-fertilizaton involving the Arabs and particularly the Sufis (during the twelfth and thirteenth centuries, when the Crusaders were returning to Europe), a number of mystics flourished who were able to use the dogmas and myths of official Christianity as foundations for the development—often after years of intense, and often dreary, search and practices—of what are usually known as "mystical experiences." These usually temporary, but in some instances often repeated, experiences were interpreted by the mystics themselves as the attainment of a "unitive state" of consciousness. The attainment of such a state was said to require a more or less total detachment of the consciousness from biological drives and personal attachments, and to involve a seemingly total identification with the supreme symbol of the mystic's religion, Christ (or in some cases Christ's mother)—or even a

---

*The term "planetary" refers to the concept according to which the earth is not only a globe of physical matter, but also a biological, mental, and spiritual system of activity and consciousness.

spiritual absorption into an ineffable and altogether transcendent and immutable "Reality," subsuming all religious symbols and divine personages.

The mystical path and mystical experiences have been described extensively, as much as they can be. Descriptions often rely upon the use of strictly negative terms to convey the experiences' utter transcendence from all that (to use the terminology of old India) has "name and form." However, what usually is not stressed, or even made clear, is that the mystics *of all countries* (in the strict and precise sense of the term "mystic") always *emerge from* and are *sustained* in their strivings by *both* their respective religions and all that is fundamental in their cultures. A St. Theresa of Avila would not have been possible without the Catholic church and the racial-cultural background of Spain; nor a Ramakrishna without his early absorption in the very concrete form of the particular type of Hinduism surrounding and conditioning his youth. Nevertheless, the apologist for the mystical way is correct in saying that in spite of the differences in various mystics' cultural and religious backgrounds, what mystics experience during their subliminal and ecstatic state of consciousness is remarkably similar. It may be similar, however, mainly insofar as intellectual words and concepts can relate the experience. Thus, the similarity may characterize the nature of the human mind *as interpreter of what is beyond its normal state* as much as the nature of the experience itself. Moreover, the written or recorded interpretations we possess refer to experiences which human beings have had *in relatively recent times*—that is, during the last three millennia, and at most since 3102 B.C., the traditional start of Kali Yuga and the incarnation of Sri Krishna. What are five thousand years in the probable millions human beings have been on earth?

Granted, however, that the "end" of the mystical way is similar whatever the culture and religion (and in general the collective and personal conditioning) from which the mystic started, this end could not have been attained without the original conditioning, the symbols, and the psychological (and even more psychic) support of *a* religion and culture. Even if the priesthood, and entrenched interests of the official religion and culture, often made the mystic's path arduous, they did so simply because it seemed to challenge the rigorously set ecclesiastic or even political structures of the society. Mystics need their culture and religion as psychic support, even if this support is used to rise beyond the culture's and religion's limits, to proclaim a reality beyond the sociocultural and religious symbols and forms. The great Catholic mystics of Europe prayed in the more or less traditional manner, and implicitly believed in the indisputable validity, power, and efficacy of the Christ mythos, the church, and its sacraments. This is true of all mystics who have ecstatic experiences of "unity" and/or identification with the divine by following a path which begins at the level of their ancestral, traditional religion. Because they represent the "flowering" of a religion and culture, great mystics are very different from the "leaves" representing their more ordinary coreligionists. But these leaves (or in the case of trees, branches) must develop *before* a mystic arises; without them the mystic would not be possible.

Another type of unusual human being also plays a significant and primary role in the evolution of societies and their cultures and religions— the seed persons mentioned earlier. I shall deal with them again presently, but first we should consider what has been happening in the Euro-American culture after it began to divorce itself from subservience to the forms of institutionalized Christianity.

Christianity having been split into conflicting ideologies, Christendom became increasingly dominated by empiricism—that is, by a scientific methodology which made the perceptions of the human senses and the interpretations of a strictly rationalistic intellect (using a specific, but by no means the only possible, kind of logic) *the sole valid means* for the acquisition of knowledge. This type of knowledge also has special, indeed revolutionary, characteristics: it has to be so obtained and formulated as to be available to *anyone* who wants it for *whatever purpose* their sole discretion defines. No previous kinds of knowledge had such characteristics; never before was access to or the acquisition of knowledge considered independent of the knower's degree of understanding, personal evolution, and capacity to use knowledge constructively.

During the seventeenth and eighteenth centuries, great European minds were concerned with the development of basic tools for the scientific method. The European empirical approach also took a sociopolitical form which, at least in principle, repudiated old sociocultural categories, and developed instead the concept of the social atom—the citizen of a society theoretically based on equality and individual rights. This sociopolitical philosophy inevitably implies the possibility of relatively unchecked acquisitiveness and separative existence, powered by ambition and greed (nicely called the "profit motive"). During the nineteenth century, Euro-American culture responded to the development of an increasingly materialistic and separative outlook with nationalistic separativeness, an emotional, Romantic individualism, and a struggle for power between nations and classes matching the struggle for life which Darwin had seen paramount in the biosphere.

Dane Rudhyar

AN EMPIRICAL PSYCHOLOGY

As the twentieth century began, the main field of a developing mass consciousness—a composite of pseudoindividualistic and increasingly disassociated human responses—became the field of psychology. But by psychology I do not mean *only* the Freudian, Jungian, and Maslovian types of personal psychology dealing with the problems and confusion of human beings subjected to increasingly chaotic and disintegrating social, ethical, religious, and cultural values and forms. I am also referring to the kind of international psychology having developed throughout the century which has made the international scene resemble a family struggle between masculine America and feminine Russia—with other industrial nations as collateral relatives, and the new nations of the Third World as children. This international war of nerves uses an ideological conflict—individualistic capitalism versus collectivistic socialism-communism—as a decoy, for it is essentially a power struggle between opposite but complementary types of emotional-mental responses to the results of the technological revolution. Technology, in turn, is the result of the empirical and quantitative approach of the scientific mind when this mind is focused *either* upon strictly materialistic values (comfort, progress, satisfaction of the drive for power) or upon almost exclusively personal concerns (for example, the Human Potential Movement whose roots can be found in the New Thought teachings and affirmations of the era between the two world wars).

Modern psychology since Freud is the result of applying the empirical approach of science to particular persons considered as basically separate psychic entities. These individualized psychic atoms emerged from the undifferentiated generic and collective mass of the human species and of various cultures; and the basic psychological problem of our century deals with the character of the relationship between these individual and collective factors. This relationship has become a cold war. The "peace proposal" offered by the psychologist Jung seeks to have the individual field of consciousness (the "I" realization) absorb and illumine the collective depths of the psyche (human nature and the great archetypes of a potentially all-inclusive, worldwide culture).

While Jung and Maslow seem to have opened up the field of consciousness to transcendent values and realizations, and while "transpersonal" psychology seeks to deal with the very limits of human consciousness and with what this consciousness may infer from inner experiences, taking uncertain and subjective forms in the light that floods the room of consciousness when the windows of the personality have been opened, Jung and Maslow firmly exhorted students and practitioners of transpersonal psychology: *Whatever you do, do not give up an empirical approach*. At least in his public stance and teachings, Jung never deviated from his belief that, having "assimilated" the contents of the collective unconscious and the deeper meaning of the culture's and religion's great symbols, a healthy person had to remain both psychically rooted and socially active in his or her culture and religion. Jung never seems to have believed, or at least taught, that a radical uprooting, not only from one's culture but *from the level at which cultures operate,* is the goal of spiritual development. He apparently refused to accept the possibility of the existence, within the total field of the planet earth, of beings as superior to human persons—in an evolutionary sense or in other ways—as, let us say, the human species is to a vegetable species.

Yet, in all times and in all cultures and religions, at least a small number of individuals (and in some cases whole cultures) have believed in the existence of such beings and in the possibility of mere human beings reaching such a condition. On the basis of inner experiences believed to be incontrovertible, even if not susceptible to empirical proofs, these individuals have reoriented their entire beings toward the taking of radically transformative steps that eventually would actualize the possibility of this superindividual, ultimately superhuman state of *being*—that is, of consciousness *and* activity. These individuals are true occultists. Symbolically speaking, they aim beyond the flowering of their cultures, at the evolutionary transformation which can occur only within mutating seeds. As seed persons they become separate in consciousness and inner being from the plant (culture) out of which they developed. Even while they are being slowly developed as seeds within the "fruit," they are, as Jesus stated, *in* this world but not *of* it—and this not only in consciousness, but also in terms of the quality of their activity and the character of their motivation. Nevertheless, what might be called the "other world" should not be considered a heavenly realm totally removed from and incomprehensible to human consciousness; it pervades this world of existence. The two realms constantly interact and are interrelated, one might say illustratively, as air pervades all substances of water and earth.

THE OCCULT PATH

Today the basic difference between the person who has typically mystical experiences and the true occultist is especially difficult to understand because depth psychologists, especially Jung, have attempted to reduce everything dealing with metaphysics to the level of psychology. Jung's commentary on *The Secret of the Golden Flower* is particularly definite in stating his utter lack of interest in, and even his contempt for, Asian metaphysics:

> My admiration for the great Eastern philosophers is as great and indubitable as my attitude toward their metaphysics is irreverent. I suspect them of being symbolical psychologists to whom no greater wrong could be done than to be taken literally. If it were really metaphysics that they mean, it would be useless to try to understand them.*

He objects to the criticism that his approach is merely a form of "psychologism," which he considers "as childish as metaphysics," and stresses that "it is reasonable to accord to the psyche the same validity as is given the empirical world, and to admit that the former has just as much 'reality' as the latter." Yet, when he refers to the process clearly defined in the Chinese text as the gradual formation of a "diamond body, the indestructible breath-body which develops in the Golden Flower" (which I refer to symbolically as "the seed"), Jung pompously asserts, "This body is a symbol for a remarkable fact," and proceeds to relate it to the experience of the Apostle Paul, which from an occultist's point of view is altogether different.

Space here does not permit me to quote the ambiguous discussion which follows or to discuss further Jung's convenient pushing into the "collective unconscious" of everything that would disturb his subservience to the scientific and empirical assumptions of the European culture to which he was so deeply and conservatively attached. I mention Jung's attitude solely because it has become the prototype for an emerging "new age" psychology of consciousness and the foundation for the widespread, intense concern with strictly personal problems of happiness, growth, and self-actualization that has spread throughout the Euro-American culture. Especially in the 1960s and 70s, it has aimed at an "expansion of consciousness," initiated through drugs; yet the term "drug" also can refer to repetitive psychic practices. Some types of meditation may produce a real addiction to a condition of relaxed psychobiological well-being.

When a Chinese occultist spoke of the Diamond Body, or when a Vajrayana Buddhist refers to the three "bodies" of the Buddha, there is no reason to believe they considered these *structured fields of activity and consciousness* as mere "symbols" conveniently related to certain stages of psychological unfoldment only in terms of consciousness. For the occultist, these "bodies" are *states of being*. They may be called bodies only to the extent that they refer to the ability to function effectively and consciously (in

*Wilhelm, Richard trans., *The Secret of the Golden Flower*, Commentary by C. G. Jung (New York, 1931), pp. 128ff.

a different type of consciousness!) at different levels of existence. Even the Nirmanakaya state of Gautama, while he acted as a man among men, may well have differed in quality of vibrations from that at which the strictly physical bodies of ordinary human beings operate. There are, in Sanskrit, various words to define several stages of development of the inner "vehicles" surrounding and pervading a human being's natural physical body (for example: upadhi, kosha, sharira). Yet one should speak of a "body" only when, at a particular level, density, vibratory speed, and quality of substance, an effectively organized system of functional activities is built to be the activity-aspect of a corresponding level of conscious being.

Building such a system of organization, the related aspects of consciousness (or superhuman faculties), and an effective will polarized by adequate higher-level purposes (to some extent replacing lower-level feelings and impulses) is a long, arduous, dangerous, and utterly demanding process. It is what occultists mean by "the Path." What develops on the Path is not merely consciousness *but a quality of being.* According to an individual's karma and the conditions of the society and its culture, this quality of being exteriorizes itself in varying degrees as a different and always more or less abnormal behavior (which inevitably is difficult for most people to understand), based on different feeling-responses to all types of relationships.

Certain cultures and collective forms of social organization have existed which undoubtedly were devised especially to *shelter and sustain* human beings born with a special readiness to enter upon the Path. The Tibetan culture, at least since the introduction of Buddhism, seems to have been such a sheltering envelope—a collective "fruit" wherein many "seeds" could develop. The *tulku* state, if truly genuine, stresses the attainment of a level of evolution at which the *center* of the being exists and matures at a superphysical level, even though, superficially, and in terms of cultural-religious activity, the incarnate tulku operates in and through a relatively normal and natural human vehicle (or body). The tulku is said to be a direct emanation of one of the celestial Buddhas, for instance, the Buddha of Compassion, Avalokiteshvara. This emanation "incarnates" in (or animates) a succession of human beings (even, in some instances, several at the same time).

Such human beings should not be called mystics, even though some of their experiences may be similar to or identical with those of Christian, Sufi, or Hindu mystics. The nature of experiences occurring even in the highest forms of Tibetan Buddhism is ambiguous because the Buddhist *sangha* (the religious community) is symbolically the "fruit" rather than a collection of "seeds." Tibetan Buddhism is a religion; Tibetan society is (or rather was) a culture. The outer form of this theocratic society constituted an institutional-ized *collective* system, defined by a very special geographical region and the possibilities it offered. On the other hand, the "highest" sangha is a planetary Communion which I have referred to as the *Pleroma* of humanity. It exists beyond all cultures. One could symbolize it as a planetary "granary" to which the "seeds" of all cultures find their way—but not as essentially separate units. For the Pleroma is a spiritual Communion in which what had been independent individuals *interpenetrate* in unanimity of purpose sus-tained by a common will. The Pleroma, the Many-as-One, is a soul-being that not only reflects but *is* the full, concrete, planetary actualization of what, "in the beginning" of this earth system (the divine Word or Logos), was an all-inclusive *potentiality* of being.

What we call mankind is but the long, gradual, arduous, often tragic, and always dangerous transition between the level of "life"—as we know it in the earth's biosphere, where it operates as a quasi-instinctual and compul-sive type of homogeneity—and that of the Pleroma. The highest possibility of consciousness—together with the most effective capacity for action and the purest cosmic or divine will—operate in this Pleroma state. Subcon-sciously, if not consciously, humanity aspires to such a state because it is humanity's function on this planet to be the transition between two levels of being: the vegetable and Pleroma states. Man is an animal into which the seed of divinity has been "sown"—or to use another metaphor, onto which the capacity to become divine was "grafted." This capacity belonged to superior minds (or mental beings) who, having "grafted" an "emanation" of their power onto protohuman beings, have remained involved in the result—that is, in our "human, all too human" efforts to reach the Pleroma state by following the arduous Path of discipleship or transformation.*

Today's "new age" persons have difficulty understanding this process because Indian and Sufi philosopher-mystics have emphasized a *subjective* approach stressing the practice of what has become popularized as medita-tion and the achievement of strictly subjective states, as samadhi or satori are usually understood. The true occultist also must have subjective experiences of "unitive" states, but he or she seeks to develop a *higher physical* as well as a *higher mental consciousness*. On his or her way to the fully developed Pleroma state, the disciple on the Path serves as a link between the animal-human and the Pleroma state, and this *through* what he or she has developed of a "higher mind" (which elsewhere I have called the "mind of whole-

*See my books *Beyond Individualism: The Psychology of Transformation* (Quest Books, Wheaton, Illinois, 1979), *Beyond Personhood* (Rudhyar Institute, Palo Alto, California, 1982), and *The Rhythm of Wholeness* (Quest Books, Wheaton, Illinois, 1983).

ness").** To be such an agent is what *transpersonal living* really means: individualized personhood is placed unconditionally at the service of the Pleroma. What has been called the "inner Ruler" (or the "Master within") is, in this sense, the powerful and effectual focalization of the Pleroma within (yet from above or beyond) the person.

The Pleroma is a state of total being, not only of consciousness. A Pleroma being has "his" center of being at a level beyond what our senses perceive as physical matter. At this level there is no gender, no biological imperatives, and no subservience to the patterns, symbols, and paradigms of a *particular* culture. While the *essential* level of Pleroma activity is the "world of forces," a Pleroma being seems able to act, at least temporarily and for a definite planetary purpose involving humanity as a whole, *through* what seems to be the form and substance of a physical body.

Unfortunately, the analytical mind, which the western world has developed so intently and almost exclusively, is normally able to think of anything human only in terms of separateness and individual being. Yet recently, a few progressive minds have been trying to imagine a world of interpenetrating wholes. But while it is easy to say philosophically that everything is in everything else, it is much harder to translate this concept effectively into personal-emotional and egocentric terms.

The state of interpenetration should also refer to the interpenetration of the future and the present—with humanity's dreary past (karma) acting as a negative factor (inertia). The Pleroma future interpenetrates the human present—yet each particular, rigidly separative culture, having molded individual minds and personalities, acts against this interpenetration; for, alas!, most human beings cling to their "own" culture. *Potentially,* the Pleroma is now. It is the archetypal Word, the Logos that was in the beginning yet remains changeless; yet it is this archetypal potential of being *in the process* of self-actualization in terms of human consciousness *and* human activity. Mankind *is* this process. The Pleroma *is,* yet is also in the making. Because it is in the making, it calls to all of us to participate in this making.

Theology is dualistic and doctrinaire; mysticism is nondualistic and experiential Theology is dogmatic and credal; mysticism aims at the unfathomable mystery beyond all dogmas and creeds. Theology is the rational articulation of absolute faith; mysticism encourages transition from faith to personal realization. Theology interposes an organized organi administrative hierarchy to mediate between the layman and God. Mysticism affirms the spiritual equality of all

**See my book *The Rhythm of Wholeness* (Quest Books, Wheaton, Illinois, 1983).

"Human, All Too Human" and Beyond

men and their potential for direct union with the Divine.

HARIDAS CHAUDHURI, Western Theology and Indian Mysticism

Liberation is not escapism, but consists in the conscious transformation of the elements that constitute our world and our existence. This is the great secret . . . of the mystic of all times.

LAMA ANGAGARIKA GOVINDA

. . . to Return to the Divine, one doesn't regress to infancy. Mysticism is not regression in the service of the ego, but evolution in transcendence of the ego.

KEN WILBER, The Atman Project

ON ENLIGHTENMENT

S W A M I

S I V A N A N D A   R A D H A

Enlightenment is an experience
that symbol and metaphor
can't quite capture.
The mind clings to its beliefs:
"I don't *know*, but I *believe*."

Maya is dazzling
with its colorful displays.
Emotions grip, temptations lure
and attachment—just happens?

Enlightenment is dying
to the world of concepts
accumulated ideas
ignorance and darkness.

WHAT IS ENLIGHTENMENT?

AT A PUBLIC lecture a member of the audience asked, "Do you have enlightenment?"

In a flash I realized that everybody in the room would have a very different concept of enlightenment. I responded, "See me after the lecture and you can tell me what *you* mean by enlightenment. Only then can I answer your question."

Can anyone describe how wine tastes to a person who has never tasted wine? The precondition of the tastebuds, the eating habits, and the underlying imagination about how wine *might* taste will all influence the listener's theoretical understanding. In the same way we can give no definite answer to the question "What is enlightenment?" There is also no "psychology" of that particular state of consciousness called enlightenment. There is a psychology of personalities, yes, and a path of character development to move toward enlightenment. But enlightenment itself—Cosmic Consciousness—and doesn't need any psychology.

I am reminded of a Chinese story, very well-known in the East. The Master shows some students a piece of beautiful brocade, woven in very intricate patterns, and then asks, "Have you seen the perfection of the brocade?"

The students all enthusiastically exclaim, "Yes! You have just shown it to us."

The teacher smiles and says, "You have seen only the back, where the threads are knotted together. You must desire to see the brocade in its perfection."

If a mother tells her daughter what it is like to be pregnant and to give birth, theoretically all the knowledge is transmitted, including the "psychology of experience." But the daughter will only know what it means to give birth when she has the experience herself. And her experience may be quite different from her mother's.

Another example: A man and woman are in love. It is a wonderful spring day with buds coming to flower, the sun penetrating through new leaves, and a wonderful feeling pervading the air with happiness, fulfillment, a sense of having it all.

Now you ask them, "Why are you in love with *this* person?"

They respond with superlatives of beauty, intelligence, aesthetics, behavior, knowledge, personality, and so on. With each quality you offer to introduce them to someone who has even more of that quality. But no—no other will do.

In the same way we can never interfere with any seeker's perception of enlightenment. It is an entirely personal experience that he or she will not even be able to give a full account of.

Although we can't define enlightenment precisely, can we expect certain actions or behavior from a person we believe to be enlightened? Do students have a right to demand the kind of moral example that the Teachings talk about? I think you cannot teach anybody surgery unless you have learned it, performed it, and become skillful in it. In the same way, if I want a beautiful cabinet, then I have to choose a cabinetmaker who can build it.

But at all times cultural background has to be considered. If a rabbi, a swami, a priest, or a minister has an illicit affair, we in the West consider him very immoral. But the following Tibetan story gives a different view: A young woman, coming home from the farm, was seduced by a yogi. She told her experience to her mother, who instead of comforting her, exclaimed that this was the most blessed moment of her daughter's life because now she would give birth to an enlightened being.

Is the story made up as an excuse, or is there some validity to the assumption that yogic practices affect the brain, and those effects can be inherited? This is a question for modern science.

Is a rabbi who is thought to be very holy and above everything still enlightened despite the fact that he has remarried four or five times and has many children from many different women?

If we look at Mahatma Gandhi, was he an enlightened being? *Mahatma* means *great soul*. Was he a great soul, but not necessarily enlightened? Mahatma Gandhi often slept with young women, one on each side of him, to practice control of his sexual urges. Was this right? Was it wrong? Was it moral or immoral? Only the person who performed the action can answer that question.

If a yogi says "I am beyond karma," it may be a clever excuse to fulfill personal desires. A yogic teacher once said, "Divine Mother brought this woman into my house, and because she missed her flight she had to stay here with me." Was this truly a provision of the divine forces or was the man simply falling victim to temptation because he lacked discrimination?

People who claim enlightenment may do so in many different ways: by their outer appearance, their mannerisms, and activities. Do we see only our own idealized idea in another individual and then assume—because we are impressed by appearance, by the manner of speaking, by the sacred texts, and for the sake of our own needs—that this individual is enlightened?

Are our personal ideas about morality and wisdom good enough tools to help us understand enlightenment? And if we cannot recognize enlightenment with only the help of our five senses, what are we left with? Our concept of enlightenment will grow as we ourselves grow. A child in kindergarten develops a certain awareness, which changes with further schooling, and changes more with college education. But even after college, the student has acquired only the tools. The essence of what has been learned will only be known through experience.

DIFFERENT PATHS, DIFFERENT WORDS

We can see that to *discuss* enlightenment is difficult. And if you were to find many enlightened people and ask them how they attained that state, each would describe a different approach, and in very different terms.

In the Christian tradition, Jesus said, "Be ye therefore perfect even as your Father which is perfect" (Mt. 5:48). Who is this Father in Heaven?

And what did Jesus mean by perfection? Where is Heaven? In modern times we can travel into space and visit other planets, but it is very difficult to find Heaven. Is it a state of mind? Is it a state of interaction of the five senses? How do you imagine Heaven? How would you describe it? What would you like to see there? How would you like to be there? What would you feel? Hot, cold, pleasant, summer all the time? Bored? Or if you seek Heaven, will you be a wanderer over this world and many other worlds, one after another? Will you eventually find your place in the universe or will you not?

The scientist, searching for objective evidence, says, "In all my experiments with the brain, I have never found a soul."

"But," I would have to ask, "have you ever found the mind? Where is that?"

The answer would have to be, No, because the mind cannot be located. Does it mean the mind does not exist? If you had never heard of the word *soul*, would you have had to find a word to describe that force? Many descriptions are basically different expressions for the same thing: whether it is called the *soul*, the *Buddha nature*, the *inner Light*, the *Kingdom within*, the *innate Energy*. Like the physicist whose search for the smallest particle or wave requires building extraordinarily complex mechanisms to explode atoms, there is no means for us to follow consciousness comfortably, exactly, visibly, perceptibly. And only the traces tell us that something is there.

Perhaps it will be easier if we look at the enlightened being as a genius in the spiritual field. How does anyone become a genius, and how can others, who are not, recognize it? What do you expect from a genius? How do you measure genius? Think of Einstein, who broke all previous conceptual limitations of physics. The genius in the spiritual field, too, must break through all limitations, to go beyond the mind's present horizon.

The adventurer who travels the road to enlightenment cultivates a taste for the adventure, and nourishes an expansion of hope and possibility. But even when we find our place in the universe, we are incapable of stating it directly. The greatest wonders must be clothed in symbol and metaphor. How did consciousness get here? We can take the moon as a symbol for individual consciousness. Then we have to ask, What is the greater source of Light, like the sun, that this consciousness reflects?

As human beings functioning in three dimensions, we are tempted to take excursions into the fourth. But many people have a difficult and painful time accepting even what exists within three dimensions. Searching for more dimensions will not provide answers if you are unable to lift your mind into that Light.

In the meantime, let us approach enlightenment by finding out what is the purpose of our life, each in our own way.

AWARENESS: THE STEP TOWARD ENLIGHTENMENT

To approach enlightenment you need to develop awareness. Enlightenment, in that sense, has as many levels as awareness. If you can liberate yourself from your own limitations, and if you welcome anyone who helps you to liberate yourself, then you already have some degree of enlightenment.

The degree of your self-understanding is a good measure of the degree of your enlightenment. This understanding can eventually become more than psychological. By your own efforts, you can open yourself to Divine Inspiration and the Wisdom that radiates from other sources.

Enlightenment, even in the first stages, gives you more insight. Then it is your duty to see the spiritual potential in other people and to do what you can to further it, within the limitations of your understanding. If you pursue someone because you see that person hurting himself and you want to help, or because you see that the individual could really have great spiritual experiences—you are acting out of compassion. The enlightened motivation is to bring as many as you can to the Divine.

And if someone turns against you, will you still be willing to help? You may need time to assess the situation, but will you dismiss a person entirely? Only when there is an accumulation of negativity (or to use the Western term *evil*) that is too overpowering for you to handle, should you stay away. But that doesn't mean you should reject that person.

What is important is your interaction with people. How do you interact? Accept or reject? Condemn or help? Bind or liberate? That says a lot about your level of awareness.

The more you really know yourself, to that degree you are enlightened. If you really know yourself, you might not be able to put everything into perfect action to the satisfaction of other people. But then you realize it is not your purpose to please other people or to project an image.

As you move toward self-knowledge, you may feel like a stumbling child. Keep struggling, even if you get bruised through criticism. You may find it extremely difficult, but still persist.

The greatest obstacle is not so much physical temptations as your will. If you make a mistake and feel remorse, you may be forgiven. You can say to the Divine, "You hold onto me—you know I cannot hold onto you." But if you don't ask, and if your ego finds excuses to justify yourself, why should you be forgiven?

Enlightenment exacts a high price. So while there is inspiration in spiritual life, there are also many hurdles to jump. Staying with spiritual life really means dealing with your ego and self-will. It's as simple as that. And there is nobody and no power that can release you from that battle. You are on the path of evolution. You can *retard* your evolution severely or you can advance it.

As for morality, the power you obtain through spiritual practice is neutral. What you *do* with that power is entirely your responsibility, and it's an awesome one. If you don't know that you have the capacity, at any moment, to flip the power in the opposite direction, then you don't really know yourself. You can be a Christ or the Devil. The power is neutral, it is what you do with it. That is why commitment is so important, because the intensity of your commitment is the source of grace that will come back to you. In proportion to your commitment, grace will sustain you. Your commitment has to be to the Divine, not to any person.

Many people have very strong, powerful personalities but if all the power they have acquired is hooked into the ego and hooked into self-will, it means nothing. The ego cannot be enlightened.

If there is a moment when a spiritual teacher indulges in personal enjoyment of the recognition or worship, a price is paid for that. Jesus said, "Lay not up for yourselves treasures upon earth . . . But lay up for yourselves treasures in heaven . . ." (Mt. 6:19–21) In other words, if you have your reward on earth, there is nothing to look forward to—your ego received its full satisfaction. If you did not have your reward here, you will find it somewhere else. You have to decide: where do you want your reward? Why seek recognition from those who don't even know what you are doing? Such recognition is neither useful nor satisfying. If you have awareness, then you don't need recognition.

The basic struggle is that you live in the world of the mind and you live in the world of the physical. You must reach up to the Light. Instead of indulging emotions and feelings, indulge in Divine Light. That's the only indulgence that will give a blessing in return. Otherwise you will run after things that continuously elude you, while the Light will not. Everything else is impermanent. The Light is permanent. It is the life force that permeates the whole universe. The same Energy can take *all* shapes and forms. You give it the shape and form. See what an awesome power you really have?

When you decide to use that Energy to take you back to your divine origin, then you fulfill the purpose of your life. Evolution—the individual development of awareness toward enlightenment—is the true purpose of life.

THE MOOD OF ENLIGHTENMENT

A Talk Given by Master
Da Avabhasa to His Devotees

I regard Da Avabhasa (formerly Da Free John) as an authentic religious genius who clarifies and unifies the entire spectrum of issues and experiences that concern spiritual seekers and consciousness researchers. His teaching about enlightenment seems to be unsurpassed by any spiritual teacher of any time; it leads to an inclusive realization and inspection of the entire human condition—just as he himself has lived it.

Da Avabhasa views human development as unfolding in seven stages that range from the development of the body to the highest spiritual realization. An important part of that teaching is his criticism of "conventional" or "ordinary" mysticism which he sees as characteristic of the fifth and sixth stages of life. Such mysticism belongs to the ego and is based on the same kind of psychology as popular "downtown" religion, he says. There is a kind of enthusiastic believing and attachment to a sect, to "secret" practices, and, often, to an individual. There are various kinds of pleasurable, consoling experiences that can be cultivated by turning attention inward, but these are not enlightenment; they are really egoistic creations that distract us from God. Certain internal sounds, lights, visions—these are the phenomena of conventional mysticism. Do not mistake them for reality, he warns; they are not genuine self-transcendence or God-realization. They are only stages of Becoming to be passed through on the basis of prior recognition of Being.

The seventh and ultimate stage in Da Avabhasa's map of reality is radical intuitive identification with Divine Reality, the Condition of all conditions, the Radiant Transcendental Being. (He capitalizes certain words to emphasize their special meaning in his teaching.) This he calls sahaja-samadhi, "Ecstasy with open eyes." That is *true* mysticism. While in this Condition, with energy and attention totally freed, all phenomena that arise—even the universe itself—are simply recognized as nonbinding modifications of the Divine Being Itself.

The God-realized spiritual master or Adept, Da Avabhasa says, is devoted to awakening humanity to its true nature and destiny—a condition that transcends not only the past and present, but also the future of all evolution of self, of humanity, and of the entire cosmos. Da Avabhasa's teaching ultimately exceeds all evolutionary prescriptions. God-realization here and now is his principal concern. Thus, although the Way he teaches acknowledges Becoming, it is nevertheless grounded in recognition of unconditional Being—the prior God-nature of all creation—and the need for moment-to-moment surrender and sacrifice of all self-sense to the Great Being which lives in us all.

For a fuller description of the seven stages of psychospiritual development by Da Avabhasa, see Appendix 1.

MASTER DA AVABHASA: While you are live, everything seems important. Even despair is important, an acknowledgment that something important to you has not happened. Thus, life, while you live it, is full of importances. On the other hand, the entire universe conspires to make you surrender what seems important, because everything in the universe comes to an end. All experience is conspiring to move you to transcend experience while at the same time demanding that you fulfill experience. Every instant of your life contains both of these urges.

Life is completely absurd. Every particle of it would move you toward some experience or other, and yet all experience conceals the ultimate message of the necessity for transcendence or freedom from experience. That one must attain freedom from something that is unnecessary to begin with is utterly absurd. Why bother with it to begin with?

Enlightenment is to Awaken from the seriousness of experience. It is not to despair or to destroy oneself. Despair is serious, and so is suicide. Self-indulgence is serious, stressful effort is serious, discipline is serious, interest is serious, knowledge is serious: death, sex, food; everything is completely serious. This movement or tendency to survive, to continue in independent form, is profoundly serious, and it is also absurd because it must be transcended. Enlightenment is to be restored to Divine humor, to realize that nothing is necessary. No experience is necessary. You can either become distracted by experience and repeat it, or you can transcend it. One or the other. If you have transcended experience, then it is no longer necessary. In that case, whether or not experience continues makes not the slightest bit of difference to you. Experience will come to an end with death in any case.

We are under the incredibly absurd illusion that there is an objective world "outside" Consciousness. There is not a shred of truth in this presumption. There is no world independent of Consciousness. The world is a modification of Consciousness, a play on Consciousness. It has no independent reality and no necessity. It is just possibility. What Consciousness does in terms of possibility in any moment is the drama of the seriousness of existence. When it Awakens to its true Position, which is senior to phenomena, then it is full of humor and there is no necessity to any experience. There is only Enlightenment, Divine Freedom.

You are constantly imagining that you are experiencing objective things, but you are not. You do not actually see an object—that lamp over there, for instance. It is not the object you are seeing. Isn't it obvious to you that you are experiencing a phenomenon of the brain? You cannot see the lamp. You are not inside your head looking out at the lamp. A bizarre phenomenon of the brain produces the sensation that there is a lamp over there. Where is it, anyway? A reflected image twists around in the eyeball, and nerve impulses and electrical currents flash around the meat brain in order to construct an illusion, a sensation, an idea. What is objective about it? It is just your own fascination. It is your own mind. It is your own Consciousness, modified by organs of experience. It is mind. It is harmless enough in itself, really, but you are so distracted by it that you have lost your humor. You have lost your true position. You do not have a right relationship to experience.

The right relationship to all experience is to exist as the Transcendental Consciousness, the Radiant Reality Itself, in which phenomena arise without necessity, humorously. The wrong relationship to experiential phenomena is to presume that you are a separate person, a separate consciousness, in the midst of a world that you know nothing about, that somehow encloses you, that is objective to you, that is separate from you. In that case, you see, experience is a very serious business. You have no option but to submit to it, to be distracted and tormented by it.

Spiritual life is simply the Enlightened life. There really is no spiritual life until Enlightenment, or the seventh stage of life[1]—All the stages of life before then are stages of experience wherein, as a discipline, we bring the Intuition of the Truth to experience, thereby transcending that level of experience. We engage this process stage by stage, practicing this Transcendental discipline relative to the many qualities of experience, until all possible experience is transcended. Only then have we resumed the Transcendental Position, and only then can we live the Enlightened Life. Existence is spiritual only when lived from the point of view of Enlightenment. Previous to the Awakening of that Disposition, existence is not spiritual in the truest sense. It is simply a struggle with the impulse of experience, the humorlessness of experience, the motive to survive as this moment with all of its parts and implications and motives.

The motive to continue, the motive to fulfill desire, the motive to remain self-conscious, to remain yourself, to remain embodied, is basic to your sense of existence. Surviving as experience is what you are chronically doing, you see. You are not existing as the Transcendental Reality. You are just being this body-mind. You are moved to continue as that, and to

---

[1] Editor's note: For an elaboration of the seven stages of life, see Appendix 1.

glamorize it, and to have as much pleasure as possible while being the body-mind. Consequently, if you can temporarily manage to acquire a great deal of pleasure as this body-mind, you begin to think that pleasure itself is Enlightenment! As soon as you get a little physical or emotional or mental pleasure, right away you think that you are existing in the highest state that one can realize. But in true Enlightenment there is no struggle whatsoever for the continuation of phenomena. There is no fundamental or binding effort to make phenomena continue. There simply are phenomena, these conventions of experience, but they are unnecessary, temporary, harmless modifications of Consciousness. That Consciousness, Realized in Enlightenment, is not an independent person. It is without qualification; Transcendental. It is Enlightenment. The Enlightened individual is no longer fitted to the separate soul-consciousness, the individuated self struggling to survive as itself or to become something else. In Enlightenment, the motive to survival dissolves. Continued bodily existence is spontaneous, no longer dependent upon a psychological motive to continue. It simply continues, and then at some point bodily existence also simply comes to an end. It is neither necessary nor ultimate.

Likewise, the universe is not ultimate. It does not hide a great Fact. It is perfectly ordinary and unnecessary. We could just as well be having any one of an infinite number of other possible experiences at this moment. It happens that this one is arising, but anything else could also arise. However, you are determined that this experience continue to arise more or less exactly as it is now arising. If you could relax that demand just a little bit, something entirely different would happen. But you are afraid of something entirely different. You are afraid to die. You are afraid to allow things to change. Therefore, you hold on to your present experience. But if you could give up everything, not through negative, reactive effort, but through Transcendental Realization, then your humor would be restored, and a different sense of existence would quite spontaneously arise. Then you would realize that there is no necessity to this present experience, except that it is set in motion through ordinary causation and will therefore continue for its term.

We are not present in our experience. In other words, acting, or experiencing, is not a present activity. It has nothing to do with the present, the absolute Moment of Existence. It is the past. All experience is the past. There is nothing new, and there is nothing real about the mind that experiences. The mind is simply memory, past association. It is not perceptive, nor truly sensitive to anything. It is just the mechanical record of patterns. The body is exactly the same as the mind, but because we think so much we imagine that the mind is something different from the body. Actually, the body-mind is one, a simultaneous coincidence. Just as the mind is past associations, the body is past associations.

The body is the past. It is like a star—the rays of light that we now see were generated light years before now. The present form of that star is not visible, because it is so far away that the light it generates today takes eons to arrive. Likewise, these bodies are the reflections of the distant past. They have no present significance. They must be transcended before we can Realize the Present, or the Transcendental Reality.

Such a Realization, however, occurs only in the seventh stage of life. Many people read and think about spiritual teachings, and their minds prattle the traditional ideas to the point that they think they are already Enlightened. Yet they have never become the bodily Sacrifice that is essential for this Realization. Enlightenment, or the Realization of God, is not just a conceptual understanding. It is not just a relatively calm state of mind. Enlightenment is an absolute Condition of existence that literally transcends the body-mind. It is not just an idea the body-mind has that makes it feel better. From the radical, Enlightened point of view, there is no body-mind! Thus, in order to enter into the seventh stage of life, one must pass through the most profound and even terrifying transformation. That event cannot be casually created by a little thinking. One must come to the point where there is literally no necessity to the body-mind, to the psyche, or to experience.

Countless silly people think that they are Enlightened when, at best, they feel good today. That mediocre sense of pleasure is not Enlightenment. Enlightenment involves no thinking whatsoever. There is no rational justification for Enlightenment, no logical sequence of thought that leads to it. Enlightenment is a spontaneous, absolute, transcendental Awakening that is free of all the seriousness and necessity of bodily and mental existence. Therefore, death, the cessation of experience, the cessation of states of mind, the cessation of the body, the cessation of the world, is no longer a threat. So much the worse for it! There is complete freedom from the implications of all that dreadful destiny that everyone fears so profoundly. The Enlightened being is not at all threatened by all of that. He is laughing. He is free.

But one must pay the price for this Freedom. It is not simply an attitude toward the world that one enjoys from some conventional position of separation. There is the Radiant Transcendental Consciousness, the Absolute Divine Reality. That truly is Existence, and It must be Realized if Enlightenment is to be true. In that Realization, the Divine Person is tacitly obvious, as concrete as any object that you now associate with bodily life and experience. Once this Realization is Awake, there is no necessity to the phenomena of experience. They simply continue in this moment, but they have no power to deceive.

All the stages of life leading up to the seventh stage are stages of distraction by the seriousness of one or another kind of experience. The process of the transcendence of experience begins at the lowest level, where experience involves the fear of loss of the body and the profound connection to food, and the craving for sexual self-indulgence. These experiences characterize the ordinary person, the lowest kind of person in the spectrum of existence. Yogis, mystics, and saints all cling mightily to experiential inwardness: visions, flashing lights in the brain, vibrations in the middle of the head, exotic, many-armed works of art that they create in imagination, infinite peacefulness without a single thought, or even seeing and thinking nothing and having no experience at all. But these are all, high and low, merely the possibilities of human beings in the first six stages of life.

In the Way of Divine Ignorance, what makes these possibilities spiritually significant is that in each stage of life, in the midst of each stage of distracting experience, whether high or low, we must realize self-transcendence and whole body surrender into the Radiant Transcendental Consciousness, or Divine Person. Apart from such self-transcendence, however, the first six stages of mere maturing in the structural possibilities of Man are absurd, humorless, fundamentally very serious. Something in each of the first six stages is taken profoundly seriously by ordinary human beings. The body and food, sex, thinking, psychic awareness, higher mental hallucinations, even blissful, internal silence—there appears to be something profoundly serious and meaningful to one's hallucinated existence in each of those stages.

But the seventh stage, the Enlightened stage, is not serious at all. In that stage we Realize our native Transcendence of everything. There is the tacit Realization that there is nothing serious whatsoever about experiential existence. It could end in this moment, casually; and that cessation in itself would not have the slightest significance. Or, it could continue for infinite eons of time, through infinite permutations and transformations of experience; and its continuing would not have any significance either. That is the Disposition in Enlightenment—Realization of the nonnecessity of everything. Absolutely nothing is of serious consequence or of ultimate necessity—absolutely nothing.

The ordinary reactive personality, who is basically in despair and hysterical, can also say that life is meaningless, but such a person is very serious. The Enlightened man, however, Realizes total Freedom. He is no longer serious, but neither is he self-destructive. He has passed into Ecstasy. He has not suppressed or separated from himself—rather, all that he is has been transcended in the Radiant Transcendental Consciousness. Thus, he is full of humor and delight. He is not aggressively opposed to the world, nor is he clinging to it. All the tension in his heart has been released. To speak of Enlightenment without that sign is nonsense. There is no Enlightenment without the release of the heart from all of its seriousness, all of its clinging to phenomena, high and low.

From the point of view of Enlightenment, even mystical phenomena are nonsense. They are not serious. They are hallucinations, brain phenomena, psychism, permutations of your own body-mind. They are just more of your seriousness. They have no necessity and they are not the source of Bliss. Whether they are higher phenomena, viewed from the mental or subjective point of view, or lower phenomena, viewed essentially from the bodily point of view, all phenomena are serious and unnecessary. They do not bring happiness, fundamentally. Happiness is inherent in the Radiant Transcendental Consciousness. When that Reality is Realized, its inherent Bliss is obvious, and phenomena are seen not to contain any independent Life or Consciousness, nor to grant Freedom or Bliss. From the Enlightened point of view, all phenomena are simply the theatre of Eternal Blissfulness, a theatre that may or may not continue.

Therefore, all one's serious occupations while alive are absurd expressions of the past. They are all ways of serving limitation in oneself and limitations in others. Better that they all fall apart—but not in the negative, nihilistic sense. We must simply be given up in God, the Current of Radiant Bliss. We must become Radiant. We must be allowed to manifest the Radiant Blissfulness of the Absolute Consciousness. We must be allowed to become love, to be free, to be humorous. Then everything that is past will dissolve. The mind is the past, and so the mind dissolves. The body is the past, and so the body dissolves.

For the usual man, the body is the past, moving into the future. There is no present in the usual life. We are too busy having experiences to be Awakened in the present. The present is the Transcendental Reality Itself, for which we have no time because we are so occupied. Thus, you must Awaken from your vulgar disposition of clinging to vital desires themselves. You must Awaken from your romantic nostalgia for life and your desire for experiences. You must Awaken from your coolness of mind, whereby you inspect the world and find logical consistency and meaning. You must Awaken to your true Position, wherein all the locks on the heart are dissolved and all the tension in the heart is released.

It is the tension in the heart that produces obsession with vital experience, with reactive and illusory emotional experience, with mental forms and inner psychic forms: all the subjective distractions. When the tension in the heart is released, there is no clinging to the body-mind or its experiential possibilities. If the body-mind arises, that is fine, and if it does not arise, that too is fine.

When you begin to come to rest in the native Blissfulness of God, you realize freedom and you receive Grace. Grace is the humor you enjoy by always already resting in God. Grace is not ultimately a matter of achieving all kinds of successes in life. Success may come also, but that is just part of the game of experience. Grace is the liberation that comes when we rest in God. Then the locks in the heart are loosened, and the seriousness of experience is dispelled. We feel Radiant. Our occupations become Blissful. Our capacity to enter into the spiritual process is clarified and intensified. We have energy for spiritual life. The process of self-transcendence is quickened, and we move into higher stages of the transforming process until Enlightenment is Radical or Perfect, uncaused and unsupported. In that case, there is simply rest in God, or Grace Absolute, and the world and the body-mind are allowed to float in Infinity. There is no tension in the body-mind, and no illusion.

The moral of this talk is that all devotees must realize Humor, Freedom, or Distance from all the seriousness of their interests and their occupations from day to day. They must see the ordinariness of it, even the absurdity of it, without becoming ironic. They must be free of the world in itself and rest naturally in the mood of the heart, the Intuition of the Radiant Transcendental Consciousness. If you rest in God, then you have received Grace. Then Grace has entered into your daily life and only serves its ultimate transcendence. If you do not come to rest in God, the heart is like a stone or a clenched fist. It has not entered into the Infinite Radiance of Consciousness. It is fixed upon itself. It is Narcissus, self-meditative, self-protective, threatened by everything to Infinity, obsessed with possibilities and the repetition of experience in order to acquire a sense of survival, consolation, and pleasure.

The only Happiness is the release of the heart, or the differentiated self, which is not a fixed entity. The self is just like this clenched fist. Relax the fist and there is nothing inside. Relax the heart and there is no one inside. The sense of self is just the tension in the body-mind that gives it the sense of independence. Relax the tension and the body-mind becomes transparent. There is no ego. There is no ego in experience. That is why Enlightenment is not really an event in the universe. It is not associated with experience of special, so-called "Enlightenment phenomena." It would seem, from the ordinary point of view, that Enlightenment is the dissolution of this separate self. But Enlightenment is the Realization that there is no such self and that there never was; that there is no such self in all the other beings that now continue to exist, and that there never was a self when one was struggling to become Enlightened or to transcend oneself.

The Disposition of the Enlightened one is paradoxical. It is a bodily

Disposition because he is, in a conventional sense, embodied, and he therefore represents the past and its movement toward the future. And, paradoxically, his obligation is to somehow serve the Enlightenment of other beings. But from the point of view of Enlightenment itself there are no other beings, and those conventions of experience that we call other beings are not, in fact, failing to be Enlightened. They *are* Enlightenment. They are themselves only the Radiant Transcendental Consciousness. Therefore, all that we are confronting is a conventional concept of bondage and the need to survive. It is a superficial concept, and yet all beings are profoundly organized around these notions of bondage and survival. They create their daily lives around motives based in these notions. Thus, all beings appear to be tormented, and yet their torment is totally superficial and insignificant. The affair of life is unnecessary, but it is inevitable. The best description of it is that it is absurd. The entire universe and all experience exist only to be transcended.

The Spiritual Master is absurd, like everything else. He is a Function that serves to Enlighten or Awaken beings from this condition that is absurd and unnecessary to begin with. The occupation of the Spiritual Master is as absurd as anything anyone else does, you see. Therefore, it requires a Sense of Humor, or the Enlightened point of view. Likewise, people must be obliged to be responsible in their approach to me. Irresponsible people cannot be Enlightened, cannot be Awakened, cannot hear the Teaching. That obligation for responsibility having been met, then there is the right circumstance for our meeting, and then our meeting is truly Enlightening.

The true way is the one that is blissful now. The true teaching turns you to present bliss and does not require you to create it. All ways that turn you to paths, goals, gradual attainments, and the idea of a necessary and ultimate future that is an evolutionary and revolutionary state unknown in the present are false. They are patterned after the model of separation and are only forms of seeking. Understanding is present bliss, unqualified freedom and reality, consciousness itself without motion or necessity. Bliss, which is conscious reality, is the ground of all creativity, transformation and evolution.

DA AVABHASA, *The Knee of Listening*

THE ULTIMATE STATE OF CONSCIOUSNESS

K E N   W I L B E R

The foremost theoretical psychologist in the field of transpersonal and spiritual studies is Ken Wilber. His writings present a major conceptual breakthrough in consciousness research. His approach is grounded in a profound understanding of the nature of enlightenment, as this essay demonstrates, and is supported by incisive scholarship and a graceful literary style.

The dimensions of his achievement cannot be overstated because he offers a "unified field theory" that is utterly brilliant and compelling. It qualifies Wilber as the Einstein of consciousness research. The "fields" he unifies are fields of knowledge, and they offer the foundation of a new paradigm for science and society. His first book, *The Spectrum of Consciousness,* neatly integrated different systems of psychology and psychotherapy from East and West into one seamless continuum that illuminated them all while transcending them all. His second book, *No Boundary,* is a more popular presentation of the spectrum model than the scholarly *Spectrum* that nevertheless contains new insights. *The Atman Project* is an exposition of the stages of consciousness unfoldment in an individual from birth to enlightenment; its companion, *Up from Eden,* describes the same process operating in the human race throughout history. Altogether, Wilber advances a perspective that he calls *psychologia perennis,* a universal and unanimous view of human consciousness which expresses the very same insights as the perennial philosophy—human nature is ultimately identical with the One-in-All—but in more decidedly psychological language.

"The Ultimate State of Consciousness" was chosen to end this book because it is both simple and elegant. It comes as close as words have to describing the indescribable—that Great Being which lives in us all and which is the alpha and omega of all cosmic Becoming. That Great Being, Wilber says, is the ultimate state which, paradoxically, is so *right now,* even though a "part" of it is working itself out on a universal scale through eons of time. As he puts it in *The Atman Project,* "it is not that an individual is first an ego and then may become a Buddha—it is that he was first Buddha and then became an ego."

In other words, your human beingness is an expression of the Great Being which manifests itself in the countless realms of creation with endless diversity of forms and phenomena. But before any of those realms existed, your "original face" was none other than the Great Mystery which is your true condition at *this very moment,* has

196

always been and always will be. There is no state which is apart from it in any way whatsoever. You are *already* enlightened. Realize it.

IN THE CHANDOGYA UPANISHAD, Brahman—the absolute reality, the ultimate state of consciousness—is described in glaringly simple and disconcertingly straightforward terms: the Absolute is "One without a second." That inspired Upanishadic text does not describe the ultimate as the creator, controller, ruler, or lord of a second; neither does it speak of One opposed to a second, nor One outside a second, nor over, above, or beyond a second—but One without a second. The Absolute, in other words, is that which has nothing outside It, nothing apart from It, nothing other to It, a fact expressed in Isaiah as "I am the Lord, and there is none else." All of which means that there is really nothing outside Brahman, nothing outside the Absolute. In the words of an old Zen Master:

> All the Buddhas and all sentient beings are nothing but the One Mind, beside which nothing exists. Above, below, and around you, all is spontaneously existing, for there is nowhere which is outside the Buddha-Mind.

Of course, if there were anything outside the Absolute, that would immediately impose a limitation on It, for the Absolute would then be one outside a second instead of One without a second. And so it is in this sense that Brahman, the Buddha-Mind, the Godhead, is called absolutely all-encompassing, all-inclusive, and all-pervading. When the *Upanishads* say "All the world is Brahman," and "This, too, is Brahman"; when the *Lankavatara Sutra* proclaims that "The world is nothing but Mind," and "All is Mind"; when the *Awakening of Faith* states that "All things are only of the One Mind"; when the Taoist texts insist that "There is nothing outside the Tao; you cannot deviate from It"—well, they mean just that. To quote the apocryphal *Acts of Peter:*

> Thou art perceived of the spirit only, thou art unto me father, thou my mother, thou my brother, thou my friend, thou my bondsman, thou my steward: thou art All and All is in thee: and thou ART, and there is nought else that IS save thee only.

This being true because, as Christ said in the *Gospel of St. Thomas:*

> I am the Light that is above them all, I am the All, the all came forth from Me and the All attained to Me. Cleave a piece of wood, I am there; Lift up the stone and you will find Me there.

Now the statement that all the world is really Brahman usually fires up in overly imaginative minds such fancies as uniform, all-pervading, feature-

197

less but divine goo; the instantaneous and total evaporation of all diversity and multiplicity, leaving behind an immaculate but amorphous All-knowing, All-merciful, celestial Vacuum. We flounder in such mental frenzies only because we expect the statement "All is Brahman" to be a logical proposition, containing some type of information or data about the universe, and taken thus, we can only picture its meaning to be the reduction of all multiplicity to uniform, homogenous, and unchanging mush.

But "All is Brahman" should not be mistaken as a philosophical conclusion, a logical theory, or a merely verbal explanation of reality. For the sages of every time and place have unanimously maintained that the Absolute is actually ineffable, unspeakable, utterly beyond words, symbols, and logic. And not because it is too mysterious or too sublime or too complex for words, but rather because it is too simple, too obvious, too close to be caught in the net of symbols and signs. Because there is nothing outside It, there is no way to define or classify It. As Johannes Scotus (Erigena) remarked, "God does not know Himself, what He is, because He is not a *what;* in a certain respect He is incomprehensible to Himself and to every intellect." Or, as Shankara, the Master of Vedanta Hinduism, explains:

> Now there is no class to which Brahman belongs, no common genus. It cannot therefore be denoted by words which signify a category of things. Nor can it be denoted by quality, for it is without qualities; nor yet by activity because it is without activity—"at rest, without parts or activity," according to the Scriptures. Neither can it be denoted by relationship, for it is "without a second" and is not the object of anything but its own self. Therefore it cannot be defined by word or idea; as the Scripture says, it is the One "before whom words recoil."

This, indeed, is also the entire point of Wittgenstein's philosophy; namely, we cannot make any valid statements about reality as a whole because there is no place outside it where we can take up a stance so as to describe it. In other words, 'We could only say things about the world as a whole if we could get outside the world, if, that is to say, it ceased to be for us the whole world. . . . [But] for us, it cannot have a boundary, since it has nothing outside it.' And having no boundary, no limits—being one without a second—it cannot be defined or classified. You can define and classify, for example, a "fish" because there are things that are not fishes, such as rocks, trees, and alligators; and drawing a mental line between what is fish and what is not fish, you are able to define and classify it. But you cannot define or say "what" Brahman is, for there is nothing It is not—being one without a second, there is nothing outside It and so nowhere to draw the classifying line.

Hence, the Absolute, the real world as it is, is also called the Void, since all definitions and propositions and statements about reality are void and meaningless. Even such statements as "Reality is the Limitless" won't quite do, for the "limitless" excludes that which is "limited." Rather, the Absolute is totally void of all conceptual elaborations, and so even the word "void," if taken to be a logical idea, is to be denied validity. In the words of Nagarajuna:

> It cannot be called void or not void,
> Or both or neither;
> But in order to point it out,
> It is called "the Void."

Since all propositions about reality are void and invalid, the same, of course, holds true for the statement "All is Brahman," *if* this statement is taken as a factual, logical proposition. If, for instance, Brahman were taken as a concrete and categorical fact *among other facts,* then "All is Brahman" would be sheerest nonsense: to predicate something of everything is to predicate it of nothing. But Brahman is not a fact among other facts, as any logician will tell us, but the Fact of all facts. "All is Brahman" is not merely a logical proposition; it is more of an experiential revelation, and while the logic of the statement is admittedly quite flawed, the experience itself is not. And the experience of All-is-Brahman makes it quite clear that there is not one thing outside the Absolute, even though when translated into words, we are left with nonsense. But, as Wittgenstein would say, although It cannot be *said,* It can be *shown.*

Now the insight that there is nothing outside of Brahman implies also that there is nothing *opposed* to It; that is to say, the Absolute is that which has no opposite. Thus, It is also called the Non-dual, the Not-two, the No-opposite. To quote the third Patriarch of Zen:

> All forms of dualism
> Are ignorantly contrived by the mind itself.
> They are like visions and flowers in the air:
> Why bother to take hold of them?
> When dualism does no more obtain,
> Even Oneness itself remains not as such.
> The True Mind is not divided—
> When a direct identification is asked for,
> We can only say, "Not-Two!"

But, as Seng-t'san points out, "Not two" does not mean just One. For pure Oneness is most dualistic, excluding as it does its opposite of Manyness.

The single One opposes the plural Many, while the Nondual embraces them both. "One without a second" means "One without an opposite," not One opposed to Many. Thus, as we have already hinted, we mustn't picture the Absolute as excluding diversity, as being an undifferentiated monistic mush, for Brahman embraces both unity and multiplicity with equanimity.

Now, the import of what has been said thus far is that since there is really nothing outside the Nondual, there is no point in either space or time where the Absolute is not. And it isn't that a *part* of the Absolute is present in each and every thing—as in pantheism—for that is to introduce a boundary within the infinite, assigning to each thing a different piece of the infinite pie. Rather, the *entire* Absolute is completely and wholly present at every point of space and time, for the simple reason that you can't have a different infinite at each point. The Absolute, as St. Bonaventure put it, is "a sphere, whose center is everywhere and whose circumference, nowhere," so that, in the words of Plotinus, "while it is nowhere, nowhere is it not."

Yet notice that the Absolute can be entirely present at every point of space only if It is itself spaceless. Just as, to use Eckhart's example, your eyes can see things which are colored red only because your eyes themselves are without red color, or "red-less," so also the Absolute can embrace all space because It is itself without space, or "space-less." This, incidentally, is why so many angels can fit on the head of a pin—they don't take up any room!

At any rate, the infinite is not a point, or a space—even a very big space—or a dimension among other points, spaces, and dimensions; but is rather point-less, spaceless, dimensionless—not one among many, but one without a second. In just this fashion, the *whole* of the infinite can be present at all points of space, for being itself spaceless, it does not contend with space and so is free to utterly embrace it, just as water, being shapeless and formless, can fill containers of all shapes and forms. And since the infinite is present in its entirety at every point of space, *all* of the infinite is fully present right HERE. In fact, to the eye of the infinite, no such place as *there* exists (since, put crudely, if you go to some other place over *there,* you will still only find the very same infinite as *here,* for there isn't a different one at each place).

And so also with time: the Absolute can be present in its entirety at every point of time only if It is itself timeless. And that which is timeless is eternal, for, as Wittgenstein rightly pointed out, eternity is "not infinite temporal duration, but timelessness." That is to say, eternity is not everlasting time, but a moment without time. Hence, being timeless, *all* of eternity is wholly and completely present at every point of time—and thus, all of eternity is already present right NOW. To the eye of eternity, there is no *then,* either past or future.

Point without dimension or extension, moment without date or duration—such is the Absolute. And while It is nowhere, nowhere is It not. That, simply, is the meaning of omnipresence—the Absolute is simultaneously present everywhere and everywhen in its entirety. "Who sees not God everywhere sees him truly nowhere."

With all of the foregoing, it won't be hard to understand that all metaphysical traditions have universally claimed that the Absolute is literally unattainable. For if it were possible for a person to *attain* the Absolute, this would imply moving from a point where the Absolute is not to a point where It is—yet there is no point where It is not! In other words, it's impossible to attain It because it's impossible to escape It in the first place. And so it is important to realize that since the Absolute is already one with everything everywhere, we can in no way manufacture or attain to our union with It. No matter what we do or don't do, try to do or try not to do, we can never attain It. In the words of Shankara:

> As Brahman constitutes a person's Self, it is not something to be attained by that person. And even if Brahman were altogether different from a person's Self, still it would not be something to be attained; for as it is omnipresent it is part of its nature that it is ever present to everyone.

Or read carefully the following from the great Zen Master Huang Po:

> That there is nothing which can be attained is not idle talk; it is the truth. You have always been one with the Buddha, so do not pretend you can attain to this oneness by various practices. If, at this very moment, you could convince yourselves of its unattainability, being certain indeed that nothing at all can ever be attained, you would already be Bodhi-minded. Hard is the meaning of this saying! It is to teach you to refrain from seeking Buddhahood, since any search is doomed to failure.

Or, just to push the point home, consider the words of Sri Ramana Maharshi:

> There is no reaching the Self. If Self were to be reached, it would mean that the Self is not here and now, but that it has yet to be obtained. What is got afresh will also be lost. So it will be impermanent. What is not permanent is not worth striving for. So I say the Self is not reached. You *are* the Self; you are already That.

Thus the Absolute, the Buddha-Mind, the real Self cannot be attained. For to attain union with the Absolute implies bringing together two things, and yet in all reality there is only One without a second. The attempt to bring the soul and God together merely perpetuates the illusion that the two are separate. As the above quotes make clear, the Self is already present, and we're already It.

Now it is sometimes said that whereas we are indeed already one with the Absolute, most of us, nevertheless, do not realize that this is so; that whereas union with God cannot be attained, *knowledge of that union can be attained;* that whereas we cannot manufacture the Supreme Identity, we can realize it. And that realization, that attainment of the knowledge of our Supreme Identity, is everywhere said to be the very ultimate state of consciousness, enlightenment, satori, moksha, wu, release, liberation.

Now there is certainly some degree of truth in the statement that we are all Buddhas but don't know it, and that we must therefore attain this knowledge for complete liberation. But on closer inspection, this is not entirely satisfactory. For by the truth of nonduality, to know God is to be God: the two are not at all separate. As is clearly stated in the *Mundaka Upanishad,* "Verily, he who knows the supreme Brahman, becomes Brahman." So there is not one thing called God and another thing called knowledge of God. Rather, it is that knowledge is but one of the names of God. And, if we cannot attain God, neither can we attain knowledge of God—since the two are actually one and the same. Put it another way: since the ultimate state of consciousness *is* Brahman, and since Brahman cannot be attained, neither can the ultimate state of consciousness.

If this conclusion seems a bit odd to you, then go ahead and suppose, on the contrary, that the ultimate state of consciousness could be attained, or reached, or entered. What would that imply? Only that that state of consciousness which you *entered* would necessarily have a beginning in time; that that state of consciousness is therefore not timeless and eternal; and that, in short, that state of consciousness is precisely not the ultimate state of consciousness. The ultimate state of consciousness cannot be entered because it is timeless, without beginning or end, and conversely, any state of consciousness you can enter is not the ultimate state of consciousness.

Hsuan-tse heard of a meditation master named Chih-huang, and when he went to visit him, Chih-huang was meditating.

"What are you doing there?" inquired Hsuan-tse.

"I am entering into a samadhi, a highest state of consciousness."

"You speak of *entering,* but how do you enter into a samadhi—with a thoughtful mind or with a thoughtless mind? If you say with a thoughtless mind, then all non-sentient beings such as plants or bricks could attain samadhi. If you say with a thoughtful mind, then all sentient beings could attain it."

"Well," replied Chih-huang, "I am not conscious of either being thoughtful or being thoughtless."

Hsuan-tse's verdict was swift coming. "If you are conscious of neither, you are actually in samadhi all the time; why do you even talk at all of

202

entering into or coming out of it? If, however, there is any *entering* or *coming out*, it is not the Great Samadhi."

So what does it mean that you can't enter the ultimate state of consciousness? What does it mean that never, under any circumstances, at any time, through any effort, can you enter the ultimate state of consciousness? Only that the ultimate state of consciousness is already fully and completely present. And that means the ultimate state of consciousness is in no way different from your ordinary state of consciousness or from any other state of consciousness you might have at this or at any moment. "Your ordinary mind, just that is the Tao," says Nansen. Whatever state you have now, regardless of what you think of it and regardless of its nature, is absolutely It. You therefore cannot enter It, because you have always been in It from the very beginning.

Of course, this should have been obvious all along. Since the ultimate state of consciousness is Brahman, and since Brahman is absolutely all-inclusive, the ultimate state of consciousness is equally all-inclusive. That is to say, the ultimate state of consciousness is not a state among other states, but a state inclusive of all states. This means most emphatically that the ultimate state of consciousness is not an altered state of consciousness, for—being one without a second—there is no alternative to It. The ultimate state of consciousness is perfectly compatible with each and every state of consciousness and altered state of consciousness, and there is no state of consciousness apart from or outside of It. As René Guénon explains it, "The state of *Yoga* is not then analogous with any particular state whatsoever, but embraces all possible states as the principle embraces all its consequences."

All of this points inescapably to the fact that you not only are already one with the Absolute, you already know you are. As Huang Po said, "The Buddha-Nature and your perception of It are one." And since, as we have seen, the Buddha-Nature is always present, then so is your perception of It. If you maintain that you are Buddha but don't know it, you necessarily introduce a very subtle dualism between the Buddha Nature and your perception of It, imagining that the one is while the other is yet to come, and such is not possible. Truly, as we cannot manufacture the Absolute, we cannot manufacture knowledge of the Absolute. Both are already present.

> Rekison Roshi was asked by a monk, "What is this 'apprehending of a sound and being delivered'?" Rekison took up some fire-tongs, struck the firewood, and asked, "You hear it?" "I hear it," replied the monk. "Who is not delivered?" asked Rekison.

That the ultimate state of consciousness is not a state apart, or in any way different from the present state of consciousness, is the point so many people seem to miss. Hence, they misguidedly seek to engineer for themselves a "higher" state of consciousness, radically different from their present state of awareness, wherein it is imagined that the supreme identity can be realized. Some imagine that this particular and exclusive "higher" state of consciousness is connected with specific brain wave patterns, such as predominant amounts of high amplitude alpha waves. Others maintain that an individual's neurological system must undergo several changes, evolving, as it were, to a point where this "higher" state of consciousness can finally emerge. Some even believe that physiological stress has to be removed through meditative techniques and *then* the "higher" state of consciousness will result. But all this chatter totally overlooks the inescapable fact that *any* state of consciousness that can be entered, or that emerges after various practices, must have a beginning in time, and thus is not, and could never be, the timeless and eternal ultimate state of consciousness.

Moreover, to imagine that certain steps can be taken in order to realize the ultimate state of consciousness and attain liberation is actually to make the ultimate state an *effect*. That is to say, to believe certain stages or various steps or particular practices can lead to liberation is inescapably to make liberation the *result* of these steps, the *consequence* of these stages, the *effect* of these causes. Yet long ago Shankara saw the utter absurdity of such a notion:

> If Brahman were represented as supplementary to certain actions, and release were assumed to be the effect of those actions, it would be temporal, and would have to be considered merely as something holding a preeminent position among the described temporal fruits of actions with their various degrees.
>
> But as release is shown to be of the nature of the eternally free Self, it cannot be charged with the imperfection of temporality. Those, on the other hand, who consider release to be the effect of something maintain that it depends on the action of mind, speech, or body; so likewise, those who consider it to be a mere modification. Non-eternality of release is the certain consequence of these two opinions; for we observe in common life that things which are modifications, such as sour milk and the like, and things which are effects, such as jars, etc., are non-eternal.

And what of the opinion that we all have Buddha Nature, but as yet just don't know it? And that through some sort of action, such as meditation, we can attain to this knowledge? Shankara is decisive:

> It might be said that release might be a quality of the Self which is merely

hidden and becomes manifest on the Self being purified by some action; just as the quality of clearness becomes manifest in a mirror when the mirror is cleaned by means of the action of rubbing. This objection is invalid, we reply, because the Self cannot be the abode of any action. For an action cannot exist without modifying that in which it abides. But if the Self were modified by an action, its non-eternality would result therefrom; an altogether unacceptable result.

In short, since the ultimate state of consciousness is your present state of consciousness, there is obviously no way to cause, produce, effect, or manufacture that which is already the case—and even if you could, the result would be noneternal. But when we imagine that the ultimate state of consciousness is different from the state of consciousness we have now, we then foolheartedly seek ways to usher in this supposedly different and miraculous state of "higher" consciousness, totally ignorant of the fact that even if we get this "higher" state of consciousness, it is not the ultimate state because it is the result of certain steps, and therefore has a beginning in time. And yet, think we, some knowledge of the Absolute awaits us in this particular higher state of consciousness. But as Eckhart so forcefully explained, if we imagine God can be found in a *particular* state of consciousness, then when that state slips from us, that god slips with it.

"Contrary to widespread belief," writes Alan Watts, "the knowledge and contemplation of the infinite is not a state of trance, for because of the truth that there is no opposition between the infinite and the finite, knowledge of the infinite may be compatible with all possible states of mind, feeling, and sensation. [This] knowledge is an inclusive, not an exclusive, state of consciousness."

In fact, it's only because we keep insisting that the ultimate state of consciousness be different from the present state of consciousness that makes it so hard to admit to ourselves that we already know our Buddha Nature. We imagine, for instance, that nirvana is different from samsara, that enlightenment is different from ignorance, that Brahman is different from maya (illusion). Yet Nagarajuna clearly states: "There is no difference whatsoever between nirvana and samsara; there is no difference whatsoever between samsara and nirvana. There is not the slightest bit of difference between these two." And Hsuan-chueh begins his celebrated *Song of Realizing the Tao:*

See you not that easygoing Man of Tao, who has abandoned learning
*   and does not strive?*
He neither avoids false thoughts nor seeks the true,
For ignorance is in reality the Buddha nature,
And this illusory, changeful body is the body of Truth.

And pure Vedanta has never understood maya or illusion to be different from Brahman, but rather as something Brahman is doing. And yet, we seek to escape samsara as if it weren't nirvana; we try to overcome ignorance as if it weren't enlightenment; we strive to wipe out maya as if it weren't Brahman. Fénelon, Archbishop of Cambrai, has the only acceptable comment on this state of affairs: "There is no more dangerous illusion than the fancies by which people try to avoid illusion."

Hence, all seeking, spiritual or otherwise, is profoundly irrelevant; and viewing the ultimate state of consciousness as a particular altered state of consciousness is absolutely unacceptable. I am not at all denying that some very miraculous altered states of consciousness can certainly be attained—they can be attained for the simple reason that they are partial and exclusive, and hence can be developed and perfected. But what has that to do with the all-inclusive ultimate state of consciousness? You can surely train yourself to enter alpha states; you can develop your abilty with a mantra; you can learn to halt all thoughts from rising—but only because these are exclusive and partial states of consciousness apart from other states, and for that very reason can selectively be given more attention and effort than the others. But you cannot train yourself to enter that state of consciousness which you have never left and which includes all possible states of consciousness. There is just no place outside the ultimate state of consciousness where you can take up a position to train yourself in It. Listen to Huang Po once again:

> Bodhi (knowledge of the Buddha-Nature) is no state. The Buddha did not attain to it. Sentient beings do not lack it. It cannot be reached with the body nor sought with the mind. All sentient beings are already of one form with Bodhi.
> If you know positively that all sentient beings are already one with Bodhi, you will cease thinking of Bodhi as something to be attained. You may recently have heard others talking about this "attaining of the Bodhi-Mind," but this may be called an intellectual way of driving the Buddha away. By following this method, you only APPEAR to achieve Buddhahood; if you were to spend aeon upon aeon in that way, you would only achieve the Sambhogakaya (blissful states) and Nirmanakaya (transformed states). What connection would all that have with your original and real Buddha-Nature?

Upon hearing this, many of us nevertheless feel that "Yes, I do understand that somehow I must already be one with the Absolute, but I still just don't know it!" But that is manifestly not true. The very fact that you are now seeking Buddha shows that you already know you are Buddha. "Console thyself," wrote Pascal. "Thou wouldest not seek Me if thou hadst not found Me." And St. Bernard expressed the very same sentiment, "No one is able to seek Thee, save because he has first found." Or, as Blyth put it, "In order to be enlightened, we must first be enlightened."

Of course, an individual might indeed feel that he doesn't really know It, despite all the best assurances of the masters. And the reason It might not seem evident to him is the somewhat peculiar nature of this ever present Bodhi-knowledge; namely, it is nondual. A person doesn't seem to know It only because he is so used to seeing things dualistically, where he as subject holds out and looks at an object, either mental or physical, and feels that, yes, he sees that object very clearly, with "he" and "that object" being two different things altogether. He, as subject, then naturally assumes that he can also see Brahman in the same way, as an object out there to look at and grasp. It thus seems that he, the grasper, should be able to get Brahman, the grasped. But Brahman won't split into getter and got. In all of reality there is only One without a second, and yet out of habit the person tries to make It two, to split It so as to finally grab It and exclaim, "Aha! I've got It!" He tries to make it an experience to be grasped among other experiences. But Brahman is not a particular experience, being One without a second, and so he is left grasping at ghosts and clutching at smoke.

And so it is that we all inevitably end up feeling that we just can't see It, no matter how hard we try. *But the fact that we always can't see It is perfect proof that we always know It*. In the words of the *Kena Upanishad*:

> If you think that you know Brahman well, what you know of Its nature is in reality but little; for this reason Brahman should still be more attentively considered by you. . . . Whoever among us understands the following words: "I do not know It, and yet I know It," verily that man knows it. He who thinks that Brahman is not comprehended, by him Brahman is comprehended; but he who thinks that Brahman is comprehended knows It not. Brahman is unknown to those who know It and is known to those who do not know It at all.

That is, the very state of not knowing Brahman IS the ultimate state of consciousness, *and that is exactly how you feel right now!* Says a Zen poem:

> *When you seek to know It, you cannot see It.*
> *You cannot take hold of It,*
> *But neither can you lose It.*
> *In not being able to get It, you get It.*
> *When you are silent, It speaks.*
> *When you speak, It is silent.*
> *The great gate is wide open to bestow alms,*
> *And no crowd is blocking the way.*

Since you are Brahman, you obviously can't *see* Brahman, just as, for instance, an eye cannot see itself and an ear cannot hear itself. The *Brihadaranyaka Upanishad* says, "Thou couldst not see the seer of sight, thou couldst not hear the hearer of hearing, nor perceive the perceiver of perception, nor know the knower of knowledge." And the *Zenrin* puts it simply, "Like a sword that cuts, but cannot cut itself; like an eye that sees, but cannot see itself." In fact, if your eye tries to see itself, it sees absolutely nothing! Likewise, the void is what you right now don't see when you try to look for Brahman. That void is exactly what you have always been looking for and have always never found nor seen. And *that* very not-seeing is It! And since you always don't see It, you always know It. Because any individual, explains St. Dionysius, "by the very fact of not seeing and not knowing God, truly understands Him who is beyond sight and knowledge; knowing this, too, that He is in all things that are felt and known."

Still don't see It? How right you already are.

When a person rediscovers that his deepest Nature is one with the All, he is relieved of the burdens of time, of anxiety, of worry; he is released from the chains of alienation and separate self-existence. Seeing that self and other are one, he is released from the fear of life; seeing that being and non-being are one, he is delivered from the fear of death.

KEN WILBER, *Up from Eden*

. . . unfreedom, aggression, and anxiety are not characteristic of the *nature* of humanity, but character of the *separate self* of humanity. It is not man's instincts that undo him, but his psychological appetites, and those appetites are a product of *boundary*, not of biology.

KEN WILBER, *Up from Eden*

And so proceeds meditation, which is simply higher development, which is simply higher evolution—a transformation from unity to unity until there is simply Unity, whereupon Brahman, in an unnoticed shock of recognition and final remembrance, grins silently to itself, closes its eyes, breathes deeply, and throws itself outward for the millionth time, losing itself in its manifestation for the sport and play of it all.

KEN WILBER, *The Atman Project*

THE SECRET OF HAPPINESS

J O H N   W H I T E

AS I MADE a cup of tea the other day, I read my fortune on the teabag's label. "The secret of happiness," it said, "is not in doing what you like but in liking what you do." This thought-provoking adage immediately reminded me of another with the same insight: "If you can't change your fate, change your attitude."

Both express a profound paradox, but neither expresses it in full. The necessary follow-on question to my teabag teaching is: "How can I learn to like what I do—my job, my marriage, my social obligations, whatever—if they are boring, difficult, frustrating?" Or, in terms of the other saying: "What attitude should I take and how will that affect my life's course?"

The answer to both is the same: selfless service. It was perhaps best stated centuries ago in the *Bhagavad Gita*. There, in chapter 18, Krishna counsels Arjuna to live in a spirit of complete surrender to the Divine, with no thought for self-interest. "Perform every action with your heart fixed on God. Renounce attachment to the fruits [of your actions]. . . . Work done with anxiety about results is far inferior to work done without such anxiety in the calm of self-surrender to higher destiny."

St. Paul, in his first epistle to the Corinthians (10:31), said it similarly: ". . . whatsoever ye do, do all to the glory of God."

When you perform every action with your heart fixed on God, you cannot help liking what you do, no matter what it is, no matter how previously distasteful it was, because everything is worship. At the very least, the action you have to perform will be bearable, if not actually pleasant. You see the light of God shining in all things because you know all things to be manifestations of God, the Self of all. Whether it's doing the dishes, mowing the lawn, [going to the office or factory,] visiting your mother-in-law, or any other presumably unwelcome or unpleasant situation, if you do it for God and see it as God, there is no aversion and no suffering. Instead, there is release from self-pity, anger, and all the corrosive scheming you "e-go" through to escape your circumstances. Your energy and intelligence are freed to make heavy work light and to be creative in your

209

tasks and relations. Thus, circumstances previously regarded as a problem now become a challenge, even an exciting opportunity to learn and to grow and to relieve a bit of the world's burden.

Happiness is a function of your state of consciousness. So long as there is an "other" in your consciousness, there will be a limit to your happiness. Suffering is directly proportional to the amount of ego or self-interest present in you. But when there is no one but the One, when you are the Self of all, you are infinitely fulfilled, infinitely happy. In such a state, existence itself is seen to be inherently blissful. Then whatever occurs in your life and whatever you are required to do is perfectly acceptable. There may be pain, but there is no suffering.

This is the key to a life without problems, fears, complaints, or regrets. This is the secret of happiness. This is enlightenment.

Appendix 1

MAPS OF REALITY

AT THE END of my introduction to *The Highest State of Consciousness*, I attempted to describe that "highest state" by making this statement: "I am the universe; I am Universal Mind." To put it another way, I meant that the utterly clear perception of ultimate reality sees cosmos and consciousness as a living One-Without-a-Second and "Thou art that" union of outer and inner space. A few years after the book was published, I happened to discuss my statement with a teacher of Vedanta. He said to me, "No, John, the highest state of consciousness is not Universal Mind. It is the *source* of Universal Mind."

I appreciated his comment.. It gave further refinement to the explorations in consciousness I'd been making. It was another way of saying that Ultimate Reality is beyond anything describable by human beings. We can experience it, we can identify with it, but we cannot equal it. Even the most elevated people have found that there are states of development beyond their present level of attainment, that new experiences await them in those states. Even in cosmic consciousness there are planes, levels or graduations that range as far beyond the "entry level" as does the spectrum of levels for egoic or self-consciousness, from infant to adult. Enlightenment is an endless process. The Growth of the self never stops until it reaches universal proportions.

But what happens then? Even the evolution of consciousness to universal dimensions—to a universe supremely conscious of itself as a unified, living entity—is not the end. Beyond that, what can be said?

There are all kinds of intriguing cosmological and theological statements. Science fiction, for example, offers Piers Anthony's *Macroscope* and Olaf Stapledon's still-unsurpassed *Star Maker*. In philosophy and metaphysics, there are many; three notable titles are *The Urantia Book*, *A Rosicrucian Cosmo-conception*, and Itzhak Benton's recent, posthumous *A Cosmic Book*. For the prepared mind, books of this sort can be extremely valuable. For most people, however, such works are confusing, even distracting and detrimental to what is really necessary for them at the time: to become grounded and functional on the earth plane before venturing into higher worlds.

This book has offered glimpses of the destination of the spiritual journey through all worlds, high and low. But it necessarily had to exclude much material. If you think of it as a guidebook, it left out descriptions of most towns and cities along the way, and the scenic vistas and the tourist traps as well, not to mention the roadblocks, highway bandits, and other dangerous situations that might be encountered.

But for me to ignore all that completely would be a disservice. This appendix, therefore, is an overview of some of the best maps of reality accessible to spiritual travelers. All are legitimate approximations of the ground to be covered. However, there are some differences to be noted among them such as terminology, degree of resolution used in projecting the map, and emphases of various features of the terrain. For example, one map might be intended for rockhounds interested in geology, another might be for mountain climbers, and a third, for naturalists, might focus primarily on flowers and wildlife. Which is for you? Only you can tell.

But as East meets West in transcendental fashion, a powerful fermentation and enrichment is taking place. The western emphasis on physical science, objectivity, and outer space is blending with the eastern emphasis on spiritual science, subjectivity, and inner space. The result is a proliferation of increasingly useful statements about the relationship between cosmos and consciousness. Contemporary consciousness researchers are elucidating that relationship with greater detail and precision, thanks to their grounding in both eastern and western traditions. Earlier maps of consciousness are being restated with exciting relevance to modern life, and new maps are being created.

Now, as general semantics states repeatedly, the map is not the territory. Reading about the territory is not the same thing as actually traveling there. But for those who intend to travel the planes of Being, the following can be tremendously valuable. Nevertheless, all of it, *all*, is inadequate to describe that Great Mystery called God and none of it, *none*, can ever substitute for the noetic realization of the Ground of Being which comes in silence beyond all form, image, symbol, and sound.

One useful map of reality is available in Daniel Goleman's *The Meditative Mind*. A contemporary rendering of the classical Buddhist text, *Visuddhimagga*, Goleman describes this 2,500-year-old map of inner space as "probably the broadest and most detailed traditional psychology of states of consciousness." According to this ancient book of wisdom, there are two broad paths of meditation: the Path of Concentration (or absorption) and the Path of Insight (or mindfulness). The book describes in detail various stages of concentration or absorption. These states lead from what is called the "access state," or ordinary consciousness, through higher states, with their feelings of bliss and one-pointedness, to the highest formless states of absorption.

However, Goleman points out, the *Visuddhimagga* sees mastery of states of concentration, and tasting their sublime bliss, as of secondary importance to discriminating wisdom. The Path of Insight is the path to Nirvana, the highest realization. That path is also described in detail there.

Another time-tested map of consciousness can be found in yoga. Many classical and modern yogic texts describe states of growth through higher states of consciousness. The best known is the ancient text by Patanjali, the codifier of yoga, whose teachings are known simply as his *Yoga Sutras*. The words of a modern yogi, Swami Kriyananda, in his autobiographical *The Path*, give us a useful statement of the yogic view of consciousness unfoldment:

> Liberation from ego does not come with the first glimpses of cosmic consciousness. Present, at first, even in an expanded state of awareness, is the subtle memory, "I, the formless but nevertheless still real John Smith, am enjoying this state of consciousness." The body in this trance state is immobile; one's absorption in God at this point is called *sabikalpa samadhi:* qualified absorption, a condition that is still subject to change, for from it one returns to assume once again the limitations of ego. By repeated absorption in the trance state, however, ego's hold on the mind is gradually broken, until the realization dawns: "There is no John Smith to go back to. I am Spirit!" This is the supreme state: *nirbikalpa samadhi,* or unqualified absorption—a condition changeless and eternal. If from this state one returns to body-consciousness, it is no longer with the thought of separate existence from the ocean of Spirit. John Smith no longer exists. It is the eternal Spirit now which animates the body, eats through it, teaches through it, and carries on all the normal functions of a human being. This outward direction of energy on the part of one who has attained *nirbikalpa samadhi* is sometimes known also as *sahaja,* or effortless, *samadhi.*
>
> Divine freedom comes only with the attainment of *nirbikalpa samadhi.* Until that stage the ego can still—and alas, sometimes does—draw the mind back down into delusion. With *nirbikalpa samadhi,* one becomes what is known as a *jivan mukta,* free even though living in a physical form. A *jivan mukta,* however, unimaginably high though his state is, is not yet *fully* emancipated. The subtle memory, "I am John Smith," has been destroyed; he can acquire no new karma, since the post of ego to which karma is tied has been broken. But there remains even now the memory of all those prior existences: John Smith in thousands, perhaps millions of incarnations; John Smith the one-time bandit, John Smith the disappointed musician, John Smith the betrayed lover, the beggar, the swaggering tyrant. All those old selves must be made over, their karma spiritualized, released into the Infinite.

Meher Baba's map of consciousness is one that embraces all time and space within an understanding of their limits and what is beyond those limits. According to him, creation emanates from God in an inscrutable state—formless and colorless—that he describes as God in the Beyond State. Even more mysterious is the "final" state of God: Beyond the Beyond State. About that nothing can be said. But from the Beyond State of God, God's creative and impulsive imagination to know Itself as omnipresent, infinite, and eternal brings forth creation. The primeval form of the cosmos is called the gross sphere and involves gaseous forms—the countless stars. Gradually, through evolution, the solid elemental and mineral forms of creation emerge—planets and other astronomical bodies—followed by the vegetable and animal forms on countless worlds. At the level of human life, a new sphere of creation is attained—the subtle. This sphere contains four planes which the spiritual seeker traverses through many lifetimes until, finally, he attains entrance into the third great realm of creation, the mental sphere. This sphere, containing two planes, is transcended when the seeker realizes himself as infinite and none other than God. This experience occurs in the seventh plane. And beyond that? God in the Beyond State—and Beyond the Beyond State.

The maps of reality found in sacred traditions and esoteric/transpersonal psychologies have gained depth and refinement over millennia. Do these "official" forms—Christian, Buddhist, Hindu, Sufi, kaballist, kundalini yoga, etc.—mark our ultimate understanding? Is there nothing new under the sun? Or does our understanding of human transformation and Ultimate Reality continue to unfold?

Yes, it does—and no, it doesn't. As I have said, enlightenment is an endless process. It is a state of perfect poise and balance between Being and Becoming, nirvana and samsara, time and eternity. As T. S. Eliot put it at the end of his *Four Quartets,*

> *We shall not cease from exploration*
> *And the end of all our exploring*
> *Will be to arrive where we started*
> *And know the place for the first time.*

In expressing our understanding of the journey, over the millennia we have gained greater and greater detail, depth and comprehensiveness in our reality mapmaking. So, thanks to the collective efforts of sages and psychologists alike, there are increasingly useful maps of reality.

The most brilliant and extended modern map is to be found in Ken Wilber's *The Atman Project.* It is a tour de force through the major eastern and western psychologies and spiritual traditions. It presents the nature of the major states of human consciousness from birth to enlightenment, and the development processes through which the different structures, or states of consciousness, unfold in the psyche. A breathtaking synthesis of knowledge, *The Atman Project* is this century's most important work of psychology.

Wilber writes as an enlightened transpersonal psychologist. In the work of Da Avabhasa we have an equally brilliant map of unfolding human consciousness that is original but religiously oriented, though fully compatible with Wilber's psychological orientation. His statements about the seventh stage of life are especially important because they give *new* knowledge about enlightenment.

The seventh stage has three phases, Da Avabhasa says: transfiguration, transformation and translation. *Transfiguration* is the pervasion of body and mind by Transcendental Radiance or the Light of God. Bodily and mental *transformation* involves the arising of supernormal signs or abilities, such as healing power, longevity and psychic capabilities. Divine *translation* is the ultimate evidence of God-realization, wherein the limited psychophysical body, mind and world are no longer noticed—not because the consciousness has withdrawn from all such phenomena, but because it has entered into such profound absorptive realization of the divine condition that all phenomena are "outshined," as he puts it, by that Light. This, he declares in *The Bodily Sacrifice of Attention*, is bhava-samadhi, "about which nothing sufficient can be said, and there is not Anyone, Anything, or Anywhere beyond it to be realized."

The following appendix succinctly summarizes Da Avabhasa's teaching about the stages of human development and the states of consciousness associated with them. It was compiled from his writings by the editorial staff of his community. I present it as the most insightful and accurate brief map of reality for the contemporary spiritual seeker.

THE SEVEN STAGES OF LIFE

THE ULTIMATE IMPORT of our human birth is to discover or Realize the Truth of our life. To do so, however, we are required first to observe, understand, and transcend ourselves. Master Da Avabhasa's "seven stages of life" prove a valuable key to our self-understanding. But before we are able to put his Enlightened scheme to use, we must first enter into the culture of self-transcendence.

> We can know or Realize what is only through self-understanding that becomes not merely self-information but self-transcendence. Therefore, we must first become capable (through self-understanding and self-

215

transcendence) of self-submission and free participation in what is prior to our own self-contraction.

I do not merely propose the idea of God, or soul, or Transcendental Being. Such propositions cannot be rightly believed or presumed by the separate and separative ego. Therefore, the ideas of religion that occupy egos and the egoic culture of self-abstracted scientism are themselves false views, representing a poignant and inevitably frustrated longing for love, release, and ultimate Happiness. On the contrary, I propose self-observation, true self-understanding, and perfect self-transcendence. And if the Way of self-transcendence is magnified as the fullness of participatory capability, then what is will be discovered to be Divine, unbound, eternal, Transcendental Happiness.[1]

The model or scheme of the seven stages of life provides a structure whereby we might fully examine and rightly evaluate our spiritual and human growth, as well as the mass of spiritual teaching and experience that presently informs the psyche of today's man and woman. Thus, the seven stages are means for gauging our human and spiritual growth, free of the taboos and prejudices of conventional society that tend to reinforce and even propagate many false views, and thus prevent us from Realizing the Truth of our existence.

As is made clear again and again throughout his Teaching, Master Da is a Spirit-Baptizer, one who transmits the Way, or "Living Current," to prepared aspirants. When the individual consciousness, established in self-understanding, combines with "Grace" or the Power of Spiritual Blessing, the individual is drawn through and beyond the hierarchy of earthly (gross) and cosmic (subtle) illusions or forms of knowledge and experience. Thus, the seven stages of life can be viewed as a spiritual school offering seven lessons about self-transcendence. When we have completed the course of self-observation, self-understanding, and self-transcendence through all the possibilities of the first six stages of life, the Adept, who is the Master of this school, reveals a hidden "doorway" that grants passage, via sacrifice, beyond all limitations, into the perfect Realization of the Divine Domain.

STAGE 1 *(Years Birth to 7)*

The first stage of life, occupying the years from conception and birth to age seven, is the stage of the human individual's vital-physical adaptation to the world into which he or she is born. In this first stage, the being learns "simple" skills like focusing with the eyes, grasping and manipulating objects, walking, talking, assimilating and converting food and breath

[1]Da Free John. *The Dreaded Gom-Boo, or the Imaginary Disease That Religion Seeks to Cure*, p. 93.

into energy, and controlling bladder and bowels, with only minimal responsibility for thinking conceptually and relating to his fellow beings.

STAGE 2 *(Years 7–14)*

The second stage of life is the stage of the development, integration, and coordination of the emotional-sexual or feeling dimension of the being with the gross physical. The young personality grows in the awareness of himself or herself as a social being, sharing life in an expanded sphere of relations. Just as in the first stage we learn about and become responsible for the assimilation and elimination of elemental food, in the second stage we must likewise learn about, adapt to, and engage a new dimension of sustenance of food. When breathing is combined with feeling and bodily relaxation, we awaken to the Universal Life-Current or Energy that pervades the body and all of life. In the second stage of life we learn to align body, emotion, feeling, and breathing in a functional realization of the disposition of relational sacrifice or love. Thus, we learn to transcend reactive emotion, tendencies toward neurotic inversion, and habits of self- and other-destructiveness.

We should understand that the emotional-sexual growth in the second stage of life is the development of the individual's glandular and hormonal system. "Sexual communion," or the yoga of sexual love, is a responsibility suggested to individuals only when full development, responsibility, and harmony of the first three, or lower vital, stages of life have been accomplished, and the individual is awakened to the feeling dimension of the heart, or the fourth stage of life (described below).

STAGE 3 *(Years 15–21)*

The third stage of life is the stage of the development of the thinking mind and the will and of the integration of the vital-physical, emotional-sexual, and mental-intentional functions. This stage marks the transition to truly human autonomy wherein the first two stages of life are adapted to a practical and analytical intelligence, and an informed will or intention, and the individual gains responsibility for and control over vital life.

> This third stage is not an end in itself, or the completion of potential human growth. Indeed, it only marks the awakening of self-conscious intelligence and a movement toward personal and individualistic survival motives. Man in the third stage of life is not yet truly human. He only brings individual force and form to the vital and elemental experience and world. He tempers and also extends the frenzy of feeding and sexing by submitting these to the

processes of the verbal and analytical mind. Man in the third stage of life is characterized by the frenzy of mind, the frenzy of problems and solutions.

The truly human being appears only in the fourth stage of life, wherein the vital, elemental, emotional-sexual, and lower mental functions come into the summary and unifying dominion of the heart, the psyche of the whole bodily being. Such is the awakened moral and spiritual disposition, in which Truth becomes the Principle in consciousness, and higher structural growth becomes the benign, nonproblematic possibility. Thus, the Law in the truly human realm is sacrifice as the individual, whole, and entire human body-mind, through love, founded in prior intuition of the Divine Reality. The human sacrifice is the spiritual practice of love and intuition of the Real under all conditions of experience and higher growth.[2]

STAGE 4

The first three stages may generally be associated with the first twenty-one years of life (three periods of seven years), but the last four (which grow beyond the limits of the grosser elements and functions) may not truly be considered in terms of limits of time, whether brief or long. Each stage develops as a process of adaptation (or readaptation) to a specific, functional point of view relative to the totality of experience.[3]

The fourth stage, and all the later stages, cannot be conceived within fixed periods of time. The duration of the higher stages of life depends entirely upon the individual's qualities and his or her spiritual practice of self-transcendence.[4]

The fourth stage of life marks the beginning of our humanity. In this stage the psychic depth of our being is awakened and adapted to profound intimacy with the Spirit or the "Living Current," in Master Da's language, of the "Great One or Divine Reality." This fourth stage is the stage of "free religion," or the stage of "whole bodily surrender and adaptation to the universal Life via Love-Communion (the disposition of the heart or deep psyche of pure energy)."[5]

The realization of the physical, emotional, mental, and moral responsibilities of the first three stages of life provides the necessary foundation for the testing and transformation that inevitably accompany true spiritual life. Without that basis we may come to enjoy yogic and mystical experience, for example, but remain unable to exercise real intelligence, freedom,

---

[2]Bubba [Da] Free John, *Love of the Two-Armed Form*, p. 75.
[3]Bubba [Da] Free John, *The Enlightenment of the Whole Body*, p. 192.
[4]*Ibid.*, p. 186.
[5]Da Free John, *Scientific Proof of the Existence of God Will Soon Be Announced by the White House!* p. 155.

and love under the most ordinary of human circumstances. If the elementary functions of our bodily, mental, and emotional adaptation to life have not been learned and tested during our first twenty-one years, we linger, egoically bound, in the lesser stages. Inevitably we must submit to the wisdom of self-transcendence.

However, to mature through and beyond the mechanics of the first three stages of life is not a casual, conventional matter of "growing older and wiser." Rather, the individual's entrance into the fourth stage of life begins with the awakening of the "psychic heart," which is marked by a clear sensitivity to the Life-Current. In this stage, the Divine Presence or Life-Force is felt to exist independent of, or senior to, the body-mind. By cultivating a conscious relationship to this Presence, the spiritual practitioner begins to demonstrate and enjoy the spiritual qualities of faith, love, and surrender. Thus, devotional surrender to the Living Reality is the essential feature of the fourth stage of life. The individual is obliged to persist beyond religious conventions and traditions, as Master Da himself emphasizes, by means of "continuous and concentrated self-devotion via heartfelt feeling-attention to the Ultimate Reality."[6]

STAGE 5

The fifth stage is associated with the mystical aspect of spirituality. The individual's attention is inverted away from the theatre of outer-directed attention to the inner or subjective experiences of the "subtle physiology" of the brain-mind. The mystical ascent through the psychic centers of the body-mind is conditioned by the nervous system. Experience in this stage reaches its peak in the state of "conditional nirvikalpa samadhi" or formless ecstasy.[7] At the apex of the fifth stage, the individual has transcended his or her fascination with mental forms and images. Master Da comments further:

> In the fifth stage of life, yogic mysticism raises attention into the extremities of subtle experience—or the heavens of ascended knowledge. But Liberation in God is not Realized at that stage or by such means. In order for the Life-Current to cross the Divide between the body-mind and Infinity, the gesture of attention and the illusion of an independent conscious self must be utterly Dissolved in the true Self.

[6]Da Free John, *Nirvanasara*, p. 188.
[7]In his Teaching Master Da distinguishes between the fifth-stage phenomena of conditional nirvikalpa samadhi (the yogic Self-Realization and the traditional epitome or highest possible reach of the process of yogic absorption of attention in the rising force of the bodily Current of Life) and Translation, or Unconditional Nirvikalpa Samadhi, the ultimate stage of the seventh or God-Realized stage of life.

The highest extreme of the ascent of attention is called "nirvikalpa samadhi," or total Absorption of self-consciousness in Radiant Transcendental Consciousness. But, in fact, the seed of differentiated self remains in such ascended Absorption of attention. Attention is yet extended outside the heart, or the root of self-consciousness, as a geature toward an independent Object, and, therefore, such "samadhi" is not only temporary, but it remains a form of subject-object Contemplation.[8]

STAGE 6

The sixth stage of life is the profound stage of "ego-death or the transcendence of mind, all sense of 'I,' and primal fear." It marks the transition from the "esoteric meditation" (subject-object Contemplation) of the fifth stage to the transcendence of attention, and thus the transcendence of the sense of being a subject (egoic consciousness) over against objects (the world and all relations). It is the Awakening to Transcendental Consciousness. The practice in the sixth stage of life is a deepening of the sense of identification with consciousness prior to attention to objects.

Through the Graceful Transmission of the Spiritual Master, a felt Current of Bliss is awakened at an "unfathomable Space in the right side of the heart." It is at this locus in the right side of the heart that "the Radiant Transcendental Consciousness is continually associated with the impulse of life in the individual body-mind."[9] Master Da refers to this "Space" as the "Location of Happiness," or the doorway to the Divine Domain of Radiant Transcendental Consciousness and the seventh stage of life. As Master Da explains:

> The sixth stage is the last of the progressive stages previous to Transcendental Awakening. It is the basic stage in which the transition is made from terrestrial and cosmic conceptions of the Divine or Real Being to conceptions of the Ultimate as the Transcendental Reality and Condition and Identity of all apparent beings and conditions. And the process of self-sacrifice is thus transformed from an effort that serves the development of knowledge and experience in the planes of the psycho-physical personality to a direct effort of utter self-transcendence.[10]

And:

> In the sixth stage of life, the body-mind is simply relaxed into the Life-Current, and attention (the root or base of the mind) is inverted away from gross and subtle states and objects of the body-mind, and toward its own Root, the

---

[8]Bubba [Da] Free John, *The Enlightenment of the Whole Body*, pp. 422–23.
[9]*Ibid.*, p. 401.
[10]Da Free John, *Nirvanasara*, p. 189.

ultimate Root of the ego-self, which is the "Witness" Consciousness (when attention is active) and also simple Consciousness (prior to objects and self-definition). The final result of this is conditional Self-Realization or the intuition of Radiant Transcendental Being via the exclusive self-essence (inverted away from all objects).[11]

STAGE 7

In the seventh stage of life, the liberated "individual" recognizes everything as a modification of the Radiant Transcendental Being. Now the Transcendental Self is no longer pitted against the phenomenal world. Instead, the world is recognized as continuously arising in the Ultimate Being, which is coessential with the Self. This last act of self-sacrifice continues into infinity. Master Da summarizes the seventh stage as follows:

> In the seventh stage of life there is native or radical intuitive identification with Radiant Transcendental Being, the Identity of all beings (or subjects) and the Condition of all conditions (or objects). This intuitive identification (or Radical Self-Abiding) is directly Realized, entirely apart from any dissociative act of inversion. And, while so Abiding, if any conditions arise, or if any states of body-mind arise, they are simply recognized in the Radiant Transcendental Being (as transparent or nonbinding modifications of Itself). Such is Sahaj Samadhi, and it is inherently free of any apparent implications, limitations, or binding power of phenomenal conditions. If no conditions arise to the notice, there is simply Radiant Transcendental Being. Such is Bhava Samadhi, about Which nothing is sufficient can be said, and there is not Anyone, Anything, or Anywhere beyond It to be Realized.[12]

Master Da's Teaching relative to the seven stages of life often refers to the demonstration or Signs of Whole Bodily Enlightenment—Transfiguration, Transformation, and Translation. Once fully Realized, the seventh stage of life becomes the perpetually Enlightened foundation of existence, even beyond death, and in any future lifetimes. The gross body-mind is progressively Transfigured in Divine Radiance, and the subtle or higher mind becomes the vehicle of Transformation, wherein that Radiance manifests extraordinary powers and faculties (such as psychic and healing capacities, genius, longevity, etc.) as spontaneous expressions of Divine Self-Abiding. Ultimately, for periods during this lifetime, this continuous

---

[11]Da Free John, *The Bodily Sacrifice of Attention*, p. 30.
[12]*Ibid.*, p. 30.

God-Realization leads to Divine Translation, or conversion of the individuated being beyond all phenomenal appearances into the "Divine Domain"
of Radiant Life-Consciousness.

The seven stages of life thus mark the natural, or structurally inevitable, evolutionary development of human existence from ordinary egoic
birth to the ultimate stages of God-Realization. In the Way of Radical
Understanding, which is the Way that Master Da Avabhasa Teaches, the
Awakened disposition of the seventh stage is made the foundation of life
and spiritual practice through each individual's cultivation of Cummunion
with the Divine via Master Da Avabhasa. Thus, in this Way all growth and
evolution are relieved of the dilemmas of un-Happiness, seeking, and the
illusions that characterize the first six stages of life when lived apart from
the instruction and Transmission of a seventh stage Adept.

Appendix 2

WOMEN AND ENLIGHTENMENT

SWAMI VIVEKANANDA, who brought Vedanta to the West, once wrote: "There is no chance for the welfare of the world unless the condition of women is improved. It is not possible for a bird to fly on only one wing."

As human evolution enters a new phase, characterized by transcendence of ego and recognition of the unity of all life, it seems appropriate here to address one of the great needs of this time of transition. I refer to the relative lack of models and literature for women entering spiritual life. As I surveyed sacred history and religious literature to find appropriate selections for this book, I was saddened to see the extent to which women have been kept "outside the temple." Spiritually aspiring women have very few examples of the fully liberated female, either historical or contemporary, to serve as models or examples. Likewise, spiritual literature directed to women is much more rare than that for men.

Of course, liberation has traditionally been recognized as being fully human first, and then male or female. That is how it was, mythically speaking, in life before the Fall into duality and the sexes; that is how it will be in the coming new age, when androgyny characterizes the sexual psychology of men and women. There will be a fullness and fusion within an individual's consciousness of the best traits traditionally considered masculine and feminine. Genuine spiritual literature recognizes that and transcends the division into genders; it speaks the truth alike to men and women's hearts and minds, urging liberation from all partial identities and from bondage to that which is less than ultimate. The emphasis is on God, not gender; on spirit, not sex roles.

Although equality between the sexes has been advocated or tacitly approved earlier in history by a few rare individuals—Jesus and the Buddha were two—it obviously has not been practiced. In a sense, then, it is a new idea or at least an idea whose time has come. I know of no society before the present where men and women have psychologically and culturally regarded each other as equals. All societies have been preponderantly either patriarchal or matriarchal. The last three thousand years have been, by and large, the Age of Man in the patriarchal sense. Prior to that, the religion of the Great Mother dominated world affairs, even though those affairs were largely tribal or local.

As the age of priestesses gave way to the age of priests, for whatever reasons—I think Ken Wilber best explains the situation in *Up from Eden*—women generally took a back seat in social and spiritual affairs. True, there were exceptions, both individually and culturally. But the general thrust of human development brought men to the foreground, and spiritually aspiring women were allowed only secondary or subservient roles. That status was overcome by just a handful of hardy and courageous female seekers of God, who most often had to go outside the established religious institutions in their thirst for spiritual growth and understanding of ultimate reality.

With the rise of patriarchal society on a global scale, recorded history became essentially male history—and therefore tended to exclude half the world's population! Women were denied positions of authority and opportunities for spiritual unfoldment, or at least not encouraged by the male-dominated institutions. And just as they were excluded from positions of authority in religious institutions, so also were they excluded, by and large, from the written records of those institutions. Thus, recorded history offers almost no female figures as role models of the mystic or the enlightened teacher, and almost no spiritual literature written by or for women. This has led to a one-sidedness and blindness in modern society as the "sins" (i.e., ignorance) of the fathers are visited on their sons and daughters.

But lack of evidence is not evidence of lack. If recorded history is distinguished from "lived" history, one finds there are little-known examples of spiritually liberated women in religious and sacred traditions. Women today, therefore, should not make the mistake of thinking they are incomplete and need a male mediator—priest, teacher, or role model—in their journey to God. That is not to say women should reject men as teachers or role models in their spiritual life; it is only to say they are not absolutely necessary and that there are other—female—resources at hand. Also, bear in mind that liberation does not eliminate distinctions; it eliminates inequalities.

This brief survey is intended primarily for spiritually aspiring women who do not want to deny or ignore their femininity, but want to fulfill it on the spiritual path. Although liberation transcends all sexual/gender roles, it is nevertheless right and proper for God-seeking women, if they are so moved, to pattern their lives after enlightened women, until they have grown beyond the need for such patterns altogether.

A word of caution, however. Before liberation, there must be deliberation. Careful discrimination is necessary because not all the women mentioned here were—or, in the case of living figures, are—equally evolved in consciousness. As with men in the spiritual world, not everything they said or did is necessarily divine wisdom. Saints can be dogmatic about bad dogma; mystics can suffer from skewed metaphysics. Moreover, even highly developed people, regardless of gender, can have quirks of personality and flaws of character. These eccentricities may be mistaken for high-level spirituality when they are actually no such thing. Even worse, naive spiritual aspirants may fall victim to unscrupulous teachers of alluring or mystifying demeanor who seduce them—figuratively and sometimes literally—under the guise of offering special "initiation into the mysteries."

A word of disclaimer, also. I have deliberately omitted references to women in magical and pagan traditions such as witchcraft, astrology, tarot, and so forth. I did so because I do not consider them to be major spiritual traditions. There undoubtedly are spiritually inclined women in them, and I don't mean any slight or insult. Those traditions are indeed valuable because anything that deepens self-knowledge is valuable. But they are founded *in* Nature rather than the transcendental source *of* Nature. The "self" as they define it is not the Self of religious and sacred traditions. Therefore, I have no sense of them as paths to enlightenment, nor am I aware of any enlightened women, historical or contemporary, whose stature is directly attributable to them.

Having said that, I must also disclaim omniscience. I am grateful for the guidance and support given me by several women who commented on an earlier draft of this appendix. And I welcome further comments from those who can correct me where I may have erred and inform me where I am ignorant. Thankfully, the dearth of spiritual literature and role models for women is now being rectified. There are contemporary females of great stature who speak and write from the depths of their hard-won wisdom. And there are scholarly studies disclosing long-hidden material about previous women of spirit that brings recorded history into truer alignment with lived history. I hope such works multiply so that the following overview might soon become a footnote in a long, rich history of women in spiritual life.

Christianity. The Christian tradition records many women saints and mystics in its long history. There are Joan of Arc, several Catharines, Blessed Angela of Foligno, Dame Julian of Norwich, Madame Guyon, and the founder of a holy order, Teresa of Avila, author of the mystical *Interior Castle.* Her name lives on in the work of the holy woman of Calcutta, the Nobel Prize winner, Mother Teresa. Mother Cabrini is another whom many consider to be a contemporary saint. The female par excellence in the

Christian tradition is of course the Blessed Virgin Mary, whose life exemplifies perfect submission to God, and is the origin of the Madonna ideal of Christianity. Likewise, Elizabeth, the mother of John the Baptist, deserves mention. Last of all, there is the "fallen woman," Mary Magdalene, whose story of selfless devotion and service to Jesus has touched the hearts of millions. A basic source text here is Evelyn Underhill's *Mysticism*, as is the anthology *Women Saints—East and West* by Swami Ghanananda.

Judaism. Judaism records several women of spirit during the biblical period. Among the ancient figures are Sarah, priestess of light, and Miriam, a prophetess and seer. Chana (Hannah) is credited by Jewish tradition as having been the first to pray from the heart, speaking directly and extemporaneously to God. Ima Shalom (Mother of Peace) was renowned during the period of Roman occupation of Judea for her wisdom. There is said to have been other females who were poets, kaballists, scholars, or prophetesses. Outside the biblical period, however, Judaism is almost devoid of recorded saintly or mystical women. The only female mystic known in the tradition was Hannah Rachel, also called the Maiden of Ludomir. She was a nineteenth-century lay Hasidic rebbe (spiritual leader) who counseled men and women as part of her work. Because of patriarchy she was obliged to sit behind a curtain as she counseled men. The daughter of the twelfth-century Gaon of Baghdad, Samuel Ben Ali became a religious authority because her father had no sons to educate and succeed him. (Perhaps she was the original Yentl?) *Women Saints—East and West* mentions Henrietta Szold as "Jewish, born in America, and a saint" who devoted herself for sixty years to saving lives.

Hinduism. Hinduism and other Indian sacred traditions have an ample roster of God-intoxicated women, ancient and modern. There was Lalla, a fourteenth-century Kashmiri yogini-poetess, who composed song-poems to God and sang them in the marketplace. In the sixteenth century, a poetess-saint of North India, Mirabai, likewise expressed her devotion through hundreds of song-poems. The nun Yogeshwari, also known as Bhairavi Brahmani, was a woman of high spiritual attainment in the last century who taught tantric meditation to the great yogi Ramakrishna. Ramakrishna's wife, Sri Sarada Devi, is also said to have been a very elevated, saintly person. In this century, Anandamoyee Ma is considered by many to be one of India's saints. Two other elevated women in this broad tradition are Srimata Gayatri Devi of the Vedanta Centre in Cohasset, Massachusetts, whose story is told in her *One Life's Pilgrimage*, and Indira Devi, a yogini and coauthor with Dilip Kumar Roy of *Pilgrim of the Stars*. Another living teacher accessible today is Swami Sivananda Radha of the Yasodhara Ashram in Kootenay Bay, British Columbia. Her book, *Radha: Diary of a*

Woman's Search, is an absorbing account of her 1955 journey to India where she was initiated into a yogic holy order.

Buddhism. Buddhism is said to have many highly evolved women, but they are far less known than the men. Although the Buddha did not exclude women from holy orders (Buddhism has no priesthood), he forbade women from being wandering monks when a female monk was raped. The order of Buddhist nuns ceased by the fifth century A.D. In Chinese Buddhism, Kuan Yin, the bodhisattva of compassion, is female but mythical. The only historical female figures in Buddhism who have come to my attention are Yasodhara, or Gopa (the Buddha's wife while he was a prince), Gautami (the Buddha's younger sister), and several others described in *Women Saints—East and West.* One modern figure is abbess Jiyu Kennett of the Shasta Abbey at Mount Shasta, California. She is roshi (spiritual teacher) to several dozen Zen monks and has written about her life in the two-volume *The Wild White Goose.* Another contemporary female Buddhist, recently deceased, was Claire Myers Owens, who came to Buddhism late in life but with a great and noble soul ripe for satori. She wrote of her experiences in *Zen and the Lady.*

Islam. There is only one female mystic, Rabi'a, recorded in the Sufi tradition, the mystical stream of Islam. *Women Saints—East and West* describes this eighth-century woman as "an inspiring example to all ordinary women who also can aspire to a height of spiritual perfection." There may be other God-realized women in Islam who are unknown to the public, however, because there are a few hints of this in the otherwise blank record. Mohammed's wife, Kadijah, was also his first disciple and therefore it can be assumed she had some degree of spiritual insight. Furthermore, on the day of his death, Mohammed gave advice to his daughter Fatima and his aunt Safiya: "Work ye out that which shall gain acceptance for you with the Lord: for I verily have no power with him to save you in any wise." Again, this indicates they were spiritually aspiring women with some degree of insight.

Jainism. *Women Saints—East and West* notes several female saints in the Jain tradition whose spiritual caliber included scholarship and composition of sacred texts. Notable among them was Arya Chandana, a contemporary of Mahavira, founder of Jainism. Described as deeply religious, she became his first disciple and the head of his order of nuns. Another contemporary of Mahavira was Jayanti, the sister of a King. Jayanti listened to Mahavira's discourses and discussed all sorts of spiritual matters with him. Eventually she left her life in the palace to become a nun. The order of nuns in Jainism continues today.

Native American Traditions. Native American mythology names various females of a divine nature, or who helped establish spiritual traditions, but I can find no historical figures. There are contemporary ones, however: Brooke Medicine Eagle, a medicine woman of Euro-Native American ancestry; O Shinnah Fast Wolf, whose special skill involves healing through crystals and gems; Twylah Hurd Nitsch, a granddaughter of the last Seneca medicine man; and Wabun (born Marlise James of Welsh ancestry), who is medicine partner of Sun Bear, founder of the first interracial/New Age tribe and medicine society.

Contemporary Spiritual Traditions. As if breaking with history, the modern era has seen a proliferation of spiritual traditions in which women have had a leading role. Mary Baker Eddy founded Christian Science; Ellen G. White began Seventh Day Adventism; Myrtle Fillmore and her husband Charles cofounded Unity; Alice A. Bailey started the Arcane School; occultist Helena P. Blavatsky founded Theosophy and was ably succeeded by Annie Besant.

One modern figure of exceptional stature was a Frenchwoman, Mira Richard, better known as The Mother. Early in this century she became the spiritual collaborator of Sri Aurobindo. The life story of The Mother is inspiring, and the content of her teaching and Sri Aurobindo's—called Integral Yoga—is worthy of profound study.

Another notable woman in contemporary spiritual affairs is the recently-deceased Murshida Ivy O. Duce, successor to Meher Baba and his organization, Sufism Reoriented.

In the still-new tradition of Da Free John, notice was given in recent months that two female devotees entered the seventh stage of life—direct realization of the Radiant Transcendental Being. The women were conferred names by him in honor of the event. Their names, drawn from the Hawaiian Islands where they were located on the occasion, are Namale-Ma and Nananu-I-Ma.

As I said earlier, not all the women named here are of equal elevation in consciousness. I have offered this survey with the caution that discrimination is needed by those who seek female role models for their spiritual growth. I also emphasize that the women noted here are not the sole guideline to spirituality for females. Spirituality is simply seeing God in all things, regardless of whether the thing is great or small, ordinary or extraordinary, and then expressing that insight through selfless service. When God-consciousness is one's state, everything is blissful, including washing dishes, doing laundry, raising children, and other traditional forms of "women's work" because one constantly beholds God as the world-process of life.

From that point of view, it doesn't matter whether you are a commoner or a king—or queen. All that matters is to act in loving service to the world which is none other than your true self, whether you do it quietly in humble, everyday circumstances, or you do it in bold headlines across the arena of global events.

So enlightenment doesn't require withdrawal from the world or rejection of traditional male/female roles (although those roles should be voluntarily adopted, not coerced). Rather, it requires self-transcendence. That, and that alone, is the path to liberation. As a Buddhist scripture puts it:

> *With neither a male nor female body*
> *Will enlightenment be attained.*

For a list of books on "Women and Spiritual Life," see the end of Appendix 3.

Appendix 3

SUGGESTIONS FOR
FURTHER EXPLORATION

First you go toward the light,
Next you're in the light,
Then you are the light.

IN ADDITION to the sacred texts of the world (such as the *Holy Bible, Koran, Bhagavad Gita, Tao Te Ching,* etc.) and the works from which the preceding selections have been taken, the following are recommended. Although reading about enlightenment is not a substitute for spiritual discipline and practice, opening the eye of contemplation can nevertheless be assisted by studying works concerned with awakening insight. Hence, these suggestions. They are somewhat arbitrarily categorized and are by no means comprehensive. Moreover, there is some variation in the degree of insight or level of consciousness brought to each work by its author. But as a basic library for the serious seeker on the spiritual path, they constitute a solid, trustworthy resource.

Consciousness Research

Sri Aurobindo, *The Mind of Light*. E. P. Dutton: New York, NY, 1971. A brief and luminous introduction to the evolutionary possibilities envisioned by Sri Aurobindo, based on the Supermind.

Paul Brunton, *The Wisdom of the Overself*. Samuel Weiser: New York, NY, 1970. The masterwork of a modern consciousness researcher, this book deals with topics such as the development of intuition, the infinity of time and space, and God and the universal mind.

Arthur Deikman, *The Observing Self: Mysticism and Psychotherapy*. Beacon Press: Boston, MA, 1982. Deikman shows mysticism's contribution to western psychology and psychotherapy, and argues that mysticism is a science of higher psychological development.

Thaddeus Golas, *The Lazy Man's Guide to Enlightenment*. The Seed Center: Palo Alto, CA, 1972. A brief, witty, and wise discussion of what enlightenment means in psychological and behavioral terms.

Edward Hoffman, *The Way of Splendor*. Shambhala Publications: Boulder, CO, 1981. A study of Jewish mysticism and the kaballistic tradition that elucidates its relationship to modern psychology, especially parapsychology and transpersonal psychology.

Da Free John, *Scientific Proof of the Existence of God Will Soon Be Announced By the White House!*. Dawn Horse Press: Middletown, CA, 1980. A monumental study of popular cults and mass culture that exposes the fundamental flaws of organized religion, science, and politics, and gives clear indications for establishing an enlightened culture based on wisdom and love.

————, *Easy Death*. Dawn Horse Press: Middletown, CA, 1983. A remarkable examination of the relationship between death and enlightenment, with detailed revelations of the after-death states of consciousness.

Gopi Krishna, *Higher Consciousness,* Julian Press: New York, NY, 1974. Clear, direct answers to questions about the nature of higher consciousness and the kundalini experience.

————, *Kundalini, The Evolutionary Energy in Man*. Shambhala Publications: Berkeley, CA, 1971. An autobiographical account of the awakening of kundalini and its significance for human evolution.

Barry McWaters, *Conscious Evolution*. Institute for Conscious Evolution: 2418 Clement Street, San Francisco, CA 94121, 1981. A clear, simple, and sensible discussion of personal and societal transformation through conscious participation in the evolution of the cosmos.

John Niendorff, *Listen to the Light*. Science of Mind Publications: P.O. Box 75127, Los Angeles, CA 90075, 1980. Short, stunningly poetic essays on higher consciousness. "About the One" and "Celebration" are gems.

Dane Rudhyar, *Beyond Individualism*. Theosophical Publishing House: Wheaton, IL 60187, 1979. Subtitled "The Psychology of Transformation," this work discusses human growth from a transpersonal and transcultural perspective rich in insights and provocative new concepts.

————, *Rhythm of Wholeness*. Theosophical Publishing House: Wheaton, IL 60187, 1983. A comprehensive and articulate discussion of the relationship between Being and Becoming on a cosmic scale that brings it home in individual terms. Rudhyar, who was the first to use the term "transpersonal" in English (in the 1930s), clarifies the role of transpersonal activity in human evolution.

————, *Beyond Personhood*. Rudhyar Institute for Transpersonal Activity: 3635 Lupine Avenue, Palo Alto, CA 94303, 1982. A booklet-length discussion of the evolutionary transition humanity is now undergoing and the role of the Pleroma in that process of psychological change.

Charles T. Tart, ed., *Transpersonal Psychologies*. Harper & Row: New York, NY, 1975 and reprinted by Psychological Processes, 1675 Visalia Avenue, Berkeley, CA 94707. A textbook on the psychologies associated with various sacred traditions and consciousness-expanding systems.

Frances Vaughan and Roger Walsh, eds., *Beyond Ego: Transpersonal Dimensions in Psychology.* J. P. Tarcher: Los Angeles, CA, 1980. A collection of articles and essays on higher human development by leading transpersonal psychologists.

Ken Wilber, *The Atman Project.* Theosophical Publishing House: Wheaton, IL, 1980. A transpersonal view of human development that brilliantly maps the stages of growth from birth to enlightenment, and extends modern psychology through a synthesis of eastern and western insights.

————, *Eye to Eye.* Doubleday: New York, NY, 1983. A collection of closely focused essays on the quest for a new paradigm of humanity's relation to the cosmos. The first two chapters alone are a milestone in science and intellectual history.

————, ed., *The Holographic Paradigm.* Shambhala Publications: Boulder, CO, 1983. A collection of articles, essays, and interviews on the relationship between science and mysticism.

————, *No Boundary.* Shambhala Publications: Boulder, CO, 1981. The best introduction to Wilber's work and to consciousness research in general.

————, *Up From Eden.* Doubleday: New York, NY, 1982. A transpersonal view of human evolution that reveals the divine within history in a way that is wholly compatible with modern science and spiritual traditions, and that demonstrates the evolution of consciousness as the driving force within humanity.

Meditation and Prayer

Pandit Usharbudh Arya, *Meditation and the Art of Dying.* Himalayan International Institute: Honesdale, PA, 18431, 1979. A review discussion of the finest yogic teachings on the nature of the death experience, offering sound advice and instruction on the relationship between death and enlightenment.

Grace Brame, *Receptive Prayer.* CBP Press: St Louis, Missouri, 1985. An insightful book about Christian prayer and meditation with valuable instructions for practice.

Ram Dass, *Journey of Awakening.* Bantam Books: New York, NY, 1978. A meditator's guidebook which contains a useful listing of groups that teach meditation and offer retreats.

Daniel Goleman, *The Varieties of Meditative Experience.* E. P. Dutton: New York, NY, 1977. An illuminating look at the meditative approach to enlightenment in major religions and spiritual traditions, it demonstrates the essential unity of experience among diverse pathways to God.

Joseph Goldstein, *The Experience of Insight*. Shambhala Publications: Boulder, CO 80302, 1983. Clear instruction for the practice of Buddhist meditation, with a discussion of basic topics such as karma, the four noble truths, and the factors of enlightenment.

Anagarika Govinda, *Creative Meditation and Multi-Dimensional Consciousness*. Theosophical Publishing House: Wheaton, IL, 1976. An insightful book on the transformation of all life into enlightened spirit through meditation.

Tom Sampson, *Cultivating the Presence*. T. Y. Crowell: New York, NY, 1977. An excellent manual for Christians and others involved in the spiritual practice of a living awareness of God in daily affairs.

John White, *What Is Meditation?* Anchor Books: New York, NY, 1974. A survey of meditative traditions by experienced meditators of those traditions.

Mysticism and Sacred Traditions

Anonymous, *A Course in Miracles*. Foundation for Inner Peace: P.O. Box 635, Tiburon, CA 94920, 1975. A channeled teaching of remarkable quality which emphasizes the role of relationships and forgiveness as a method of awakening to God as Love and Self-of-All.

Haridas Chaudhuri, *Integral Yoga*. California Institute of Asian Studies: 3494 21st Street, San Francisco, CA, 94110, 1965. An introduction to the yoga of Sri Aurobindo that succinctly but clearly explains the methods and metaphysics of the sage.

Christopher Hills, *The Christ Book*. University of the Trees Press: Boulder Creek, CA 95006. One of the few books among many about Jesus which offers real insight into his life and teaching.

Da Free John, *Enlightenment and the Transformation of Man*. Dawn Horse Press: Clearlake, CA 95422, 1983. An introduction to Da Free John's *Way of Radical Understanding*, using selections from talks and essays on the spiritual process and God-realization.

————, *Nirvanasara*. Dawn Horse Press: Clearlake, CA 95422, 1983. A critique of the principal spiritual traditions, particularly Buddhism and Hinduism, that results in an illumined understanding of their limitations while formulating a new spiritual tradition for both their continuation and their fulfillment.

Swami Kriyananda, *The Path: Autobiography of a Western Yogi*. Ananda Publications: Nevada City, CA, 1977. The inspiring story of an American-born man's search for God through the path of yoga and the wisdom he learned. His guru was Paramhansa Yogananda (see below), hence the subtitle.

Lobsang P. Lhalungpa, *The Life of Milarepa*. E. P. Dutton: New York, NY, 1977. The story of Tibet's most beloved saint, the eleventh-century Milarepa, this inspiring translation details his growth to enlightenment.

Swami Sivananda Radha, *Gods Who Walk the Rainbow*. Timeless Books: Box 60, Porthill, ID 83853, 1981. Informational and inspirational sketches of the gurus of Swami Radha, who is herself a highly evolved spiritual teacher, and her interactions with them on the spiritual path.

Swami Rama, *Enlightenment Without God*. Himalayan Publishers: Box 88, Honesdale, PA 18431. An expansion of the terse messages contained in the Mandukya Upanishad and a commentary on Vedanta, offering guidelines on personal self-unfoldment without reliance on external supports.

———, *Living with the Himalayan Masters*. Himalayan Publishers: Box 88, Honesdale, PA 18431. Stories related by Swami Rama about the teachings and often-miraculous accomplishments of various holy people he lived with or met during his travels in the Himalayas.

———, *Yoga and Psychotherapy*. Himalayan Publishers: Box 88, Honesdale, PA 18431. Provides an in-depth analysis of western and eastern models of the mind and their differing perspectives on such functions as ego and consciousness within a comprehensive theory of personal evolution.

Huston Smith, *Forgotten Truth*. Harper & Row: New York, NY, 1976. An excellent commentary on the transcendent unity of religions, esotericism, and the perennial philosophy.

W. T. Stace, *The Teachings of the Mystics*. New American Library: New York, NY, 1960. A survey of the characteristics, nature, meaning, and value of mystical experience as it has been described by the great mystical writers of the world throughout history.

Rudolf Steiner, *Occult Science*. Anthroposophic Press: Spring Valley, New York, NY, 1972. A basic work by a giant in the western metaphysical tradition. It describes the supersensible nature of the human being and the higher worlds.

———, *Knowledge of the Higher Worlds and Its Attainment*. Anthroposophic Press: New York, NY, 1947. Steiner's fundamental work on the path to fully conscious experience of supersensible realities. It explains in detail the exercises and disciplines a student must pursue in order to attain full spiritual knowledge.

Chogyam Trungpa, *Cutting Through Spiritual Materialism*. Shambhala Publications: Berkeley, CA, 1974. Spiritual materialism is the ego's attempt to appropriate spiritual teachings and ideas for its own purposes. Trungpa describes this subtle "conspiracy" and shows how meditation can expose it and awaken higher mind.

Vitvan, *The Christos*. School of the Natural Order: Baker, NV 89311, 1951. A little-known but profound study of human development—individually and as a race—to enlightenment that clarifies the significance of

Christianity as a spiritual discipline.

Alan W. Watts, *Behold the Spirit*. Vintage Books: New York, NY, 1972. A study of Christian mysticism that gets to the esoteric heart of the tradition while illuminating the exoteric "body," the institutional church.

———, *Psychotherapy East and West*. New American Library: New York, NY, 1961. One of the seminal books of the consciousness revolution, it discusses the nature of ego and egolessness with great lucidity.

Paramhansa Yogananda, *Autobiography of a Yogi*. Self-Realization Fellowship: Los Angeles, CA, 1946. The memoirs of a sage yogi who introduced westerners to the realities of the yogic life of self-mastery.

Roger Zelazny, *Lord of Light*. Avon Books: New York, NY, 1969. A science fiction novel about a future Buddha. Chapter 3 is a high point in English literature.

Women and Spiritual Life

(I have not read all of these books and therefore cannot comment on every one. Some are listed because various sources have suggested the titles as appropriate for inclusion herein.)

Tsultrim Allione, *Women of Wisdom*. Routledge & Kegan Paul: London, 1984. A biographical account of six Tibetan women saints/yoganis, with commentary by the author about her personal experience of spiritual life.

Miriam Arguelles and Jose Arguelles, *The Feminine, Spacious as the Sky*. Shambhala: Boulder, CO, 1977. A study of the feminine principle's relevance to both men and women in their search for self-understanding.

Carol P. Christ, *Diving Deep and Surfacing: Women Writers on Spiritual Quest*. Beacon Press: Boston, 1980.

Srimata Gayatri Devi, *One Life's Pilgrimage*. Vedanta Centre: 130 Beechwood Street, Cohasset, MA 02025, 1977. The autobiography of the first Indian woman to teach Vedanta in the west, it is an inspiring record of her activity and spiritual unfoldment.

Indira Devi and Dilip Kumar Roy, *Pilgrims of the Stars*. Delta Books: New York, NY, 1973. Reprinted by Timeless Books: P.O. Box 60, Porthill, ID 83853, 1985. The autobiography of a remarkable artist-couple's spiritual evolution. Indira Devi was a psychic, mystic poet, and classical Indian dancer.

Anne Fremantle, *Woman's Way to God*. St. Martin's Press: New York, NY, 1977. An examination of the intense religious experience of nineteen women, some famous, some lesser known.

Swami Ghanananda and Sir John Stewart-Wallace, eds., *Women Saints—East and West*. Vedanta Press: 1946 Vedanta Place, Hollywood CA 90068, 1955. A collection of essays on great saints and mystics among women of different religions and countries.

Mary E. Giles, *The Feminist Mystic*. Crossroad/Continuum: New York, 1982.

Elisabeth Haich, *Sexual Energy and Yoga*. George Allen and Unwin: London 1971.

Frances Horn, *I Want One Thing*. Devors: Marina Del Rey, CA, 1981. The autobiography of a spiritually questing woman, written at age 74, after five generations of searching for Wholeness.

Jiyu-Kennett, *The Wild White Goose*. Shasta Abbey: P.O. Box 199, MI. Shasta, CA 96069. 1977 and 1978 (two vols.) The autobiography of a woman teacher of Zen who is head of the Shasta Abbey.

Irene C. Morelli, *The Feminist Mystic and other Essays on Women and Spiritual Life*. Crossroad/Continuum: New York.

Julian of Norwich, *Julian of Norwich: Revelations of Divine Love*. Penguin Books: London, 1966.

C. Niehammer, *Daughters of the Earth*. MacMillan: New York 1977. The lives and legends of American Indian women.

Swami Nikhilananda, *Holy Mother*. Rama Krishna Vivekananda Center: New York, 1982. An account of the saintly life of Sarada Devi, the wife and first disciple of Ramakrishna.

Javad Nurbakksh, *Sufi Women*. Vedanta Press: Hollywood, 1990. Brief surveys of the lives and teachings of more than 100 Sufi women through the ages.

C. Olson, ed., *The Book of the Goddess*. Crossroad/Continuum: New York 1983.

Claire Myers Owens, *Small Ecstasies*. ACS Publications: Box 16430, San Diego, CA 92116, 1983. The story of a woman's search for cosmic consciousness by an early advocate of women's rights.

———, *Zen and the Lady*. Baraka Books: New York, NY, 1977. Claire Owens began to practice Zen at 72. Her memoirs after a decade of on-the-Zen-path are a remarkable record of spiritual struggle and victory.

Hanumanprasad Poddar, *Gopis' Love for Sri Krishna*. Dawn Horse Press: Clearlake, CA, 1981. The story of the Divine Play of Krishna and the devotional way of Love-Communion with God.

Swami Radha, *Radha: Diary of a Woman's Search*. Timeless Books: P.O. Box 60, Porthill, ID 83853, 1981. The account of a pilgrimage to India in 1955–56, during which a spiritually questing woman tested the meaning of spirituality and was initiated into the order of swamis by her guru, a renowned saint.

Bernadette Roberts, *The Experience No-Self.* Shambalha: Boulder, CO, 1984. A personal account of an American woman's spiritual odyssey within the Christian tradition to ego transcendence and God-union.

Rosemary Ruether and Eleanor McLaughlin, *Women of Spirit: Female Leadership in the Jewish and Christian Traditions.* Simon & Schuster: New York, 1979. A collection of essays that discusses women as charismatic leaders, holy women, dissenters, martyrs, renewers, and reformers within the structure of centralized authority and theological images of the feminine.

Catherine of Siena, *Catherine of Siena—The Dialogue.* Paulist Press: Ramsey, NJ, 1980. The fourteenth-century Italian saint intended this book to instruct and encourage all those whose spiritual welfare was her concern.

Charlene Spretnak, ed., *The Politics of Women's Spirituality.* Anchor Books: New York, NY, 1982.

Merlin Stone, *When God Was a Woman.* Harcourt Brace Jovanovich: New York, NY, 1976. A historical study of the religion of The Great Goddess.

St. Teresa of Avila, *Interior Castle.* Doubleday: New York, 1979. A sublime work expressing St. Teresa's deep experience in guiding souls toward spiritual perfection.

———, *The Way of Perfection.* A classic practical guide for the practice of prayer.

Mother Teresa, *A Gift for God: Prayers and Meditation.* Harper & Row: New York, 1980.

Swami Tapasyananda and Swami Nikhilananda, *Sri Sarada Devi, The Holy Mother.* Vedanta Press: 1946 Vedanta Place, Hollywood, CA 90068, 1980. A more detailed and interpretative account of Sarada Devi's life than the one by Swami Nikhilananda noted above.

St. Terese of Lisieux, *The Autobiography of St. Therese of Lisieux.* Doubleday: New York, 1957.

Evelyn Underhill, *Mysticism.* Dutton: New York, NY, 1961. First published in 1911, this is a classic work in its field and a rich source of information about women (and men) of spirit in the Christian tradition.

ABOUT THE AUTHORS

Sri Aurobindo (1872–1950) is widely regarded as one of India's greatest yogis. He was born in Calcutta but raised and educated in England. He returned to India at 22, throwing himself into the drive to rid the country of British rule. Because of his stance, he was jailed for a year in solitary confinement at Alipore. During that time he underwent a profound spiritual transformation, ignited by several progressive mystical experiences that unveiled new dimensions of reality and sent him in another direction than political action. Thereafter until his death he worked steadfastly for the transformation of humanity, developing a teaching he called Integral Yoga that combined the major traditional lines of yoga in a manner suited for the modern temperament. He was joined in his work in 1929 by a Frenchwoman, Mira Richard, who came to be known as The Mother. Central to Sri Aurobindo's teaching is "the descent of the Supermind"—a concept of spiritual evolution that sees the human race returning to godhead while transforming everyday life rather than escaping from the world. Among his numerous writings are the monumental *The Life Divine, The Synthesis of Yoga, Essays on the Gita, The Mind of Light* and the long poem *Savitri*. Information about him and his books is available from the Matagiri Sri Aurobindo Center, Mt. Tremper, NY 12457.

Meher Baba (1894–1969) described himself as an avatar or god-man, one who is fully conscious of himself as God. His name means "Compassionate Father" and his devotees accept him as the reappearing Christ, Messiah, Prophet, or Messiah of this age. He was born in Poona, India as Merwan Sheriar Irani; his parents were of Persian extraction. In 1913, while in his first year of college, he met an aged Muslim saint, who was instrumental in revealing to him his state of God-realization. In 1921 he gathered his first disciples and started his avataric mission. Four years later he began to "observe silence," thereafter communicating only by pointing to letters on an alphabet board or by gestures. His work nevertheless proceeded vigorously. He travelled widely, discoursing to people numbering in the millions during the five decades of his ministrations. His *Discourses, God Speaks, Beams* and *Life at Its Best* cover various topics of spiritual development and practice. Information about him and his centers is available from The Meher Spiritual Center, P.O. Box 487, Myrtle Beach, SC 29577 and from Sufism Reoriented, 1300 Boulevard Way, Walnut Creek, CA 94959.

Richard Maurice Bucke, M.D., (1837–1902) was a Canadian doctor and

239

psychologist. His spontaneous experience of cosmic consciousness in 1872 at age 35 led to a life concerned with understanding the nature of transcendent realization or illumination. He led an active and productive professional life, serving as superintendent of an asylum for the insane, as Professor of Mental and Nervous Diseases at Western University in Ontario, and as President of the Psychological Section of the British Medical Association and President of the American Medico-Psychological Association. His 1879 book, *Man's Moral Nature*, examined the relation between the sympathetic nervous system and morality. He also authored the 1901 classic study of the evolving human mind, *Cosmic Consciousness*, which has deeply influenced consciousness research and transpersonal psychology.

Allan Y. Cohen, Ph.D., is a practicing psychologist and Executive Director of the Pacific Institute for Research and Evaluation, with headquarters in Bethesda, Maryland and Walnut Creek, California. He earned his doctorate in clinical psychology at Harvard in 1966, after working with psychedelics explorer Dr. Timothy Leary and beginning serious study of consciousness and mysticism. Cohen has held teaching positions at Harvard, the University of California (Berkeley and San Francisco), and is currently Adjunct Professor of Parapsychology and Mysticism at John F. Kennedy University in Orinda, California. After giving up psychedelic chemicals, he explored many metaphysical paths and became committed to Meher Baba. Since 1967 he has been associated with Sufism Reoriented, a Sufi order chartered by Meher Baba. Cohen's professional work has centered around national drug abuse prevention projects. He is on the editorial board of the *Journal of Psychoactive Drugs* and is Associate Editor of the *Journal of Primary Prevention*. He has written widely in the fields of substance abuse and mysticism, and has lectured internationally on the subjects. He can be reached at the Pacific Institute, 1777 North California, Walnut Creek, California 94596.

Master Da Avabhasa (Da Free John) is a living Adept and founder of The Free Daist Communion, the spiritual fellowship of practitioners of the Way taught by him. He was born on Long Island, New York in 1939, graduated from Columbia University, attended several Christian seminaries, and practiced yoga under several yogis, notably Swami Muktananda. In the course of this, he experienced the full spectrum of psychic and mystical phenomena, and found it less than ultimate. In 1970 he consciously realized his identity with Transcendental Consciousness or Reality. Thereafter, he began his teaching function in the world. His first book was the autobiographical *The Knee of Listening*. Among his numerous source texts are *The Enlightenment of the Whole Body, Scientific Proof of the Existence of God Will Soon Be Announced by the White House!, Easy Death, The Dreaded Gom-Boo or the Imaginary Disease That Religion Seeks to Cure*, and *The Transmission of Doubt*. A renunciate, he lives in seclusion in the Fiji Islands with a small group of devotees, but visits followers of his Way on occasion at sanctuaries around the world. For more information, write to The Laughing Man Institute, P.O. Box 836, San Rafael, California 94915.

Lex Hixon, Ph.D., has studied philosophy and religion at Yale University, the Graduate Faculties of the New School for Social Research, Union Theological Seminary, and Columbia University, where he received his doctorate. He has practiced meditation for many years, primarily under the guidance of Swami Nikhi-lananda and Swami Prabhavananda of the Ramakrishna Order, and under Zen Buddhist, Tibetan Buddhist, and Islamic meditation masters. He was recently named a senior in the Zen Community of New York by its sensei Bernard Tetsugen Glassman. From 1970 to 1982, he produced and moderated *In the Spirit*, a weekly two-hour radio documentary, over WBAI-FM in New York City, interviewing various spiritual teachers and seekers, including Alan Watts, Mother Teresa of Calcutta, Swami Satchidananda, Ram Dass, Rabbi Shlomo Carlebach, and others. The author of *Coming Home*, Hixon has made pilgramages to Mecca and Bodh Gaya. He is presently studying Orthodox Christianity at St. Vladimir's Seminary in Crestwood, New York. He can be reached at 5443 Palisade Ave., Bronx, New York 10471.

Aldous Huxley (1894–1963) was a novelist, essayist, intellectual mystic. He was born in England but resided most of his life in southern California. One of the major mind-explorers of this century, it was his competition with Sir Humphrey Osmond to find a neutral term for consciousness-expanding substances that led to the invention (by Osmond in 1957) of the word "psychedelic." In that respect and many others, Huxley is a father of the consciousness research/exploration movement now underway around the world. His major books include the nonfiction works *The Doors of Perception, Heaven and Hell, Tomorrow and Tomorrow and Tomorrow* and *The Perennial Philosophy* and the novels *Brave New World* and *Island*.

Gopi Krishna (1903–1984) was a yogi-scientist philosopher, and founder-director of the Central Institute for Kundalini Research in New Delhi, India. He was born near Srinagar, Kashmir. In 1937, after 17 years of meditation, he awakened the kundalini energy in himself and began a transformative process that eventually resulted in illumination. The dozen years that immediately followed, however, were a severe ordeal filled with pain, prolonged illness, near-death, bewilderment, and doubts about his sanity. Through it all he continued to work as a humble civil servant in the Indian government and to fulfill his role as husband and father, while seeking to understand the change he was undergoing. Now in his eighties, Gopi Krishna is author of many books and articles, including his autobiography, *Kundalini, the Evolutionary Energy in Man*, and various works on kundalini research such as *The Secret of Yoga, Higher Consciousness, The Dawn of a New Science* and *The Biological Basis of Religion and Genius*. He is represented in America by the Kundalini Research Foundation, 475 Fifth Avenue, New York, NY 10016.

J. Krishnamurti (1895–1989) was an internationally-known teacher and phi-losopher. During six decades of public work, he spoke to tens of millions of people, expounding no doctrine but constantly examining the working of the human mind. He was born in South India in 1895 to an impoverished Brahmin family and was educated in England and France under the tutelage of prominent Theosophists, who saw a quality of future spiritual leadership in him. He was hailed by them as the World Teacher of this age and made head of an international order with thousands of members. In 1929 Krishnamurti dissolved the order, saying that his only concern was the liberation of human beings, who have no need of spiritual authorities or organizations. His public stance is therefore not that of a guru but a lover of truth.

His writings and discourses include *The Awakening of Intelligence, Think on These Things, The Flight of the Eagle, Freedom from the Known,* and *The First and Last Freedom.* His life's story is chronicled in Mary Lutyen's two-volume biography, *Krishnamurti.* Information about his publications and recordings can be obtained from the Krishnamurti Foundation of America, P.O. Box 216, Ojai, CA 93023.

Swami Sivananda Radha is founder and spiritual director of the Yasodhara Ashram, a yoga retreat and study center in British Columbia, Canada. She is also the founder and president of the United States-based Association for Development of Human Potential. She received her training at Sivananda Ashram in Rishikesh, India, and was initiated into *sanyas* (the path of renunciation and selfless service) there. At the request of her guru, Swami Sivananda Saraswati, she returned to the West in 1956 to help disseminate yogic teachings and practices, becoming the first Western female disciple. Her writings include *Kundalini: Yoga for the West, Hatha Yoga: The Hidden Language, Mantras: Words of Power, Radha: Diary of a Woman's Search,* and *In the Company of the Wise* and *The Divine Light Invocation.* For four decades she has lectured at universities, psychological institutes and spiritual centers internationally. She can be reached at the Yasodhara Ashram, P.O. Box 9, Kootenay Bay, B.C., Canada VOB 1XO.

Dane Rudhyar (1895–1985) was born in Paris, France, but lived in America from age 21. Creatively gifted in many fields, he was self-consecrated to assisting the birth of a global society and a transformed humanity. Upon leaving the Old World, he gave up his ancestral name, Chevenniere, in favor of one whose Sanskrit root, *rudra,* implying dynamic action and the electrical power released during storms, seemed more fitting to his new way of life. He first established his reputation as an astrologer and later pioneered humanistic and transpersonal astrology. He is also a composer, poet, philosopher, painter, novelist, and freethinking occult psychologist, and has been awarded several honorary degrees for his work. Among his numerous books are the 1936 classic *The Astrology of Personality* and later works such as *The Planetarization of Consciousness, The Astrology of Transformation, Beyond Individualism,* and *Rhythm of Wholeness.* His work is carried on by the Rudhyar Institute for Transpersonal Activity, 3635 Lupine Avenue, Palo Alto, CA 94303, which offers his books, tapes and records for sale.

Satprem was born in France in 1923. He spent a year and a half in a German concentration camp during World War Two, and after the war he travelled the world in search of what he calls "true adventure." He found it in the "new evolution" visioned by Sri Aurobindo. In 1953 he returned to India, became a renunciate, and put himself at the service of Sri Aurobindo and his spiritual collaborator, The Mother. He stayed with The Mother for 19 years, becoming her confident and witness, and collecting personal conversations now being published in a 13-volume work, *Mother's Agenda.* Sri Aurobindo, or The Adventure of Consciousness was first published in 1968. Satprem's latest work, *The Mind of the Cells,* presents The Mother's views on the willed mutation of humanity, which entails a new biology and a new consciousness. His books are available from the Institute for Evolutionary Research, 200 Park Avenue, New York, NY 10166.

Huston Smith, Ph.D., was Thomas J. Watson Professor of Religion and Distinguished Adjunct Professor of Philosophy at Syracuse University from 1973 to 1983 and for fifteen years prior to that he was Professor of Philosophy at Massachusetts Institute of Technology. He is currently (during fall semesters) Hanna Professor of Philosophy at Hamline University, St. Paul, Minnesota. Born of missionary parents in Soochow, his childhood and youth in China provided an appropriate background for his ensuing work in comparative philosophies and religions. His book, *The Religions of Man*, has sold more than two million copies; his documentary films on Tibetan Buddhism, Sufism, and Hinduism have won international film festival awards (and are available through the Hartley Film Foundation, Cat Rock Road, Cos Cob, CT 06807); and his phonograph record, *The Music of Tibet*, which demonstrates his discovery of the capacity of certain lamas to sing multi-tones simultaneously, was acclaimed by *The Journal of Ethnomusicology* as an important landmark in the study of non-European musics and, beyond that, of music itself. In addition to his book on comparative religion, Smith is author of *Forgotten Truth: The Primordial Tradition* and *Beyond the Post-Modern Mind*. He now lives at 130 Avenida Drive, Berkeley, CA 94708.

Evelyn Underhill (1875–1941) was an English poet, novelist and writer on mysticism. Born in Wolverhampton and an only child, she was educated at King's College for Women, London, where she was made an honorary Fellow in 1913 and a Fellow in 1927. She married Hubert Stuart Moore, a barrister-at-law, in 1907. In 1921 she became Upton lecturer on the Philosophy of Religion at Manchester College, England. Aberdeen University made her an honorary D.D. in 1939. She found her way intellectually from agnosticism to Christianity. Between 1900 and 1920 she wrote novels and verse, but her lasting fame rests on the many books she produced on various aspects of mysticism. Her classic *Mysticism: A Study in the Nature and Development of Man's Spiritual Consciousness*, published in 1911, was an instant and lasting success. Her 1930 *Consciousness* vied in popularity with *Mysticism*. Among her other works are *The Mystic Way, Practical Mysticism, The Life of the Spirit and the Life of Today, Man and the Supernatural, The House of the Soul* and *Essentials of Mysticism and Other Essays*, which comments on a number of female mystics.

Roger Walsh, M.D., Ph.D., is on the faculty of the Department of Psychiatry of the University of California at Irvine. Trained in medicine, psychiatry, and neuroscience, he is currently focussing on the nature of psychological health, the means for developing it, and the psychologies of both East and West which describe it. His interest in the nature of psychological well-being began as a result of this experiences in psychotherapy and meditation. He is coeditor (with Deane Shapiro) of *Beyond Health and Normality: Explorations of Exceptional Psychological Well-Being* and (with Frances Vaughan) of *Paths Beyond Ego: The Transpersonal Vision*. He also coedited (with Deane Shapiro) *Meditation: Ancient and Contemporary Perspectives* and has written *Towards an Ecology of the Brain, Staying Alive: The Psychology of Human Survival* and *The Spirit of Shamanism*. He can be reached at the Department of Psychiatry, University of California Medical School, Irvine, CA 92717.

Alan W. Watts (1915–1973) was an Anglican cleric who left the church to become an author, teacher and exponent of mysticism. He was born in England but emigrated to America, where he held a post as chaplain at Northwestern University

243

in Evanston, Illinois. While there, he broke with institutional religion and went his own way, eventually settling down on a houseboat in Sausalito, California. As an orientalist, he helped to introduce Zen to the Western world. He also was a major influence in the emergence of psychedelic drug research aimed at scientifically studying the sacred dimensions of mind. He wrote many books on religion, philosophy and mysticism, including *Psychotherapy East and West, The Supreme Identity, Behold the Spirit, The Way of Zen, Beyond Theology*, and *The Book*. His life is described in his autobiographical *In My Own Way*.

Ken Wilber, widely regarded as the foremost theorist in transpersonal psychology, is author of *The Spectrum of Consciousness, No Boundary, The Atman Project, Up From Eden, Eye to Eye, A Sociable God, Quantum Questions* and other works of psychology, philosophy, religion, and consciousness research. His *Grace and Grit* is a poignant autobiography. He earned his undergraduate degree at Duke University and then went to the University of Nebraska at Lincoln, where he completed course requirements for a Ph.D. in biochemistry. Before beginning his doctoral dissertation, he took a leave of absence to write his landmark first book, *The Spectrum of Consciousness*, but later decided not to return to the university. He has been a practitioner of Zen since 1972, and has studied under several Zen and Tibetan Buddhist masters.

ABOUT THE EDITOR

John White, M.A.T., is an internationally known author and editor in the fields of consciousness research and higher human development. He has held positions as Director of Education for the Institute of Noetic Sciences, a research organization founded by Apollo 14 astronaut Edgar D. Mitchell to study human potential and planetary problems, and as President of Alpha Logics, a school for self-directed growth in body, mind and spirit.

White is author of *The Meeting of Science and Spirit, Pole Shift, A Practical Guide to Death and Dying, Everything You Want to Know about TM*, and a children's story, *The Christmas Mice*. He has also edited a number of anthologies, including *The Highest State of Consciousness, Psychic Exploration, What Is Meditation?, Frontiers of Consciousness, Future Science, Relax, Other Worlds, Other Universes*, and *Kundalini, Evolution and Enlightenment*. Articles and reviews by him have appeared in popular magazines such as *Reader's Digest, Saturday Review, Esquire, Science of Mind, Omni, Woman's Day*, and *New Age* and in professional journals and major newspapers such as *The New York Times, San Francisco Chronicle*, and *Chicago Sun-Times*. He is General Editor of the Omega Books series published by Paragon House, New York.

White holds degrees from Dartmouth College and Yale University, and has taught English and journalism on the secondary and college levels. He is on the board of various academic and spiritual organizations, and is an editorial contributor to several national publications. As a lecturer and seminar leader, he has appeared at colleges and universities and before public and professional organizations throughout the U.S. and Canada. He has also made radio and television appearances across the United States.

He and his wife Barbara have four children and live at 60 Pound Ridge Road, Cheshire, CT 06410, U.S.A.